# Modern Kongo Prophets

African Systems of Thought

General Editors
Charles S. Bird
Ivan Karp

Contributing Editors
Thomas O. Beidelman
James Fernandez
Luc de Heusch
John Middleton
Victor Turner
Roy Willis

# Modern Kongo Prophets
## Religion in a Plural Society

Wyatt MacGaffey

INDIANA UNIVERSITY PRESS
*Bloomington*

Library of Congress Cataloging in Publication Data

MacGaffey, Wyatt.
    Modern Kongo Prophets.

    (African systems of thought)
    Bibliography:  p.270.
    Includes index.
    1.  Zaire--Religion.  2.  Prophets--Zaire.
I.  Title.  II.  Series
BL2470.Z2M32 1983 299'.67 82-48554
ISBN 0-253-33865-4
ISBN 0-253-20307-4 (pbk.)
1 2 3 4 5 87 86 85 84 83

## EMMANUEL BAMBA

Muna ntandu mu kinkole yakala;
Bu yayiza, bantula diaka mu kinkole.
Mono Kimbangu niongene.
Balunungu bena nata nitu ani,
Yena kundila ku mbanza nsilu.

I was in prison upcountry;
When I returned, they imprisoned me
 again.
To Kimbangu I complain.
The justified will carry his body
To be honored in the promised city.

# Contents

# Illustrations

# Preface

The position of theory in anthropology is somewhat like that of <u>kindoki</u> in Kongo culture. It is an occult power of which everybody who is anybody should have some, although one is never sure that those who possess it will use it for good. Some anthropologists have so high an opinion of theory that they subordinate ethnography to it, believing that the function of ethnography is merely to further the cause of theory. The record of confusion and transience in anthropological theory at least partly betrays this high ideal; on the whole, ethnography lasts longer than theory. In its service, theory, as carefully crafted as possible, is an essential tool. In that sense this is a theoretical work.

Adequate presentation of Kimbanguism seemed to require revising much of the existing literature regarding it and rebuilding some of the tools of the anthropology of religion. I have been guided in this work by my teachers, Meyer Fortes, Edmund Leach and M.G.Smith. Despite their famous disagreements, they agree in their idea of social anthropology and the high standards they uphold for its practitioners. To Professor Fortes I owe a sense of structure in social relations and in the methods of anthropology. Sir Edmund taught me to see social action as communication and to be sensitive to its intrinsic ambiguities. Professor Smith's concept of social pluralism provides the explicit framework of the study, but I am more profoundly indebted to him for a sense of the political dimension of social action.

In plural societies action is guided and interpreted according to two or more cosmologies whose application is largely though imperfectly segregated. Anthropologists are aware that their science presupposes the cosmology and organization of "modern" or capitalist society and employs categories in which the experiences of members of other societies cannot always be represented as they themselves would want to represent them.

In 1969 I attended a conference convened to discuss African intellectual responses to the West.
Because the participants seemed to take it for granted that "the West" was the same phenomenon no matter
who was looking at it, I subsequently wrote a paper
(in Philip D. Curtin, ed., Africa and the West,
University of Wisconsin Press, 1972) showing that
"the West" as BaKongo understood it was a complex
entirely foreign to occidental thought. Students of
comparative religion often make insufficient
allowance for such divergence of views and permit
themselves to interpret the foreign actor's motives
as though he saw the world as they do. Some anthropologists, on the other hand, hold that the only
valid representation of events in other societies is
one that conforms to subjective or native conceptions. The criteria of "validity" remain unexamined
in this assertion, which is a relativistic reaction
against the claims to absolute objectivity of other
social scientists.

For the sake of consistency in discourse, this
study attempts to distinguish between representations
of events in the categories of social science and the
same events as understood by BaKongo. Each perspective has its value, but they are different, and in
Zaire the difference has given rise, in religious
discourse between Africans and Europeans, to a protracted and frustrating dialogue of the deaf. The
distinction is worth attempting, although in practice
no radical segregation can be maintained. No matter
how sympathetic the anthropologist, his project is
his own and not that of the people on whose behalf he
undertakes to speak. Secondly, the potential incompatibility of the two perspectives should not be
exaggerated; they are often congruent.

Ultimately this book is the theoretically guided
record of a particular personal experience of Kimbanguism. As a personal experience it would not have
been possible but for the considerate hospitality and
cooperation of many people, of whom I can mention
only a few. Among churchmen I am especially grateful
for the assistance of His Excellency Diangienda ku
Ntima, Luntadila Ndala za Fwa, Mpadi Simon-Pierre,
Nsimba Francois, Ntengo Joseph, the late Mabwaka
Mpaka, Difuene, Soka Tuti dia Mvula, Mambu Masakidi,
Nkindu Guillaume, Kathleen Brain, and the leaders of
the Dibundu dia Mpeve a Nlongo mu Afrique, the Eglise
Universelle de Douze Apotres, and the American Baptist Foreign Missionary Society. These names must
stand for hundreds of catechists, missionaries, pro-

phets, pastors and congregants with whom I have shared public prayers and private confidences.

My debts to personal friends are still more extensive. They made possible a knowledge of Kongo life and language which has been a deep source of abiding pleasure to me. I mention only Jessy Nkoba, Yankwa Raymond, Makedika Manzambi, Makima Lutete, Sandy Mahaniah, Noe and Esther Diawaku, and Mayivangwa Therese.

Colleagues who helped in the research or commented on written drafts include Janet MacGaffey, John M.Janzen, Benoit Verhaegen, Bakwa Mwelanzambi, Kimpianga kia Mahaniah, Douglas A. Davis, Judith Shapiro, Ivan Karp, Francois Bontinck, James W. Fernandez and Robert E. Smith. The book would not have been produced at all but for George and Linda Gerstein, who own the computer, and especially George, who knows how to make it work. I have also relied on Chris Kerr, Sandy Dixon, Edith Castellano, Pennie Coia, Shirley Averill, and the staff of that excellent institution, the Haverford College Library.

The pencil drawing reproduced as Plate 10, which captures the feeling of a DMN meeting better than any of my photographs, was given to me by the artist, Kazi Thomas.

I am grateful for research assistance to the Foreign Area Fellowship Program, the Social Science Research Council, the National Endowment for the Humanities, the Fulbright-Hays Program and the Faculty Research Fund of Haverford College. None of these bodies endorses the conclusions of the book nor is responsible for its failings. Most of my research was carried out in 1964-66 and 1970, with some additional observations in 1979-80.

Chapter Two originally appeared in Cahiers des Religions Africaines (Kinshasa), 10 (1976) pp.31-49. Some paragraphs have also been reproduced from my papers, "Economic and social dimensions of Kongo slavery," in S. Miers and I. Kopytoff, eds., Slavery in Africa (Madison: University of Wisconsin Press; © 1977 by the Board of Regents of the University of Wisconsin System), pp.235-57; and "African history, anthropology, and the rationality of natives" (History in Africa, 5 (1978) pp.101-20.) Permission of the copyright holders is gratefully acknowledged.

Wyatt MacGaffey
Haverford
August, 1982

# Modern Kongo Prophets

# Introduction

The prophet movements of Lower Zaire are well
known to students of religious movements, partly
because of their scale and political impact, and
partly because of the volume of published material on
them, notably Andersson's Messianic Popular Movements
in the Lower Congo. On the other hand, the numerous
interpretations of Kongo prophetism are generally
deficient in dealing with both the social and the
cultural context. The sociological deficiency is
largely a question of theory: scholars evaluate the
social context in terms of such value-laden,
ill-defined and impractical concepts as oppression,
messianism, and syncretism. Cultural interpretations
suffer from the fact that the interpreters of prophetism have been mostly either sympathetic to the
movement but without knowledge of KiKongo or, knowing
the language, have been loyal to an opposing movement.

Lower Zaire is central to a territory occupied
by the BaKongo (sing. MuKongo, NKongo), which they
call Kongo and which has been divided since 1895
among the Republic of Congo (capital: Brazzaville),
formerly French Congo; the Republic of Zaire, formerly Belgian Congo (capital: Kinshasa); and Angola,
with Cabinda, formerly a Portuguese colony. The
BaKongo number some three million people, but in
recent centuries they have not had a unitary political system, nor are their language and culture
sharply different from those of their neighbors.
They have had extensive and profound relations with
Europe since the sixteenth century, and in Zaire
(with which this book is chiefly concerned) they are
among the best educated and most influential sections
of the national population.

The title, "Modern Kongo Prophets," refers to the prophets of the colonial and post-colonial era, notably Simon Kimbangu and his successors, on whose account the term "Kimbanguism" is commonly applied to all of them. Kimbangu emerged as the first great modern prophet in 1921, and his sons now lead the largest "independent" church in Zaire, the Church of Jesus Christ on the Earth by the Prophet Simon Kimbangu (EJCSK), said to be also the largest in Africa (M.-L. Martin 1975). In the local context, however, the term Kimbanguism is controversial, and categorical use of it prejudges certain issues deserving careful attention. To circumscribe the data as the title indicates is not to deny that prophetism existed in Kongo, as elsewhere in Central Africa, long before the colonial period. One of the remarkable features of Kongo prophetism is the degree of continuity it displays with earlier religious patterns, such that the extensive similarities between the prophetism of Kimbangu and that of Beatrice in 1704 are not at all casual or incidental (MacGaffey 1977c). Full discussion of such continuities requires an analysis of pre-colonial Kongo religion and its social and cultural context too extensive for this volume, in which the main features of the classical tradition will be taken as given.

This study provides a descriptive record of the later developments of one of the world's best-known religious movements in a period (the 1960's) of routinization. Besides adding to what is already known about Kimbanguism and its offshoots, this description differs from most others in being based on extensive participant observation, obviating at least some of the distortions of a record otherwise largely based on documents. The documentary archive was constituted in the course of political struggles in which the principal parties were KiKongo-speaking Africans and French-speaking Europeans. This record obscured rather than illuminated Kimbanguist realities, because of difficulties of translation reflecting radically different religious cultures and because the documents themselves were political instruments. As documents, drawn up, printed and disseminated in institutionalized ways, they imposed upon the historical reality the categories and the latent explanations of the European world, the bureaucratic sector of colonial society, itself politically dominant in the history of the times but not the only source of meanings, motivations or resources. Whether written by Kimbanguists or their

opponents, such documents in effect provided   answers
only  to European questions, thus distorting the content of the movement to which they referred  (JM:Part
I).
      A slight example of such distortion is   provided
by   the   ritual   use   of earth and water from Nkamba,
Kimbangu's birthplace.   In   reply   to   the   insistent
European challenge to justify their practices as legitimate, according to imprecise   standards   involving
some   correspondence   with   European   Christian practices, EJCSK replied, "It is difficult to take   up   a
stand   on   this complex issue.   Many believers seek a
cure at Lourdes, which has become a place of pilgrimage.   Can   one accuse the ecclesiastical authorities
of trickery when they tell people to go to   Lourdes?"
(Martin   1968:27).   So an ambiguous question meets an
ambiguous answer, and in the   process   the   earth   of
Nkamba   disappears   from   view, the profound connotations of the combination of earth and water in   Kongo
religious   consciousness   are   lost, and the original
issue trivialized.
      After   1960,   competition   between   prophetic
leaders   produced   a   series   of cleavages within the
movement itself, complicating the political   struggle
as   each   church,   notably EJCSK, sought to retain or
expand its membership, if possible by enlisting   support   at   home   and abroad.   At the local level these
factional conflicts were waged through kinship links,
control   of building sites, public séances and witchcraft accusations.   No   systematic   record   of   such
activities   exists;   they   are reported to us, if at
all, in occasional documents circulating, once again,
in   bureaucratic   context:   a   court   case, a mimeographed submission to a visiting dignitary,   a   press
conference.   Only   the   participant observer is in a
position to discover the realities behind these fragmentary indications.
      This report also differs   from   most   others   in
implicitly   (sometimes explicitly) rejecting the perspective not only of hostile officials but of much of
missiology   and the anthropology of religion as well.
The carefully worded and mutually contradictory   distinctions   drawn by E.Andersson, M.-L.Martin and many
other commentators on religion in Lower Zaire between
true   and   syncretic   Christianity could only acquire
interest and validity if we were   to   apply   them   to
churches   everywhere,   and   not   simply to those that
come under suspicion because Africans founded them.
      This is a study of <u>kingunza</u>, which it is conven-
ient   to   paraphrase   as   Kongo   prophetism   (<u>ngunza</u>,

"prophet"). <u>Kingunza</u>, preceded in the same area of Zaire by certain somewhat similar manifestations, achieved its historical reality among the BaKongo from 1921 onwards, in the context of particular social and ideological structures. In the consciousness of its primary users, <u>kingunza</u> owed its meaning to a set of contrasts with the related terms <u>kinganga</u> (magic), <u>kindoki</u> (witchcraft), and <u>kimfumu</u> (chiefship). These concepts in turn presupposed a cosmology of divided worlds in which the holders of these powers mediated between the dead and the living. To the observer, the cosmology and the categories of mediation become apparent principally in ritual performances in which (for example) individuals are identified and humiliated as witches, or a prophet declares himself to be such and convinces other people that he has the power to tell the future, to detect witches, and raise the dead.

As priest-diviner, the prophet updates the function of the pre-colonial <u>ngang'a mbangu</u> or <u>ngang'a ngombo</u>. The system of religious roles and ritual programs is related to, and in fact part and parcel of, the precolonial socio-economic system. By 1921, Kongo society was thoroughly incorporated in Belgian Congo as the customary sector of a plural society controlled by a statutory or bureaucratic sector staffed, at that time, by Europeans. The essential feature of customary society remained the system of matrilineal descent, with its constituent distinction between slave and freeborn members of matrilineal clans. This distinction remained important in customary context after a generation of BaKongo had been educated in mission schools and inducted into the statutory sector as wage labor.

As employees, whether catechists, railroad men, houseboys or clerks, some BaKongo were much less successful than others. Many of them experienced a sharp contradiction between their actual situation and the universalism of achievement which not only the missions but the state preached as the ideology of the European <u>mission civilisatrice</u>. Some frustrated Protestant catechists, of whom Kimbangu though the most famous was not the first, discovered in the Bible which they had been taught to study the model of the prophet. In realizing this model they articulated the needs and aspirations of what became at times the majority of their countrymen but principally of those among them who were doubly losers: in the customary sector as slaves and in the bureaucratic sector as the nucleus of a developing proletariat.

The Kongo prophet, like his Biblical prototype, is an ambiguous figure, who puts as much blame on the children of God for their sufferings as on their oppressor. The prophets, like many ordinary BaKongo in the 1960's, were ready to accept the missionary accusation of moral failings as the explanation of their unhappy condition. The Kimbanguist moral code and its observance is therefore at least as strict as that of the Baptist tradition in which Kimbangu was trained. But although the verb <u>sumuka</u> nowadays means "to sin" in the ordinary vocabulary of Christianity, it retains its meaning of "to break cult taboos," derived from the indigenous religion and cosmology, which until 1970 at least had lost very little of their power to define and interpret experiential reality for the BaKongo. The motives and the objectives of Kimbanguism are thus just as ambiguous as the social context of divided worlds, European and African, in which the BaKongo now live.

Besides accusing themselves of rule-breaking, BaKongo also explain misfortune by accusing others of being witches, whose greed brings death. Calling upon their followers to restore moral integrity to their conduct, the prophets also led them in the identification and expulsion of witches. Besides many individual BaKongo, the colonial regime as a whole fell under this indictment, since the entire history of European relations with Africa, from slavery to imperialism, was popularly understood in the idiom of witchcraft.

As a social theory, rooted in a particular social system, witchcraft and its complements, divination and healing, purported to explain individual and collective experiences, from miscarriages and unemployment to generalized oppression. Prophetic practice was often effective in relieving pain and frustration, and even contributed substantially to achieving national independence. As the social context evolved, prophetism itself changed its character. In this study I show how the different prophetic churches changed, and I argue that successive generations of prophets offered different social analyses and recommendations all framed in the same set of categories, the ideological structure of Kongo religion.

Since the prophetic calling is above all a highly personal commitment, a struggle with obscure emotions and dreams as much as it is a professional career, I also attempt in the last chapter, through the use of personal documents, to analyze the

prophet's consciousness as a microcosm of its time.
In the process I reject, as unnecessary and unhelp-
ful, the view of individual and society as separate
systems, taken for granted by almost the entire
literature on shamanism.
     The units of the analysis are never Kimbanguism,
prophetism, traditional society or the like, but
always abstract relations between two or more terms
of a system of social action which is real for both
actor and observer, thus: kingunza vs. kinganga,
slave vs. free, customary vs. bureaucratic, healer
and clientele, EJCSK and DMN, and the like. The phenomenon "Kimbanguism," for example, much written
about, is not a thing but the historically given
relations between the prophets and the missions, the
prophets and other healers, and between prophets and
prophets as they contrast themselves on various
dimensions, including the reference to Kimbangu
itself. It makes no sense, then, to study a church,
even EJCSK, as though it were constituted exclusively
by the set of its own internal relations. The study
is thus consistently historical and holistic. The
results are not simply idiosyncratic and of local
significance, since the method lends itself to the
identification, and hence the comparison, of specifically similar and different structures (MacGaffey
1972a, 1977c, 1979).

## RELIGIOUS MOVEMENTS EXPLAINED

     The study of religious movements in Africa and
elsewhere has fallen into theoretical doldrums since
the themes of messianism, revitalization, protest,
and the like, popular in the 1950's, revealed their
several limitations (LaBarre 1971; Fernandez 1978).
These retrospective rationalizations apply as satisfactorily to Kimbanguism as to other examples, but
none of them illuminates specific relations between
the content and the context of Kimbanguism. It is
obvious that the BaKongo were oppressed by the colonial government, that they suffered deprivation in
various ways, and that the movement promised to
reform their condition. Labels such as nativistic,
millenary, messianic and revitalizing can all be seen
as appropriate to the historical facts, which have
also supported protracted and futile debates whether
the movement was political as well as religious,
xenophobic, nationalist, Christian or syncretic.
These labels all purport to be descriptive and classificatory, but none of them is associated with

criteria defining its empirical relevance in any precise way. Most of them conceal judgments of approval
or disapproval.

From the beginning students have also sought to
understand the movement by relating it to outside
influences, from Protestantism to Garveyism, to which
the praise (or blame) should be given. One Catholic
missionary held that the astonishingly disciplined
marching of the Kimbanguists could only result from
European training and noted that the only Europeans
with whom they had had much contact were the Protestant missionaries. He concluded that Kimbanguist
religion was nothing but a front for the Baptist Missionary Society, itself an agent of British
imperialism. "Ils rêvent d'une mainmise de
l'Angleterre sur notre colonie" (Dufonteny 1924).

The parallel Belgian suspicion of a Garveyite
conspiracy had more foundation in fact, since BaKongo
and black Americans working in Leopoldville (Kinshasa) are known to have been in contact with the
pan-African movement, circulated literature, and at
least dreamed of liberating Congo. It is reasonable
to suppose that Kimbangu had had some contact with
these people before and after his appearance as a
prophet, especially since some of the Kongo activists
are known to have been educated at the Baptist station, Ngombe Lutete (Andersson 1958:240-57). But
whereas Kimbangu's prophetic activity owed much to
Protestant teaching, there is no sign in it of Garveyism or of specifically political intentions (cf.
Feci 1972:28). Andersson suggested that a rumor
foretelling Kimbangu's return in a ship reflected
knowledge of Marcus Garvey's Black Star Line, and
that the red rag he supposedly tied to the end of his
prophetic staff might have been the best imitation of
Garvey's red, green and black flag that he could manage, lacking both green and black cloth. Both items,
however, are more plausibly explained by reference to
Kongo cosmology. Ships, like canoes, trucks, and
trains, transport people between the worlds; staffs
and batons were in 1921 and are still signs and means
of spiritual communication; red is the color of
transition; flags (mpeve) symbolize spirit (mpeve).
In the 1960's Kimbanguists thought of America as the
land of the dead; it is unlikely that what they
understood in 1921 by "the return of the Americans"
had anything to do with international relations
(MacGaffey 1968).

The descriptive labels mentioned above, and others of their kind, all attempt to render Kimbanguism

intelligible by assuming that actors and observer
perceive a common reality, to which the actors
respond in one or more modes of action which the
observer can recognize from his own experience. The
various labels, and their accompanying attributions
of motivation, take for granted the recognizability
of movements as religious. Scholars contrast Kimbanguism with Abako, the principal political party of
the BaKongo in the 1950's, and see the relationship
between the two as evolutionary, not simply as a
chronological sequence. So Crawford Young (1965:281)
distinguishes five states in the evolution of the
nationalist movement: (1) primary resistance movements, (2) messianic and syncretic sects, (3) urban
riot and violence, (4) pre-political modern associations, (5) political parties.

Few if any of the adjectives in this list and
others like it have any precise descriptive value;
they presuppose the process of evolution which is
subsequently invoked to explain the data. Scholars
presume that villages are traditional and usually
label movements centered in them "nativistic" or
"reactionary," as though such labels were automatically appropriate. Rotberg and Mazrui (1970:xxiii)
even argue that "most Africans are religious, and it
is hardly surprising that indigenous dissatisfaction
with colonial rule should have found a variety of
religious contexts within which to ... seek
redress." Associations employing bureaucratic forms
are assumed to be modern, while those that seem less
rational are called religious and pre-political. As
Young summarizes the history of protest in Belgian
Congo (1965:286), "By the 1950's, the religious channel for the venting of frustration tended to be
supplanted by the modern, secular nationalism of
Abako."

As an account of the facts this is unacceptable.
Apart from its self-identification as a political
party, Abako, with its utopian references to the
return of a quasi-mythical Kongo kingdom, was clearly
similar in some ways to Kimbanguism, and the membership of the two organizations overlapped extensively.
Bureaucratically inscribed, dues-paying members of
the political party, who supported its leaders'
maneuvers at the Belgo-Congolese Round Table prepar-
ing for independence, also sought out prophets to
protect their children against the danger of being
"sold to America" by witchcraft. From their point of
view, both actions were equally instrumental
responses to a single reality; in ordinary Kongo

usage, <u>table ronde</u> means a conclave of witches
(MacGaffey 1978). The difference between these movements is thus not in any simple sense a matter of
religion versus politics, of two different populations, or of two different states of consciousness,
one more modern than the other, but of two different
institutional contexts. Each context, or sector,
presupposed certain norms of organization and communication, and certain assumptions about space, time,
death, sex, race, and the like; in short, a certain
cosmology.

    In this perspective, the question why colonial
rule, a political and economic phenomenon, was initially opposed by a religious rather than a political
movement is at least partly false. In its commitment
to a particular cosmology, as in much of its rhetoric, the colonial regime was a religious as well as a
political complex, and its opponent of 1921, Kimbanguism, predicated upon an entirely different
cosmology, was from its inception profoundly and
necessarily political. The history of the movement
from 1921 to the present, marked by the strained and
continuous efforts of its defenders to assert, for
ideological reasons, that it was religious and not
political, itself documents the difficulty of any
such assertion.

    To explore this question further, we must con-
sider the origin of the categories social science
seeks to apply to phenomena such as Kimbanguism.

## Intercultural Sociology

    Since its emergence in the early nineteenth cen-
tury, modern social science in the European tradition
has thought of what is now called modern or Western
society as consisting of three basic institutions:
church, state and market. These institutions, organizational levels, or "instances," to use an
expression common in recent French Marxist writing,
provide social science with important corresponding
abstract, functional categories, namely: religion,
politics, and economy. Many functional analyses of
societies so constituted are possible, but the ones
that dominate discussion all exhibit the same essential structure, a dichotomy between ideal and
material realities, which is itself yet another
appearance of the mind/body distinction founded in
seventeenth century philosophy. Social scientists
argue endlessly which one of these levels is the more
important, even determinant, in social evolution,

whether religion, otherwise known as superstructure,
or material forces and relations, the infrastructure.
Politics and social relations are situated ambiguously between the poles of this system, claimed by both
sides.
    Religion, socio-political organization and econ-
omy are the functional divisions of capitalist
society analysed synchronically. The reproduction of
such a system from generation to generation, its
diachronic dimension, can be distinguished as the
corresponding functions of education (passing on of
values), law, and domesticity (reproduction and distribution of the labor force). Here then we have the
six institutions which are the usual categories of
ethnographic description and anthropological analysis, although once again it is necessary to note
that not every institutional list anthropologists
find convenient to use will be the same, nor indeed
is there any logical necessity to any particular
list.[1]
    The endless circularity and low productivity of
the long-standing debate between idealists and mater-
ialists suggests that the question is malformed.
Before we can decide which system level is determinant, it is logically necessary to show how many
levels there must be, whether two, three, or more.
No one has as yet addressed himself to this question.
On the contrary, the identity and salience of such
categories as religion and economy are taken for
granted because they are presupposed, not only by the
debate, but by the society within which the debate
takes place. In other words, these categories are
ambiguously analytical and empirical at the same
time.
    It would be naive, however, to suppose that the
analytic categories of religion, socio-political
organization and economy correspond empirically to
three necessary functions discretely allocated in
capitalist society to three separate and specialized
institutional complexes. Capitalist ideology offers
this allocation as the norm, which editorial writers
and the like uphold with arguments to the effect that
the church should stay out of politics, the government should stay out of the market, and so on. In
fact, all three institutions fulfill in varying
degree all three functions; as Sahlins observes
(1976:4), following Lukács, it was Marx's achievement
to reveal the underlying unity, as components of a
single system, of institutional parts that presented
themselves as distinct and autonomous.

When, despite its inadequacies as an account of
the system within which it itself originates, the
sociology of capitalism addresses itself to other
kinds of society and the problem of comparison, considerable difficulties arise.  In other societies,
even that approximate segregation of religious, political and economic functions that characterizes
capitalism is not apparent. We then say that other
societies are primitive, simple, undifferentiated or
generalized.  Although church, state and market are
not in evidence, the corresponding functions are said
to be present as analytically distinguishable aspects
of behavior.  So the economy is said to be embedded
in social relations and primitive societies are said
to be diffusely religious.[2]

Of course, much that is of value can be accomplished using this approach, provided that the
analysis is logically rigorous, but no amount of
diligence or rigor can overcome its intrinsic ethno-
centrism.  Though unable to resolve their own dispute
about determinacy, the competing schools converge in
a common division of societies into the West, in
which the essential functions are institutionally
differentiated, and the rest, in which they are
merged.  As Sahlins argues (1976:54), this distinction, "a translation of different integrations of
code and praxis into a radical distinction in the
nature of societies ... legitimizes the mode of
appearance of Western society as the true explanation
of it."

Insofar as they recognize institutional differentiation, anthropologists tend to see it as some
degree of evolution towards a social system like our
own and write about the emergence of true religion,
of the state, or of the market principle.  The procedure is historicist and tautological, since
evolution in a particular direction is presupposed
rather than ascertained, and the categories in which
research is cast anticipate its conclusions.

All societies are to some extent institutionally
differentiated, in structures that do not necessarily
anticipate capitalism, feudalism or any other European form.  The totality of the functions fulfilled by
such structures presumably includes those necessary
to any social system, but the distribution of this
totality among the several institutions in which
social behavior is organized distinguishes one type
of society from another.  It is to be expected that
the ideological categories of public discourse in any
society will be related to the structure of institu-

tional differentiation, though not in such a way as
to constitute an accurate model of it.

## Kongo Institutions

We may discover the self-conception of Kongo
society through the study of religion. In this case,
as in European thought, what we seek is not a set of
doctrines, the content of the self-conception, upon
which all members of the society might conceivably be
agreed - there is no such set - but the structure
within which ideological battles are fought out.[3]
If we employ the usual categories of social science and inquire into the religion of the BaKongo, we
readily discover that it centers on four kinds of
persons believed to control an occult power called
kindoki. Referring to the Ndibu area of central
Kongo, the Kongo anthropologist Buakasa lists the
kinds as follows (1968:163): 1) the clan head, who
should use his kindoki to safeguard his followers,
but may illegitimately "eat" them; 2) nganga ngombo,
diviner; 3) ngang'a n'kisi, operator of charms; and
4) "ndoki privés," private witches.
As Buakasa implies, but does not spell out, two
intersecting criteria differentiate these various
holders of kindoki: 1) the criterion of ends, public
versus private, groups the chief and the diviner
against the self-interested witch and magician; and
2) the criterion of effects, destructive versus
therapeutic, groups the violent chief and witch
against the healers, diviner and magician (MacGaffey
1970a).
In Kongo thought these four roles are so many
responses to the possibility of obtaining power from
the world of the dead and using it in this world with
violent or therapeutic effect, for altruistic or
selfish ends. The BaKongo associate the four kinds
of holders of kindoki with the four classes of the
dead as follows: chiefs and elders, heads of their
clans, are priests of the ancestors; diviners are
priests of local spirits (bisimbi, bankita);
magicians serve functionally specialized charms
(min'kisi); and witches are in league with malicious
ghosts (min'kuyu). The roles (religious commissions), that is to say, presuppose a certain
cosmology, a belief in a land of the dead and the
spirits who inhabit it.
In fact, Kongo institutions are the source of
their cosmology, not responses to it. The spirits of

the dead owe their identities to the four kinds of
ritual addressed to them, in which sociologically
distinct congregations participate (MacGaffey 1977b).
In this dysharmonic regime of matrilineal descent and
virilocal residence, the chief, representing his
clan, stands for the lineal principle in social
organization and for social reproduction in time,
from generation to generation. The priest-diviner,
speaking to the interests of local groups, represents
society's extension in space, its division into
co-resident but lineally heterogeneous units of production and consumption. The clients of a magician
seek help for individual problems. These are the
three positive cults of the dead. The fourth is a
negative and in fact imaginary cult whose members,
accused of witchcraft, are punished for their alleged
misuse of occult power for selfish ends.

Already our exploration of institutions, characterized as religious because of their ideological
orientation towards an occult world, has led us into
important political, social, legal, and medical functions in Kongo life. Since these cults all involve
more or less expensive initiation fees, prestations,
fines, and therapeutic dues, their economic function
is equally conspicuous. Control of marriage and
domesticity is carried on in the same framework. In
fact no major social function can be discussed
without reference to the religious commissions; or,
to put the same conclusion in a different
perspective: the social programs in which the four
central roles are realized are as much economic and
political as they are religious, and none of these
functions is carried on through a comparable program
lacking reference to the occult. In short, these are
the institutions of Kongo society perceived ideologically, equivalent to the church, state and market of
capitalism, and the corresponding abstract categories
are kimfumu (chiefship) kinganga ngombo (divination),
kingang'a n'kisi (magic) and kindoki (witchcraft).

Just as the categories of Western social science
can be related to the institutional structure of capitalism, so Kongo ideology can be related to the
lineage mode of production that prevailed until the
European occupation in 1885. The subordination of
Kongo society to Belgian rule in the twentieth century produced extensive changes, but the ideological
distinctions outlined above still structured public
discussion of public affairs in the 1960's, as Buakasa explains (1972:59):

> With colonization... there arises a cont-
> radiction at the level of the functioning of
> the articulation of two "civilizations" now
> confronting each other. We have in effect...
> two social formations. In their respective
> functioning and in their articulation, the
> "modern" social formation is dominant and works
> in the long run to destroy the "traditional"
> formation... To the extent that the "modern"
> social formation, though dominant, does not yet
> offer a reassuring way of "reading" its con-
> tradictions, it is the "traditional" formation
> that offers its outline for interpreting these
> contradictions.

Early in the colonial period chiefship was destroyed, as was the role of priest-diviner, also known
as ngang'a mbangu, nganga kitomi, and by various
other names. In new conditions, in which the local
community was no longer the principal unit of production (since most male labor, in particular, had been
channeled into wage employment), the role of
priest-diviner, considerably modified, was taken over
by the prophets of the new Christian movements,
beginning with Simon Kimbangu in 1921. So in 1966, a
thoughtful Kongo elder writing an essay on the social
evils of the day listed the elders of the clans,
prophets, magicians, and witches as the experts to
whom he appealed to pool their knowledge in the common cause of social reform (JM No. 13). BaKongo
commonly refer to holders of occult powers in these
categories by the French word savants.

## Intellectuals in the Modern World

One approach to the study of religious movements
that retains considerable scholarly attention is the
intellectualism of R. Horton, especially his model
of conversion (1971;1975). The present study shares
Horton's interest in the intellectual aspects of
African religion and the agency of individual thinkers in religious change, a perspective widely
accepted in recent years (Goody 1977:19-35; Ranger
1976). Nevertheless, some points of difference will
become apparent and may be briefly indicated here.
Horton says we should compare African religions
to European science as systems of ideas for the
explanation, prediction, and control of space-time
events. African religions differ from science in
that they use anthropomorphic entities (spiritual

beings) instead of physical ones as the elements of
their models because, according to Horton, in Africa
social structure provides the most stable experiences. They also differ in that European thought,
unlike African thought, admits systematic challenges
and thus makes possible the advancement of science.
This second factor perhaps takes the ideals (or ideology) of science more seriously than its actual
practice (Feyerabend 1975), but in any case neither
factor distinguishes African traditional thought from
European social science with anything like the same
clarity. Social science has religious aspects and
functions and African religions, in their analytical
and practical aspects, have much in common with
social science (MacGaffey 1981).

Traditional African religions, Horton continues,
are organized at two levels. The higher level, the
domain of the Supreme Being, contains universalistic
propositions, but is little developed because, at
this stage in history, the African thinker's experience is largely bounded by the local community.
Particularistic propositions appropriate to local
experiences, represented in terms of lesser spiritual
beings, enrich the lower level of the religious system. As the course of history breaks down the
boundaries of the local community, intellectuals need
to develop the universalistic level of their thought,
and for this purpose they draw upon Christianity and
Islam, universalistic religions with well-developed
theologies of the Supreme Being. This movement leads
to conversion. Elements of the population whose contacts and interests are broadest, such as the rulers
of kingdoms, can be expected to convert before their
isolated, rural subjects do.

The argument implies that African thinkers
select religious themes to fit their intellectual
needs as defined by their own experience and the
existing development of their thought. Horton
believes that his perspective reveals why evangelization, when not associated with "other features of the
modern situation," often fails to produce conversion,
and also why in the end many converts express dissatisfaction with Christianity, because it does not in
fact provide a theory of the modern world.

Overall, this view of conversion emphasizes continuity in African religion. The new Christians
accept such elements of Christianity as they need to
expand the particularistic religion they began with.
This continuity matches the homogeneity of their
social organization, which changes in a quantitative

sense: its boundaries expand, contacts with the rest
of the world multiply. Horton's model implies a corresponding     view     of     history     as     increasing
rationalization of human relations; small units
merge into larger ones, local commodity production
gives way to centralized production for world markets, limited local theories are replaced by powerful
generalizations. Similar schemes of history can be
found in Marx, Durkheim and Weber. They tend to conceal much of what actually happened in colonized
Africa, which was a matter of contrasts and discontinuities. The colonial world of the BaKongo, which
the prophets interpreted, was a matter of contrasting
realities, kept separate by political action.

Plural Society

An empirical approach to prophetism in Kongo  as
a  social phenomenon must recognize the plural structure of the society in which prophetic action takes
place, that is, Kimbangu's activity and the various
responses to it. BaKongo themselves are fully conscious of this plural structure. Lacking an ideology
of individualism, they are more conscious than Ameri-
ans usually are of social structure as an arrangement
of positions (sing. fulu) and standardized interac-
tions. Lacking an ideology of progress or
modernization, they are aware of the simultaneity of
the conjoined structures which organize their lives,
although their own ideology imposes an idea of it at
least as misleading as "modernization." When we
locate prophets concretely in colonial society we
observe that their activity responds to particular
conditions; it is not a function of an undifferentiated condition of repression, deprivation, or
broadening experience.

A plural society exists when two or more collec-
tivities, each characterized by its own set of basic
institutions, are differentially incorporated within
the same political framework (Smith 1974:187). All
colonial and post-colonial societies are plural, but
not all plural societies are colonial. Even colonial
societies differ considerably among themselves in
their institutional structure.

In describing and comparing societies, anthropologists, as we have already noted, find it
convenient to identify six basic institutions as common to all societies and as exhausting the major
features of each. These institutions are domesticity, economy, law, government, education and religion.

Institutions are collectively standardized ways of doing things. Each includes the several inter-connected dimensions of "activity, social groupings, norms, ideas, values, and orientations. Each institutional system also requires a material base, a social locus, and appropriate resources" (Smith 1974:211). Institutions can only be distinguished analytically, and there can be no fixed and necessary list of institutions. Empirically, an institution such as the economy is only partially and relatively segregated from the other institutions of any society, even a capitalist one.

To analyze the structure of institutional cleavages in plural societies, M.G.Smith (1974:216) also distinguishes between the politico-jural and the domestic domains of social organization.[4] Social groupings in the politico-jural domain are characteristically corporate, whereas in the domestic domain they consist predominantly of such transitory or informal aggregates as households, neighborhoods, and friendships.

Smith observes that most of the basic institutions are represented in both domains, though not to the same extent. In the domestic domain the several sectors of a plural society may or may not share the same institutions; for example, the rules and practice of marriage may be the same throughout the population. In the political domain, however, besides whatever continuities exist, radical discontinuities between the sectors will always be found, corresponding to the distinctive interests and resources of the dominant sector, as opposed to the remainder. In a colonial society the colonizers always retain control over public policy, while the colonized exercise only such political prerogatives as the colonizers grant them, willingly or unwillingly. The boundary between what is political and what is domestic is itself a public matter and may be changed by political action.

In Lower Zaire (that is, the westernmost province of the Republic of Zaire, formerly the Lower Congo Province of Belgian Congo), the contrasted institutional sets with which we will be concerned include on the one hand those introduced by the Belgians, such as the Catholic Church, the system of statutory law and the courts that administered it, standing armed forces and regular police, banks, and industrial and agricultural enterprises employing wage labor - all institutions basically familiar to Europeans; on the other hand, divination, matrili-

neal descent, chiefship, cults of affliction, and an
economy in which consumers produced most of their own
goods, having direct access to the land they worked
-- institutions which Europeans only understand
through the medium of anthropological interpretation.

Social scientists commonly accord only an oblique recognition to such plural situations, denying
the simultaneity and organic relations of the two
sectors, which they artificially distance as traditional and modern. They see the relations between
the sectors as a matter of time and mental attitudes
rather than of politics and economics, and interpret
events in the light of an assumption that modernization will inevitably be difficult. In fact, the
institutions of the customary sector are fully contemporary; they are what they are as a result of
colonial policies and Kongo responses to them
(MacGaffey 1970b; 1978). Moreover the BaKongo, more
intensively than many other Zairean peoples, have
been thoroughly engaged in the European sector as
well, though restricted to subordinate roles in
church, state, and economy. They have thus learned
to live by two sets of rules, which they clearly distinguish, and as individuals have confronted two
different although related sets of demands and opportunities.

The thesis of the second part of this book is
that the prophetic movements and the form of their
routinization as churches can only be understood by
reference to this plural context. The prophets and
their adherents were not representative of an undifferentiated mass subject to abstract processes of
oppression or modernization. Typically, they
belonged, in each of the two organizational sectors
of their social lives, to a category of losers,
defined as such by the respective institutional
processes. Having less left to lose than other
BaKongo, they were prepared to hope and work for a
revolution, social as well as spiritual, to which
they applied the verb baluka, "to turn upside down."
It is another question to what extent their understanding of their situation, the organizational form
of prophetic activity, and the resources available
had in effect a revolutionary value.

Each of the contrasted institutional sets
requires its own symbolic media, including language
(KiKongo or French), dress, other equipment, and physical gestures. Each also presupposes its own
cosmology, an organization of the world in time and
space. For Europeans (that is, Western culture), the

dimensions of time and space are defined by history and geography, supplemented by other social sciences, such as physical anthropology, which may describe the populations of different parts of the world in terms of races (black and white, for example). Kongo cosmology is expressed in myths and in such beliefs as that when Africans die they go to America and become white (MacGaffey 1968). It is evident, thus, that with respect to such fundamental categories as life, death, and race, the contrasts between Kongo conceptions and those of Europeans are as marked as the institutional and cultural cleavages between them. Despite the common European insistence that Western science and African traditional thought are radically different in quality, the truth-value of the products of neither of these processes, as applied to history and social life, is easy to ascertain; in both instances, the content of social thought and the form of social life are closely associated.

Kongo understanding of the colonial history they shared with Belgians, their experience as individuals of events and social relations, their grasp of the past and expectation of the future, were very different from those afforded by social science in the European tradition. Yet in a formal sense it is equally valid to write a history or a sociology of prophetism in Kongo terms. The third part of this book approaches this possibility, on the assumption that the categories of such a social science exist among the BaKongo and are derived from their institutional structure and its associated cosmology.

## The Prophetic Interpretation

Given their different cosmological premises, African and European participants in the plural society of Belgian Congo understood historical events and the plural structure itself in radically different terms. Two histories and two sociologies confronted each other. Inevitably, each perspective distorted the relations institutionalized in the alternative sector. The cosmology of the colonial regime is also the cosmology of social science in the Western tradition; in applying it to the study of twentieth century African social movements we adopt the perspective of actors in the European sector of the society studied, and tend to ask questions accordingly: is this activity modernizing or not, is it tribal or territorial, religious or political, a prise de conscience by the proletariat?

In historical reality, the juxtaposition of
incompatible institutional sets has been not an
abstract or academic but a political relationship;
in the colonial context, and later, definitions of
the religious and the political (also the medical,
the academic, the educational, etc.) which purport to
segregate them as distinct types of activity, permis-
sible or otherwise, are part of the apparatus of
control. Similarly, the act of relegating Kongo
social representations to the sphere of religion,
while reserving to our own the label science, is a
political act, an ideological feature of the relations between our social system and that of the
BaKongo and others like them.
    Since "much of the so-called history of coloni-
alism in Africa is myth rather than history" (Ranger
1968:xv), and since several of the major theories
found valuable by the anthropology of recent years
have turned out to be local sociological models written down by fieldworkers as though they were accurate
accounts of the organization of the societies in
which they were current, it will not do to assume
that whereas our sociology (or psychology, etc.) is
necessarily scientific, theirs is illusory. The
truth value of alternative products is not at issue
here, however, merely their formal equivalence (Sahlins 1976:220). Europeans will inevitably prefer to
apprehend the structure of events in terms of their
own cosmology and its derivatives and indeed have no
choice; an important feature of all such sciences,
African or European, is that in their own social context they work, faulty or incomplete though they may
be (Ranger 1976:133).
    Kongo prophets are aware of the institutional
structure of their society in terms of the four central roles, which they regard as expressions of real
powers emanating from the other world. However inap-
propriately, they have interpreted their experience
of colonialism in the same terms, identifying the
real forces of imperialism with the occult powers of
the dead. In so doing, and in advocating programs of
reform known to social science as religious movements, they have articulated the common consciousness
of most BaKongo, some of whom, though not prophets
themselves, have written down similar reflexions for
the use of their fellows. Prophets have not merely
thought about and interpreted their society's problems but have experienced them in a particularly
acute and personal way; the last chapter relates
their experiences, as revealed in personal documents,

both to indigenous cosmology and to the process and form of colonial pluralism. Its theme, expressed in different words by Marx and Talcott Parsons, is also that of Lévi-Strauss (1968:xx-xxi):

> In every society, therefore, it will be inevitable that a certain (variable) percentage of individuals will be located, if one may say so, outside the system or between two or more systems not reducible to one another. Of such individuals the group asks, or even requires them to represent certain forms of compromise that cannot be achieved on the collective level, to feign imaginary transitions, to incarnate incompatible syntheses. In all these apparently aberrant behaviors, the "sick" do nothing but transcribe a state of the group and make manifest one or other of its constants. Their peripheral position with respect to any local system does not prevent them, like it, from being an integral part of the total system. More precisely, if they were not its docile witnesses, the total system would risk disintegration into its local systems.

# Part One

# *Historical Ethnography*

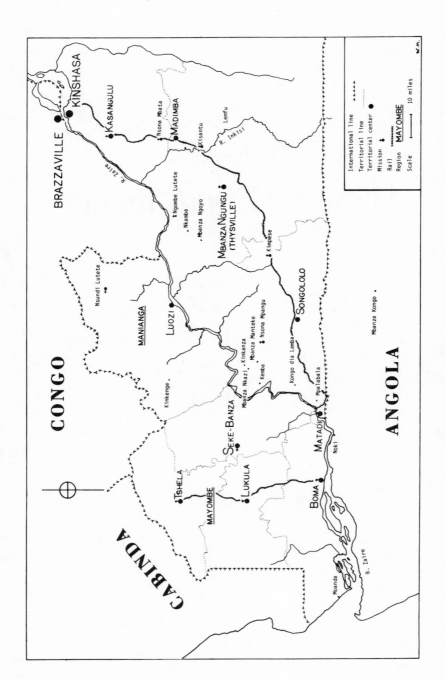

Fig.1: Map of Lower Zaire

CONGO

CABINDA

ANGOLA

BRAZZAVILLE

KINSHASA

KASANGULU

Nsona Mbata

MADIMBA

Kisantu

R. Lemfu

R. Inkisi

R. Zaïre

Ngombe Lutete

Nkamba

Mbanza Ngoyo

MBANZA NGUNGU
(THYSVILLE)

Kimpèse

SONGOLOLO

Nsundi Lutete

MANIANGA

LUOZI

Mbanza Manteke

Kinkanza

Nsona Mpangu

Mbanza Nkazi

Kemba

Kongo dia Lemba

Mpalabala

Mbanza Kongo

Kinkenge

SEKE-BANZA

TSHELA

MAYOMBE

LUKULA

MATADI

Noki

BOMA

R. Zaïre

Moanda

International line
Territorial line
Territorial center
Mission
Rail
Region    MAYOMBE
Scale    10 miles

# 1

# The Prophet Movements

The religious history of Kongo is in general
well known, though perhaps not well understood. This
chapter reviews that history for the sake of the analysis to come, adding some new information and
dwelling on three salient moments: the modern
conversion of BaKongo to Christianity, and especially
to Protestant (Baptist) Christianity; the rise, in
1921, of Kimbanguism, a movement regarded at first as
heretical but now officially recognized as Christian;
and the proliferation, in the 1950's, of schismatic
Kimbanguisms, represented here by the tiny, virtually
unknown group of the followers of Kinene.[1]

## CHRISTIAN BEGINNINGS

Portuguese missionaries first brought Christianity to
Kongo at the end of the fifteenth century. Within a
few years they had apparently converted the king and
most of the nobility of the Kongo kingdom, whose capital was at Mbanza Kongo (now São Salvador, in
northern Angola) and whose domains included much of
northern Angola and most of what is now the province
of Lower Zaire in the Republic of Zaire (Randles
1968; Cuvelier 1946).
  In general, the verdict of historiography has
been that after getting off to a good start the process of conversion succumbed to resurgent paganism in
the eighteenth century, as the number of missionaries
declined. By the nineteenth century, Christianity
survived only as pathetic fragments of mumbo-jumbo.
  On the contrary, it can be shown that Christianity was part of local religion from its first
introduction, and that it retained its vitality and

its meaning for three and a half centuries.   In Kongo
terms, Christianity was understood as a new means   of
approaching the highest of all spirits, Nzambi (God),
whose existing representative, the king, felt  when
the   missionaries   arrived that his  powers  were
threatened by the  multiplication  of  lesser  nzambi
(spirits,  shrines, charms) controlled by his nominal
subordinates.
       In the kingdom, as also throughout much of  Cen-
tral   Africa,   the  central  public cults, which also
constituted the structure  of  government,  took  the
form  of a dual regime of king and priest.  The king,
the nominee and representative of a particular matrilineal  clan, embodied the authority of the ancestors
and of the lineal principle in  social   organization.
His   responsibility  for public well-being was shared
by the kitomi, priest of a kind of "local,"  "water,"
or  "nature"  spirit,  variously  known in KiKongo as
simbi, nkita, n'kisi nsi and by other terms as  well.
(In  general,  I will  refer  to these as "local" or
simbi spirits, pl.  bisimbi.) The  kingship  was  the
highest  in  a series of ranked, quasi-magical titles
to which individuals could be initiated if they  were
eligible  by  descent  and had mustered enough wealth
and political support.  In lesser domains  throughout
the  kingdom, such titles were paired with simbi pri-
esthoods of corresponding rank, constituting a double
hierarchy.
       The  missionaries,  and  other  Europeans,  were
thought  to  be  bisimbi, partly because  they  too
apparently  came  from  the  water.   Missionaries,
without  being  aware  of  the misunderstanding, dis-
placed  many  simbi  priests  in  their  functions,
especially  rainmaking  and  the  consecration of the
king.  In  1873,  the  German  ethnographer  Bastian,
visiting  the  site  in Soyo (the northwestern tip of
Angola) of the original  baptism  on  Kongo  soil  in
1491,  recognized that the remaining traces of Christian  influence  were  integral  parts  of  a  simbi
(Chimbi) cult.  The Mani Soyo, the first convert, who
had taken Manuel as his  baptismal  name,  was  still
present  in the form of a statue, a rain charm called
Sa Manuela.  Earlier, in 1857, Bastian had noted  the
final  incorporation  of  the missionaries into Kongo
religion at Mbanza Kongo,  where  life-sized  wooden
statues  of  Capuchins  in  their habits were carried
about  on  feast  days  and  in  times  of  drought.
(Randles 1968:163-64;  Axelson 1970:192,198-99.)
       Despite these and other religious  continuities,
Kongo  (the  area inhabited by the BaKongo) underwent

profound changes during these centuries. The struggles of Mvemba Nzinga (Afonso I, 1506-1542) to
preserve his people against the exigencies and dupli-
cities of the Portuguese are famous in the history of
Africa. Eventually the fiction of an alliance, and
the kingdom itself, were broken by the battle of
Ambuila, 1665, in which Portuguese troops killed the
king of the day and more than 5,000 of his followers.
Mbanza Kongo was deserted (Randles 1968:120).[2]
    The destruction of Mbanza Kongo makes a conven-
ient date to mark the beginning of a new phase in
Kongo history. Randles calls it the age of broker
states, but it is better called the age of the slave
trade. New crops from the Americas changed the subsistence base. Portuguese demand for slaves, and
their ability to provide European goods in exchange,
reoriented trade towards the coast. The BaKongo
became middlemen in the great Congo trade, exporting
ivory, slaves and other products from the interior in
exchange for cloth, weapons, and other manufactures.
In the interior, the rivers provided the main commercial arteries, but the long series of cataracts on
the River Zaire in the 300 miles from Kinshasa to the
coast meant that goods had to be transferred from
canoes to porters when they reached Kinshasa. The
Tio (BaTeke) managed the transfer station; the
BaKongo were the porters (Vansina 1973; Sautter
1966).
    The dissolution of the kingdom accompanied this
economic transformation. A large number of autonomous polities emerged, some of them quite small,
through which the flow of trade was controlled. At
the coast, visiting ships paid trading duties to the
kings and their ministers, and specialized brokers
called ndingizi ("linguister") negotiated between the
European trading houses and Kongo caravans from the
interior (Tuckey 1818: 187; Randles 1968:201).
Externally, slaves were the principal commodity, but
internally slavery became the medium of Kongo politics and the basis for social stratification.
Slaves, though not exploited for their labor power in
distinctive relations, were the highest "denomination" in a system of exchangeable prestige goods
produced by trade and violence. The circulation of
such goods in ritual contexts, such as initiation to
titles, on terms advantageous to the wealthy and
powerful, was simultaneously a political and an
economic process that served to define and differentiate the internal and external boundaries of descent
groups and to identify the commissions and offices

(titles, cult memberships, lineage headships) through
which the groups were articulated and their regulatory processes carried on (MacGaffey 1977a).
    In the 1870's, British Baptist missionaries
settled at Mbanza Kongo (by then scarcely distinguishable from other villages) and began to penetrate
the interior of the continent. In 1879, Henry
Richards arrived in a village called Mbanza Manteke,
having made his way up the Zaire from Matadi. He
obtained a building site from the Nanga clan and was
incorporated into village life as a client whom the
Nanga chief, Makokila, thought might be useful.
    At about the same time the European powers
ceased to be content with their coastal stations and
sought to control the interior. In 1883, H.M.
Stanley, acting for Leopold II, King of the Belgians,
began to appoint officials ("chiefs") responsible for
providing porters on a new main route from Matadi to
Kinshasa, which ran through Manteke. Two years
later, the Congo Free State, comprising a vast area
in the heart of Africa which is now the Republic of
Zaire, was officially proclaimed. European powers
divided Kongo between Angola, the Free State, the
French colony of Congo to the north, and the Portuguese enclave of Cabinda. Within a few years the
Free State declared itself the owner of all land not
actually in use by the natives, the definition of use
remaining very vague. It abolished slavery but
introduced forced and clearly dependent labor for the
first time in the form of military service, contract
labor and porterage on the route to the interior.
Foreigners took over all trade except local trade and
chiefship disappeared, chiefs having been essentially
the managers and beneficiaries of the economy of
prestige goods. In due course, the local cults of
simbi spirits also disappeared, some of them as a
result of deliberate repression instigated by missionaries.
    The people of Mbanza Manteke interpreted their
new situation in religious terms and in 1886 they
began to convert to Protestant Christianity. For
seven years after his arrival, Richards had worked
without success to convert "the heathen," while his
first wife and several colleagues succumbed to
disease. In 1884 the Livingstone Inland Mission, his
sponsors, transferred their operations to the Baptist
Missionary Society of Boston, later the American Baptist Foreign Missionary Society (ABFMS) with
headquarters in Valley Forge, Pennsylvania. By 1885
Richards had acquired as his only followers a few

refugees and ex-slaves, but other missionaries began
to report that a crisis of conversion was imminent in
several of the mission stations along the trade route
that ran past Richards' door. In 1886 Richards
returned from a leave in England to find that there
were signs of an impending crisis in Mbanza Manteke
too. By now he spoke KiKongo fluently and he had
decided to change the style of his preaching (F.E.
Guinness 1890:431-32):

> At first I went to work the wrong way. My
> first idea was to teach the heathen the folly
> of idolatry and superstition, the nature of
> God, about His will as expressed in the law,
> about duty and morality and such things, as
> well as about Christ, His word, His miracles,
> and parables, His death and resurrection. But
> I found it all no use. At the end of six years
> I had not a convert.
>
> Then in bitterness of spirit I prayed and
> searched the Scriptures, and noted what the
> apostles did, and began to follow their
> example ... They preached Christ and Him cru-
> cified. They kept to the one point, and Christ
> Himself bade them do so. They were to proclaim
> repentance and remission of sins through Him.
> Not a hundred things. One thing - Christ and
> Him crucified.
>
> When I preached that, day by day and week
> by week, then I speedily saw a glorious change!
> Then I felt clothed with power, and that it was
> the Spirit of God who spoke through me. The
> results were marvelous. The stolid, stupid
> people waked up. I saw looks and whispers, and
> nudges between neighbours, astonishment, eager
> interest, and soon conviction and shame, tears
> of penitence; restless desire to hear, more
> shame, alarm, and very soon I was assailed on
> all sides with the question, "What must I do to
> be saved?" And soon the converts were numbered
> by hundreds. The thieves (and they are all
> thieves to begin with) became honest, the liars
> (and lying was customary) became truthful; the
> women became modest, and wanted dresses direct-
> ly they were converted.

"Mbanza Manteke," reported Richards to
headquarters in Boston, "is no longer a heathen country." The event became famous in missionary annals as
The Pentecost of the Congo.[3]

Since indigenous cults were all based on the idea of successful visits to the land of the dead, the new message may indeed have been more acceptable to Manteke people than the old, but other factors were clearly at work. The creation of the Free State in 1885 led rapidly to the destruction of independent Kongo trade and loosed on the villages troops of East African and other mercenaries ("Zanzibaris"), nominally under the command of young adventurers from several European countries, who looted and ravaged more or less at will while rounding up men to act as porters, soldiers and laborers (Claridge 1922; Axelson 1970:251-66). In 1886, a punitive expedition ruined Kongo dia Lemba, upon which missionaries had remarked in 1882 for its prosperity and the extent and fertility of its fields. "Some years ago," wrote Richards in 1903, "the people were afraid of the State soldiers, and to get away from oppression were scattered abroad in the woods, valleys and swamps, and many died." Many hoped that the missionary would protect them, and for years afterwards believed that allegiance to the English-speaking Protestant mission relieved them of obligations to the French-speaking government, with which the Catholic missions came to be associated.[4]

The Pentecost was nevertheless a conversion, not just a political maneuver, though it is not clear just what the people of Manteke and other areas were converted to. Contemporary missionary reports are blind to the problem, but indicate the persistence among the converts of traditional ideas. Then as later (and as before) the BaKongo regarded white people as visitors from the land of the dead. According to Catherine Mabie (1952:68), a medical missionary in Mbanza Manteke from 1898 to 1911, it was rumored there that Richards had committed a crime in his own country for which he was required to obtain heads in Congo to send home, where they would become white people. Burial grounds were watched at night. Richards' harmonium, like certain Kongo musical instruments, was believed to speak with the voices of the dead. The Bible was a sort of charm, English and literacy were the gnostic language and technique of the new cult, dresses and trousers its vestments, and a certain number of deaths among the relatives of converts was to be expected as they paid the fee for their initiation (Andersson 1968:44). His congregants believed that Richards stored in his attic the souls of those who had died of sleeping sickness before exporting them; when they were shown that the

space was empty they said, "in daytime, yes;  but at
night - ah!" Mabie herself claimed that she had been
able to persuade one mission employee that whites
were people, not spirits, and that they reproduced
just as people do.

My informants in Manteke emphasized, in speaking
of Richards, a cluster of traits appropriate to what
was later called a prophet (ngunza), and some of them
explicitly and spontaneously so labeled him. He was
known from the first as a healer;  "now that the people no longer trust in their charms and gods of their
own making for healing of the body I have to be  doctor as well as bishop, evangelist, judge, etc.," he
wrote. People believe that he could control the
weather. In 1881 he reported that on one occasion
"they asked me to pray to God for rain, as I had told
them it was no use to pray to their idols for it. I
acceded to their request, and, although we had had no
rain for a long time and the crops were suffering, a
heavy shower came on in the afternoon" (Guinness
1890:276). In 1965 I heard that, as Richards' lega-
cy, rain always falls on Mbanza Manteke on Christmas
day, even though other villages remain dry;  that
year rain fell as predicted and the people said, "We
told you so." Richards was left-handed, and a number
of Manteke parents named their children Lumonso after
this attribute. He was also blind in one eye, as a
result of a hunting accident. Such details would not
in themselves cause him to be regarded as a prophet,
but since both of them are symbols of other-worldly
connections, they may have strengthened the respect
in which he was held.

The clearest fact about the Pentecost is that it
expressed popular acceptance of a new social order
which promised forever to defend the people against
witchcraft. They burned all their fetishes, and thus
stated, in effect, that since witchcraft had been
abolished they no longer needed to try to protect
themselves individually, and that they renounced all
self-seeking activities such as might have contributed to the suffering of others. Manteke people were
invited by the missionary to renounce evil defined as
paganism and subservience to "the Devil;"  they
responded, as they had done before and would do
again, by renouncing evil as they defined it, namely,
self-seeking traffic with the world of the dead. The
ambiguity is fundamental to the subsequent history of
Christianity in Kongo.

Mass capitulations of the Pentecostal type
occurred at other Protestant stations at about the

same time, and continued into the 1930's as new areas
came under mission influence. Meanwhile, Catholic
Redemptorist Fathers, Scheutists and Jesuits made up
for their late start, working closely with the Belgian authorities (Markowitz 1973; see Plate 1).
Protestants and Catholics tolerated each other with
difficulty, not only on theological grounds but
because Protestants came to see themselves as protecting their adherents from the State; Catholics,
as defending the State against subversive tendencies
encouraged by the religious doctrine and Anglo-Saxon
affiliations of the Protestants. Missions established zone-of-influence agreements, but only within
their respective denominations. From the point of
view of this study, the most important mission
domains included the Redemptorists in Matadi (station
founded in 1899) and across the river in Mayombe;
the Swedish Evangelical Mission in Matadi and Manianga (SMF,EEMM); the American Baptist Foreign
Missionary Society (ABFMS) in Mbanza Manteke, which
it took over from the Livingstone Inland Mission
(LIM); the (British) Baptist Missionary Society
(BMS) at Ngombe Lutete, north of Thysville (Mbanza
Ngungu), the Jesuits of Kisantu, on the Inkisi River;
and the American Baptists again at Nsona Mbata,
approaching Kinshasa. Between them, the missions
converted the BaKongo, educated most of them, and to
all appearance westernized them to a greater extent
than most African peoples.

In 1908, Belgium took over the Congo Free State,
which became Belgian Congo. Administrative control
of the population, and economic control of the country's resources, were rationalized, the
administrative policy being ostensibly that of
indirect rule, advocated in British colonies by Lord
Lugard. The state encouraged missionaries, especially Catholics, and worked closely with them. By 1920,
probably the majority of the BaKongo were at least
nominally converted, and most of the men had become
accustomed to wage labor.

Unlike the Christianity of pre-colonial Kongo,
the Christianity of Belgian Congo was not a type of
territorial fertility cult, if only because the political system in which cults were paired with those
of chiefs initiated into ancestral sequences had been
destroyed and there was no longer any function for
such a cult. Mission Christianity, far more closely
supervised than the Capuchins had ever managed, and
aided by the closely linked institutions of schooling
and wage labor, successfully resisted most Congolese

attempts to assimilate it. When Kimbanguism emerged
as a public Christian healing cult, its references to
localities and their spirits were no longer central;
they echoed rather than reproduced the deep chords of
the past.

"THE GREAT THING THAT HAPPENED ON 6 APRIL 1921!"

The emergence of Simon Kimbangu as a prophet
(watelama, he stood forth) is described by his second
son Dialungana, keeper of the holy city (JM No.39):

In Nkamba a man appeared who had never studied
at a mission station, but he was a believer and
had learned to read and write a little from a
village teacher. His name was Simon Kimbangu.
He raised the dead, caused the paralyzed to
stand upright, gave sight to the blind,
cleansed lepers, and healed all the sick in the
name of the Lord Jesus. But he chased away
those who practised witchcraft.
In the twinkling of an eye this news
spread, and the whole country went wild. Like
dust the news spread that in Nkamba had
appeared a Prophet who was raising the dead.
From that time Nkamba was called the New
Jerusalem.
1. The Prophet
2. The New Jerusalem
Think well on both of them.
When the prophet was revealed, the dead in
stretchers and the sick of all kinds were
brought to the Prophet of God. But in everything, whether raising the dead, healing the
sick, or giving a blessing in the name of
Jesus, first there must be prayer, then hymns,
and then a teacher must read the Bible and
teach the doctrines that change hearts, in
order that all men should leave their wickedness; for if that does not happen, then these
blessings you have come to get become as fire
to you. Believe in the Lord Jesus, he who
saves you from your sins. For I am in obedience to him.
Now God our Father and his Son Jesus
Christ are returned to us, so cease your
wickedness. Every day the doctrine of repen-
tance must be taught, and when it is finished
the sick will be healed and the dead raised.

Now see how all the villages hastened to abandon their fetishes; see all the roads littered with fetishes of all kinds. People confessed their sins. Drums were broken, dancing forsaken. People struggled to seek out teachers. Churches were built overnight in all the villages. Those who had not cared to pray to God fought for places in church, and those who had had no use for schools fought to enter the classroom.

Thus the words of Jesus were fulfilled, when he promised: And I will pray the Father, and he shall give you another Comforter, that he may abide with you for ever; Even the Spirit of truth; whom the world cannot receive, because it seeth him not, neither knoweth him (John 14:16-17).

See now the power of the Lord Jesus revealed in his Servant, Simon Kimbangu, he having said:

Verily, verily, I say unto you, He that believeth on me, the works that I do shall he do also; and greater works than these shall he do; because I go unto my Father (John 4:12).

Because Simon Kimbangu obeyed the voice of Jesus, all things promised by Jesus were fulfilled in him, the work of Jesus was revealed, and the names of God the Father and of the Lord Jesus were glorified. Since the coming of the missionaries it had never happened that the dead arose, the lame walked, and the blind saw; or that people of their own free will threw away their fetishes, or wanted to pray to God. And only then did we the people of Kongo know that God and Jesus remembered us. The grief and suffering of our fathers were wiped away in Kongo.

From this account it appears that in Kimbanguist opinion the missionary evangelization of Kongo failed because the mercenary impulses of the missionaries caused them to corrupt the gospel and deceive their converts; "for they were hired men, and cared not for the sheep." Their failure to demonstrate the power of God in healing made this deception evident.

The corresponding missionary account of events at Nkamba, as it apeared in Congo News Letter (July 1921), resembles Dialungana's with respect to the events, but locates the element of subterfuge elsewhere. The missionary author regarded the movement

as "largely a work of deception," which therefore
"cannot be of God," although "the methods and the
immediate results seem to be good." The prophets
claim power to heal in the name of Jesus, but "in
fact differ little from the old-time witch-doctor, in
that they use the name of Jesus instead of a fetish."
In April 1922 the journal commented, "Thousands of
sick and helpless folk claimed to be perfectly whole
in consequence [of Kimbangu's healing] though they
were quite as indisposed as ever. Never have I known
such a season of lying to be abroad in the land."
Nevertheless, Protestant missionaries saw much good
in the movement, which brought them, too, many new
adherents. In the Mbanza Manteke missionary field
there were 1160 baptisms, and stocks of Bibles were
exhausted throughout Lower Congo.

Tradition says that Kimbangu received his first
spiritual call in 1918 but refused it, going to Leopoldville (Kinshasa) to work instead (JM No.39).
1918 was also the year of the great influenza epidemic, which added many deaths to the enormous toll
already exacted in Lower Congo by sleeping sickness.
By 1970 tradition had moved the date of Halley's
comet to 1918 also, so that one of the elders of the
Kimbanguist Church (EJCSK), preaching in Matadi,
could refer to 1918 as the year of three remarkable
events: the comet, the epidemic, and Kimbangu's
call.[5]

Disappointed by his experience in Leopoldville,
Kimbangu returned to Nkamba in 1921. The biography
drawn up in 1921 by his secretaries indicates that he
blamed his lack of success on his failure to obtain
the approval of the elders for his venture;[6] the
rationalization is a standard one, but more recent
tradition blames his failure to heed God's call.
This too is a standard rationalization, drawn from
the cults of affliction.[7] The biography dates the
call, and his initial refusal, after Kimbangu's
return to Nkamba. In a dream, God said to him, "I
have heard your prayer; people think it is necessary
to have spirit to do my work, but I shall give you
that which surpasses" (Raymaekers 1971:26).

The work indicated was that of healing, but Kimbangu's first efforts, we are told, were frustrated
by the unbelief of relatives of persons he attempted
to heal by laying his hand upon them (Raymaekers
op.cit., pp. 27-29; JM 39). In the course of these
efforts Kimbangu experienced a specific rivalry with
the local Protestant catechist, who represented missionary religion and its supposedly erroneous

Pl.1: The original iron Catholic church
in Boma and its modern successor

Pl.2: Kimbanguist church, Manianga

interpretation of the Bible.  This catechist, Mvwala,
sneered at Kimbangu's blessings;  meanwhile, he had a
dream of his own, and a relative of his "emerged as a
prophet."  Kimbangu  privately  knew, because of what
God had revealed to him of the matter, that this prophet's spirit was a "demon," attributable to Mvwala's
jealousy.

Mvwala's dream, which in Kimbangu's opinion he
failed to interpret properly, showed him two men carrying flags, one white and one black, and followed by
a  crowd of children.  It instructed him to preach on
the parable of the wise and foolish virgins,  holding
in  his  right  hand  a  pure and in his left hand an
impure vessel.  Kimbangu interpreted it as a  warning
to Mvwala himself to recognize the true light when it
shone in Kimbangu's own works.  One may suppose  that
Mvwala's  own  interpretation of his dream pointed to
the propriety of cooperating with white missionaries.

In April 1921 Kimbangu's  healing  was  suddenly
successful.  Among the first group of more than sixty
persons healed, the biography picks out one  who  was
paralyzed,  a  blind  man, a deaf man, and a crippled
child.  The intention of the text is to show a parallel  to  Matthew 15:30-31, "And great multitudes came
unto him ...  and he healed them, in so much that the
multitude  wondered  when they saw the dumb to speak,
the maimed to be whole, the  lame  to  walk  and  the
blind to see;  and they glorified the God of Israel."
Kimbanguists nowadays count off the  four  categories
on their fingers.  Later incidents are represented in
the biography as  fulfilling  the  prophecy  in  Mark
16:17-18 ("they shall take up serpents").

People began to seek out  the  new  prophet  but
those  who  came were mostly lapsed Christians, while
the adepts remained skeptical (Raymaekers  1971:33).
Among  his  followers the prophet dealt with an early
challenge to his authority by appearing  before  them
in a fit ("he foamed at the mouth and trembled in all
his limbs").  His spiritual  feats,  ever  more  marvelous,  included raising a child three days dead and
an encounter with a mfumu mpu, a chief consecrated on
a leopardskin, who responded with pagan obeisances to
being healed.  The prophet reproved him, saying  that
he should believe only in Christ, but the chief hank-
ered after his chiefship and  his  disease  returned.
Meanwhile  the vexatious question of "false prophets"
repeatedly arose.  The Nkamba group expected  persons
claiming  to  be prophets, who saw visions and healed
the sick, to submit themselves to Kimbangu's  inspec-
tion.  The spirit occupying many of them he declared

to be false, a "demon." The history of Kimbanguism
from this time on amply demonstrates that questions
of authority and discipline underlie judgments of
spiritual validity. Be that as it may, within a few
weeks there were prophets in villages all over Kongo.
    The local administrator, L. Morel, visited Nkam-
ba on 11 May. This description by Maquet-Tombu
(1952:140) summarizes Morel's own official report
(Archives of Cataracts District, located in Mbanza
Ngungu; cf. Ryckmans 1970:42-43).

> From a distance he saw, in the little pla-
> teau where the village was built, the noise of
> an excited crowd. He saw coming towards him  a
> strange group, yelling and gesticulating: two
> young men and two girls surrounding the princi-
> pal figure, dressed in red trousers and a white
> shirt, and holding in his hand the prophet's
> staff--Kimbangu himself! All five trembled
> ecstatically ... A crowd of people of all ages
> milled through the village, with the sick lying
> among them. No more dead bodies had been
> brought since God had told the prophet to for-
> bid it ... Kimbangu and his group continued to
> surround the white man with cries and gestures,
> and then the prophet, Bible in hand, read aloud
> the story of how David felled Goliath. To make
> quite clear what he meant, one of the girls
> showed the administrator a picture of the giant
> laid low.

    The biography's account of Morel's visit is not
very different from his own, though it has Kimbangu
reciting the 3rd Psalm rather than the story of Goliath. It describes the white man as "the enemy".
    On 18 May the BMS missionary from Ngombe Lutete,
R.L.Jennings, visited Nkamba. The biography does not
mention the event but puts in its place an encounter
at Ngombe Lutete in which the prophet trembled
violently and refused to greet Jennings, showing by
these signs that his spirit was responding to the
presence of evil. Popular traditions say that Jennings, on his visit to Nkamba, saw Kimbangu's
miracles, broke into tears, and confessed that Europeans at home exercised the same powers although in
Congo they denied them. A Manteke man who was there
at the time described Jennings' visit to me (JM No.
41). His description is consistent with Jennings'
own report, which has only recently been published.

Jennings "saw no miracles but folk who appeared demented," and was "satisfied of the falsity of it all... Barriers were raised within which the sick folk were gathered. I was asked to address the people, and kind words spoken of me as their missionary who with others had brought to them the light of God's word" (Irvine 1974).

Provoked by the general suspension of agricultural and industrial labor as most of the population downed tools to visit the prophets, by the alleged danger of disease as the sick and even the dead were carried to Nkamba, and by estimates that the prophets were anti-colonial ("xenophobic," in the colonial euphemism), the government put down the movement. As Protestants noted, the fear of anti-colonial militancy was based partly on a misunderstanding of the evangelical idiom of the hymns the prophets took from the missions. Assistant District Commissioner Dupuis forwarded to his superior a copy of two "seditious songs" then being sung in the Thysville region. One of them read in part: "Ambasi nutuyikama mu nzingu eto wau" (Angels, join with us now in our [spiritual] struggle), which Dupuis mistranslated as, "Ambassadeurs, joignez vous à nous dans notre guerre actuelle," and read as an appeal to foreign powers. Perennially jealous of their colony, Belgians were alarmed by reports that Kimbangu had foretold "the return of the Americans," which suggested to Dupuis "une intervention americaine dans les affaires de la Colonie" (Correspondence, Cataracts District, 26 July 1921; 10 September 1921). According to Congo News Letter, however (April 1922),

> There seems to have been little or nothing distinctly revolutionary in the movement. Its chief peril lay in the wonderful solidarity it effected in so brief a period among a hitherto disassociated population; also in its undoubted anti-white attitude. There was a strong tendency towards separation from missionary control and oversight in many districts. Catholic missions would seem to have suffered most.

The government's files on "l'affaire Kimbangu" show that the informants who mostly strongly emphasized the anti-governmental aspects of the movement were chiefs and village headmen, all government appointees. Missionaries seem to have turned for

information to station Christians. Europeans had
hardly any direct contact with the prophets, except
those who had been arrested.

In June Morel was instructed to arrest Kimbangu,
but the prophet escaped and remained in hiding until
September when he returned to Nkamba, apparently to
give himself up. He was tried at Thysville amid
mounting Belgian hysteria and sentenced to death but
the sentence was later commuted to life imprisonment
(Chomé 1959). Jennings and Dupuis were among the few
who defended him and argued for clemency.

Morel put the region of Mbanza Manteke under
military occupation in August 1921. The standard
text of his order forbade the use of drums as a means
of communication (it is doubtful that drum techniques
were that sophisticated in Kongo), controlled movement, forbade meetings, and declared all healthy
adults liable to forced labor. On 20 August Morel
arrested in Lundu hamlet three prophets, one a woman,
all of whom trembled at their interrogation and "in-
sulted" the government chief of Manteke (Kingalu),
calling him "Judas" (MacGaffey 1970b:267). One of
them said he had been a prophet since 5 July, having
seen during the night a bright light and a white man
who instructed him to heal the sick in the name of
Jesus. The next day Morel arrested Joshua Na Fuka,
Noah (Matanga) and Zodulwa, all of Vunda; Nsimba
Samuel and Bwela, of Bete; Johnny Lusumbu of
Kibemba; and Filipo Kayi of Manteke. Na Fuka had
built a "symbolic enclosure," that is, an arrangement
of fences to control the movement of those seeking
healing. Filipo Kayi, who had a limp and a beard,
built himself a prayer retreat on the east side of
the Manteke plateau (Yongo) to which he would repair
at dawn; informants in 1965 drew the parallel with
Richards' retreat on the west side, to which he
betook himself at sundown.

The prophet Mabwaka from Kemba responded to
Morel's interrogation as follows (text, in bad
French, by Morel's clerk; cf. JM Nos.15,16):

> First, I slept, and then God told me in my
> sleep to examine the images (examiner les
> images) for three days then later after the
> prescribed delay I sang the canticles of God
> and looked at the images which were open and I
> saw a great book from which God took various
> objects that he gave me in my sleep. Then I
> awoke, and began to tremble. I healed the
> sick.

On 25 August Morel reported to the assistant district commissioner that he had found some 100 prophets and lesser prophets and had put an end to the prophetic movements in the Manteke area, though he felt certain they continued in secret. He had given orders that the villages be cleaned up and the cultivation of rice begun.

Kimbangu died in prison in Elisabethville (Lubumbashi) in 1951. Catholic sources reported that he had died a good death, that is, that he had confessed and been received into the Church at the end; reports to this effect were circulating among Catholic clergy as early as 1939.[8] Meanwhile Kimbangu's followers continued to be arrested, the movement taking new forms under different leaders in various times and places (Andersson 1958). Among the variants we should note the north bank (Manianga) form known as ngounzisme, which eventually gave rise to the group of churches known as Dibundu dia Mpeve a Nlongo (DMN).

In 1934 the arrival of the Salvation Army, in association with the economic conditions of the day, started a new mass movement. The Army's red flag, its military idiom, and the "S" mistakenly supposed to stand for Simon all suggested that Kimbangu had returned to renew the prophetic struggle. European officers found themselves functioning willy-nilly as healers and witch-detectors. Eventually this mistaken enthusiasm found its own leader in the extraordinary figure of Mpadi Simon-Pierre, whose followers, like himself, came mostly from eastern Kongo. Mpadi called his movement the Mission des Noirs, later the Eglise des Noirs en Afrique (the Black Church, ENAF). After Mpadi's imprisonment in 1949, a disciple called Mavonda Ntangu combined Mpadism with Matswanism to form the Khaki movement, widespread during the 1950's in what was then the French colony of Moyen Congo. Matswanism was named after Andre Matswa, founder of a socio-political association deemed subversive by the French authorities; neither it nor Khakism is of direct concern in this study (see Andersson 1958; Sinda 1972). Table 1 provides a summary of these developments.

## Prophetism revived

In the mid-1950's a major resurgence associated with growing political activity against the colonial government culminated, in 1959, in official recognition of EJCSK and the return from exile, in 1960, of

Table 1.
Historical catalogue of modern prophetism.

```
1886   Pentecost of the Congo
1921   Kimbanguism
         1930   Ngunzism
                  1961   DMNA, Masamba
                  1962   Mission Prophétique
                            1964   DMN, Nlandu
                            1964   DMN, Difuene
                  1962   Eglise Prophétique
                            1963   DMN, Mbumba
                            1963   DMN, Major
         1939   Mission des Noirs, Mpadi
                  1949   Khakism, Mavonda Ntangu
         1957   EJCSK, Diangienda
                  1961   Eglise Congolaise, Bamba
                  1961?  ECUSE, Gonda
                  1963   EJCDT, Kimosi
         1960   Kinenism
         196?   DMN, Nsansi
1960   EUDA, Dizolele
```

surviving prophets such as Mabwaka and Mpadi. In
April 1960 Kimbangu's remains were brought back to
his native village, Nkamba, renamed the New
Jerusalem, and placed in a mausoleum built on the top
of the hill, near the remains of the platform from
which he used to preach and above the pool (Bethesda)
to which he sent the sick to bathe. The leaders of
EJCSK were the prophet's three sons, known as the
zimvwala, of whom the youngest, Joseph Diangienda, as
Mfumu a Nlongo, was head of the church and successor
to Kimbangu; Dialungana K.Salomon was in charge of
Nkamba; and Charles Kisolokele was a businessman and
politician, for a time a member of the government of
the Democratic Republic of Congo. Their efforts to
unite all Kimbanguists in a single national church
were unsuccessful. During the first decade of the
independent republic a multitude of churches and
would-be churches of very different character
emerged, each with its own view of its place in local
society, world history, and God's spiritual plan.
        This ecclesiastical multiplicity matched, and
was closely related to, the multiplicity of political
parties and secessionist regimes that sprang up in
the Democratic Republic of Congo after it won its
independence in 1960. A period of general instability ended in 1965 with the accession to power by coup

d'état of General Mobutu Sese Seko, who replaced all
political parties with his own Popular Revolutionary
Movement (MPR). In 1971 Mobutu forced the consolidation of most of the churches ("religious
communities") into an approved list of six (Young
1965; Willame 1972).In the years that followed, a
number of Kongo churches (including, among those discussed in the next chapter, DMNA and EUDA) sought
membership in the new national Protestant church,
ECZ. In 1977, the national synod of ECZ gave provi-
sional membership to 28 such groups from the country
as a whole. A later synod revoked it. In January
1979, amendments to the law of 1971 forbade any
church or sect to exist except as a registered
non-profit association; forbade anyone to preach
religion or receive tithes or gifts except in the
name of a registered church; denied the possibility
of registration to any church or sect whose doctrines
did not differ substantially from those of all
churches already registered; prescribed a fine for
unauthorized preaching in public or private; and
empowered the government to suspend any church whose
internal conflicts threatened the peace.

## KINENE JEAN

One of the smallest and thus most nearly typical
of the movements was founded by Kinene. In 1970 the
DMN-Kinene seemed to have remained close to the
grass-roots prophetism of the past in its direct connection with specific local problems, its equally
direct confrontations with the Spirit, and its inno-
cence in public relations. Here old hymns could
still be heard that other churches had forgotten.
Kinene Jean belonged to the Nlaza clan in Kinkanza, a large village near Mbanza Manteke. Born in
1915, he was educated at Nsona Mpangu and in the
mid-thirties he was trained as a medical assistant at
the American Baptist Mission, Nsona Mbata, where he
must have been a contemporary of Mpadi Simon. The
church he subsequently founded may have owed some of
its unusual features to the influence of Mpadi,
although the latter says he did not know Kinene until
1960. After completing his diploma, Kinene was
employed for some time as a nurse by the mission at
Mpalabala, near Matadi. Tradition says that he
sought to leave mission employ and achieved his end
by impregnating three women in the village. A few
days after his dismissal he took ship from Matadi and
spent seven months traveling abroad. By his own

account he went to Mecca, "a village near Jerusalem, where there is a house not built with hands, that descended from the sky. Any sinner entering it who does not thoroughly purge himself of evil will die on the way out." After returning to Kinkanza he was arrested for prophetism in 1953 and sent to Lowa, in Upper Congo.

On his release in 1960, Kinene knew some success as a prophet in Kinkanza, though less than Mabwaka's in nearby Kemba. It is obvious that his movement was connected with the chronic political disputes of the Nlaza clan, which in about 1960 divided, against his will, into three exogamous sections. The principal adherents of Kinenism to this day are members of his section and its allies from other clans. In 1960 Diangienda's EJCSK was trying hard to unite all the Kongo prophets into a single church; man of Kinene's followers urged him to go to Nkamba "to have his kingunza tested," that is, to have his prophetic calling authenticated. Such a course implied the candidate's recognition of the authority of Nkamba, and Kinene was reluctant to go. In 1961 he went and his followers report that when he ascended to the New Jerusalem after bathing in the pool the eyes of all present were opened and they saw a choir of twenty-one angels in the heavens. But unlike Mabwaka he did not join EJCSK; many of his followers did, and some at least appear to have been received with special favor. The death of the child born to the woman he had married after his return from exile affected him deeply; he said that his own time had come and in February 1962 he died. "He did not grow old; God called him away." His few remaining followers speak of many miracles surrounding his death, and await his coming again. The fact that nobody else takes note of the miracles is itself proof, to them, that the last great age of unbelief is already upon us.

In Kinkanza, Kinenist rituals made use of a series of structures. Ordinary services such as those still held in Matadi in 1970 took place in a church whose narthex provided separate entrances and also separate exits for each sex. At the opposite end of the church was an enclosed pulpit, also with its entrance and exit, and behind it a special door to the church for the use of the prophet alone. Men and women sat on the right and left sides, respectively, of the nave; between them sat the choir, consisting largely of children. After the service in church the congregation, or some of them, might proceed to a

spiritual cleansing and testing which began in a
second structure called the mangu, after the mango
tree standing at its center;  mangu also means "miracle." Sinners entered the mangu to confess their sins
in the presence of witnesses, who said nothing.
Connected with the mangu in some way was another
enclosure, "like a dispensary," in which sick people
could receive holy water.  The mango itself was a
tree upon which "the power of God" (wiisa kya Nzambi)
had descended and its leaves had miraculous healing
properties.

After confessing, one proceeded towards a circular enclosure, the Table Ronde, passing between the
ranks of a juvenile choir.  If they continued to sing
and did not tremble or shout "Go back! Adulterer!
Thief!" or the like, he would enter the Table Ronde,
passing by the prophet on his right, and if all went
well (vo nungini) he would arrive at another sacred
tree in the center, an African poplar
(mumpese-mpese), to which were tied palm leaves
(mandala).  This tree was a "sign" (dimbu), "the eyes
of God." On reaching it he would tremble, if he had
mpeve ("spirit"), and if so he would make his way to
the right side of the enclosure (the left, for a
woman);  if not, he would simply leave by the way he
came.  The Table Ronde was outlined with candles;  in
ordinary use, the expression table ronde refers to a
coven of witches meeting to dispose of a victim, but
in this instance a gathering of the saints is meant.
The earth from the ordeal passage from mangu to Table
Ronde, "the earth where we walked," was a powerful
purge if eaten;  "you needed no other medicine."

The stages of the Kinenist ritual corresponding
to the three principal structures--church, mangu,
Table Ronde--are similar to those of the DMN churches
(described in subsequent chapters) but details such
as the candles and the juvenile choir of spiritual
detectives recall Mpadi's Black Church.  Kinene did
not prophesy (bikula) much;  he left that to
spirit-possessed assistants, but he would listen to
one's troubles and offer advice.  At the conclusion
of the ritual he would withdraw to his house, in
front of which was another enclosure in which the
prophet entertained his followers with stories and
predictions. He told them about troubles in Pales-
tine and in America and predicted the arrival of a
messiah who was "between" Christ and Kimbangu and
superior to them.  In his wide view of the world,
acquired on his travels, Kinene once again resembles
Mpadi, but it is also likely that he had been influ-

enced by Watchtower. The messiah, he said, would
sweep away the world's institutions and replace them
with a new government. Among the portents of this
event would be the appearance of a new currency ("in
those days," said my informants, "Kasa-Vubu's coinage
had not yet been seen")[9] and a military regime
which would oppress the people ("Mobutu, obviously,"
said my informants). The prophecy was based on a
program revealed to Kinene in a dream while he was
confined at Songololo in 1953, of which he thought so
much that he had copies printed in the great enthusiastic year 1960. The program consists of eight ages
(tandu), divided into four pairs. The first age in
each pair is an age of prophets--Noah, Jesus, Kimbangu, and "ourselves;" the second is an age of apostles
in which, despite prophecies and miracles of healing,
the people follow fleshly counsels. The eighth age
is described as follows: "The time of recrimination
has come (lookula kyansembolo kilungidi). Belief in
the Lord of Heaven and his helpers is absent. People
prefer witchcraft, killing others without good reason, quarrelling, adultery, theft, dirty books,
misconduct of women in the presence of men, man with
man, woman with woman, so that procreation ceases.
For such people there is no heaven; for them dawns
only the fire of hell (i mbungulu kaka ku tiya twa
bilungi)."
        This vision of doom contains the only reference
to homosexuality I encountered in my fieldwork. In
another dream the penalties for various sins were
revealed to the prophet, in two grades, one appropriate to this age and another, usually double the
first, for the age of the messiah's reign. Most of
the sins involve the use of violence, domestic
disputes, or false witness. Harboring resentment
against another deserves two years of "punition",)
probably meaning some form of excommunication and
isolation. Wife-beating is worth one year;
husband-beating, two. Man and wife, for lack of con-
jugal affection (kolama luzolo lwakala mu fuku),
deserve three months' punishment.
        Kinenist rituals are no longer conducted at Kin-
kanza. The only active congregation (1970) is in
Matadi and even there numbers decline, as "many who
used to pray now drink instead." Two former leaders,
I was told, left after prophets (mim'bikudi) revealed
that they were leading a double life and coming at
night (in dreams) to attack members of the church.
The remainder of the faithful, daily expecting the
messiah, meet after work in a spare room of a house

near the Leopold II ravine. Both sexes use the same
two doors, one for entrance and one for exit.
Everyone removes his shoes and kneels to pray before
entering the church. The interior, or part of it, is
outlined by candles for certain events, and is sprinkled with water on every occasion. When the church
is closed, a single candle is left burning inside.
All these precautions are intended to keep off
"evil-hearted people" (bantima mbi).

At one end of the church is a small table with a
bucket of water under it. In front of the table is a
space (kinlongo) where the elders sit, three or four
men, often wearing white shirts and trousers. One of
them is the official leader, the Representative.
Other men sit in the back row of the benches that
take up the rest of the church. The congregation
rarely exceeds ten men and twenty women. The order
of service, which may vary to suit the circumstances,
includes the following phases: (1) an ordinary Protestant service, (2) Nsongolo, "showing," (3)
Nkotosolo a bougies, "entry between the candles",
that is, to the space in front of the table, the
kinlongo, delimited by a candle in each corner, (4)
Nwa maza, "drinking water," (5) Mpayikulu, "exit."

The Nsongolo is one of the central features of
Kinenism. Members recite their dreams, of which the
Representative interprets as many as he likes and
offers advice, in a quiet voice and with no spiritualist manifestations. Most of the interpretations
refer obliquely to members' relatives back home in
Kinkanza, considered to be witches; some dreams are
regarded as admonishing the dreamer on account of his
own failings. This time is also used for public confession, as when a man admitted having been angry for
three hours against a workmate who had unfairly
brought blame upon him. The dreams are often about
water. One man dreamed that he and a friend were
crossing a large river (nzadi) when a crocodile, who
was really a Kinkanza enemy, chased them, sometimes
in the shape of a crocodile and sometimes in the
shape of a man. Fortunately, as he reached the other
bank, the dreamer was inspired to sing a hymn,
whereupon the crocodile desisted. Another man
dreamed that while bathing in a pool he felt himself
drawn into the depths by the currents. After scrambling out he met someone who warned him that there
were bisimbi in the pool. When he reached his village he found that a funeral was in progress.

In principle, at least, the "entry between the
candles" follows a strict order of precedence. After

lighting the candles and sprinkling the kinlongo with
water, two elders enter it "to pray for strength from
the Holy Spirit." Afterwards they stand outside the
space, praying, while others enter, some of whom are
also sprinkled, as their condition or their dreams
dictate.   The order of precedence is (1) pregnant
women, (2) those who have had bad dreams or visions
(men first), (3) the sick, (4) the seriously sick,
(5) children, (6) married couples, "to have a blessing on their house," (7) men without wives, (8) women
without husbands, (9) girls, (10) those with fever.
The water used comes from an ordinary enamel basin
whose plain white color is regarded as important.   A
few grains of earth from the Table Ronde in Kinkanza
are added to the water.

In the next two phases of the ritual three
categories of persons take turns:   (1) those who have
mpeve, (2) those without, (3) children.   The first
category, including most of the congregation, consists of those who tremble and see visions (bitezo).
When "drinking water" these people also apply water
to their eyes to preserve their vision.   In "tram-
pling water," or "washing the feet," the participants
walk the wet floor of the kinlongo, pouring more
water on their feet.   In the last phase, more candles
are lit and everybody enters the space together for
prayers and a final hymn during which all file out.
As they go, some rub mud from the floor on their
faces and arms.

Hymns are sung at frequent intervals, some of
them being specifically associated with parts of the
ritual.   One hymn is explicitly nationalistic:

Tata Simon appeared in Kongo Africa:
Not in Europe any more,
Not the white man any more.
For the black race, in Kongo,
Jesus appeared;  the church was built.
Let me pray:  Lord Jesus, hear me.

No percussion is used, except handclapping.
Many of the hymns come from the Protestant hymnbook;
others are old Kimbanguist hymns, sung in a style
which in 1970 could scarcely be heard anywhere else.
Some, attributed to Kinene himself, owe more to the
musical traditions of Kinkanza, and the best of these
recites the tribulations of his life:

The elders of Kinkanza accused me before the
government, they conspired against me.   My

brethren, do you not know me any more?

    When I went to Lowa they put handcuffs  on
me,  they  sat  down  to  plot  against me.  My
brethren, don't you remember?

    When I went to Lowa I raised the  dead,  I
caused  the  lame to walk.  My brethren, do you
not know me any more?

    The elders of Nkamba conspired against me,
they sat down to plot against me.  My brethren,
don't you remember?

    The refrain of this song, Mu  lulendo  yi  momo
kakwizila  "In power may he come," is very similar to
the   Munkukusa   anthem.   Munkukusa   was   an
anti-witchcraft or purification rite practiced briefly in Kinkanza and elsewhere  in  1952,  just  before
Kinene's  debut  as  a  prophet (JM No.26;  Kimpianga
1981).
    Many members of the congregation, not  including
the  elders, are in a state of possession during much
of the ritual, to a greater extent than in any  other
church.   One man maintained a statuesque pose, punc-
tuating his trance with stentorian announcements such
as  "Abalahami!"  or "Adami ye Eva!," but most people
shrieked and trembled,  with  unusual  violence.    In
this state they often see "visions" which they subsequently  report  to  the  congregation,  to  the
accompaniment  of still more spiritual agitation.   On
my  first  and  last  visits  a  special  ritual  was
arranged which provoked extraordinary manifestations.
I was asked to "shake hands" (vana mbote) with everyone.   When  I  agreed  I  was  asked to stand in the
middle of the kinlongo, surrounded by candles,  while
the  entire congregation, men first, filed out by one
door, reentered by the other and came one by  one  to
shake  my  hand.   In  the  ensuing exercise (closely
resembling a  "weighing"  or  bascule  in  other  DMN
churches;   JM  No.48)  most of the participants, men
and women, trembled violently and jumped in  the  air
continuously  for  several minutes at a time, holding
me by the hand.  Most of the men were  manual  laborers,  and  since Kongo women in general  are  also
extremely muscular I found it easier, after the  last
of the congregation had passed by, to take notes with
my left hand.  While the procession continued,  hymns
were sung and many women were possessed.  The visions
they subsequently reported were filled  with  conventional  evangelical  imagery:  Bibles, tables, bright
lights, halos, rainbows, hands reaching from  heaven,
and beautiful shining strangers standing behind me.

In fulfilling to some extent the congregation's
expectations I was governed by my sense of what pol-
iteness required. The secretary afterwards explained
to me that he had had a vision, some time before, of
one of Christ's messengers visiting in the form of a
white man who shook hands and gave a blessing. He
asked if I were authorized to give blessings, but I
said I was not. The handshaking was regarded not as
a test, as the "weighing" is, but as a spiritual
strengthening. As such it had much in common with
the other rituals of the Kinenist kinlongo, which
together exemplify the proposition that spiritual
healing, fortification and greeting are ritual
efforts to affirm social categories and relationships.

# 2

# *Churches in Modern Kongo*

Popular accounts of the origins of churches in Lower Zaire resemble the traditions associated with chiefship or an old-fashioned charm (<u>n'kisi</u>). They describe the miraculous circumstances in which power was first communicated by the spirit to the founder, and trace the line of his successors down to the present day in such a way as to emphasize the uniqueness and authenticity of the heritage of this particular congregation, while discrediting the claims of others. The adherents of each tradition see their spirit as not only authentic but universal; like the heirs of the chiefs, they are infinitely optimistic about the horizon of their due respect, which extends from any little village to "Zaire, to Africa, and indeed the whole world." They quickly point out the local roots and parochial appeal of all competing traditions.

The spokesmen for such traditions seek to co-opt the fieldworker and the casual enquirer alike. The ethnography and the local-level political history of Kongo both testify to the success some have had in persuading foreigners that theirs is the one authentic chiefship, or that their charm has been handed down in unbroken succession from Mbanza Kongo. In Mbanza Manteke in 1965 I sought to avoid their individual seductive appeal, making a point of collecting traditions from all descent groups and treating none of them as a privileged document whose "truth" defined the "falsehood" of the others. In 1970 I sought the structure of Kimbanguism in the same way, choosing the port city of Matadi as a sample population. It is central to the KiKongo speaking area of Zaire and large enough to include representatives of all the regions of that area and of most of the

churches active among the BaKongo, to whom the findings can reasonably be generalized. Matadi is
described in more detail in the next chapter.

The problem was to compare two natural
universes, the population of the town as a whole and
the list of churches supported by that population, on
the assumption that any church establishes its identity not only by what it stands for but by what it
stands against. Why is it that people with some
degree of choice join one church and not another?
The data are not nearly complete, but are sufficient
to show the importance of regional, occupational, and
other variables. They also permit a classification
of the churches in ideological terms appropriate to
them, that is to say, that are intrinsic or endo-
genous. The inventory of churches also represents
the history of public religion since 1921 to the
extent that it has been a process of institutional
differentiation.

Studies of African religious phenomena usually
proceed by taking one such as Kimbanguism in isolation, as though it were a fabricated object, listing
its apparent attributes, labeling it and depositing
it in a category of similar objects. The partisans
of each of the sets of categories competing for
attention in the field of comparative religious studies argue that a little further research will show
that all the phenomena in question fall neatly into
one or other of the categories proposed. No such
project has yet succeeded, and the reason is not far
to seek. The categories proposed--nativistic, messianic, modernizing, witchfinding, and the
like--refer to motivations attributed to the actor.
Verification of motives is necessarily a difficult
task and the results will always be arbitrary and
intuitive unless the actor is seen concretely as an
individual choosing between a limited set of possibilities open to him. What these possibillities are
can never be determined a priori, but must be ascertained on the spot by a sufficiently comprehensive
inquiry. They are established within a given cultural milieu at an historically specific period by the
interaction of churches and other organizations which
compete for the loyalty of potential recruits among
the public and must therefore differentiate their
several personalities in the public eye. A Kimbanguist church, that is to say, should be examined not
only for what it is but what it is not. Such differentiation is both collective and ideological; it
cannot be expected to reveal either the objectively

real functions of a church or the actual motivations
of individual members.

## A SURVEY OF CHURCHES IN MATADI

We began by compiling a list of churches from communal records.[1] The records referred only to such
organizations as came to the government's notice, but
in fact most churches and many individual religious
specialists (healers) asked for government recognition to reduce the possibility that in the event of
trouble the government would regard them as threats
to public order. It is likely that a number of very
small organizations, churches recruited from only one
or two villages, escaped our attention, particularly
those originating in the northern and coastal regions
of Mayombe, where we had few personal contacts. One
such church, the small Kinenist group (DMN-Kinene)
described in the previous chapter, was contacted only
after persistent enquiries based on prior knowledge
of its existence.

Other organizations not contacted by us but
probably or certainly represented in Matadi included
the following: Islam, whose mosque in Mvuzi Commune
was attended by Senegalese traders and by a group of
Kongo converts from nearby Mpalabala; the Eglise
Evangélique Congolaise au Mayombe, formed by schism
from the Christian and Missionary Alliance of Boma;
the Eglise Sainte de Jésus par le Prophète Simon Kimbangu, a Yombe group which recently seceded from
EJCSK; and the Angolan church of Simão Toco. The
term "church" is intended simply to translate the
KiKongo dibundu. I distinguish below the different
kinds of organization to which this word was applied
by the members, and comment on the significance of
membership.

## Numerical strength of the churches

Many of the smaller churches had very similar
names; government correspondence often mentioned how
difficult it was to tell them apart. In what follows, some churches are referred to by initials.
Since some of them have also changed their names from
time to time, Table 2 also gives the name of the
founder or official representative as an aid to identification.[2]

The figures in the table vary greatly in
reliability. The Apostles[3] and the Salvation Army
were efficiently organized and the figures given for

Table 2. Adult Church Membership in Matadi,1970.

| Abbrev. | Full Name; founder or leader. | |
|---|---|---|
| DMNA | Dibundu dia Mpeve a Nlongo mu Afrique (Eglise du Saint Esprit en Afrique), Masamba Esaie. | 100 |
| DMN-Difuene | Mission Prophétique Ngounzisme, Difuene Emmanuel. | 100 |
| DMN-Kinene | Dibundu dia Mpeve a Nlongo, Kinene Jean. | 50 |
| DMN-Major | Mission Prophétique Congolaise, J.B.Batiaka-Kibenga. | 50 |
| DMN-Mbumba | Eglise Prophétique Congolaise, Mbumba Philippe. | 280 |
| DMN-Nlandu | Eglise Nationale Ngounziste du Congo, Nlandu Nathaniel. | 250 |
| DMN-Nsansi | Eglise Mpeve a Nlongo, Félix Nsansi. | 100 |
| Catholic | Eglise Catholique. | 12,000 |
| EC-Gonda (ECUSE) | Eglise Chrétienne Union Saint Esprit, Gonda André. | 200 |
| EJCSK | Eglise de Jésus Christ sur la Terre par le Prophète Simon Kimbangu, Joseph Diangienda ku Ntima. | 3,544 |
| ENAF | Eglise des Noirs en Afrique, Mpadi Simon-Pierre. | 100 |
| EUDA (Apostles) | Eglise Universelle de Douze Apôtres, Isaac Dizolele | 185 |
| Protestant (EECK) (ECZ) | Eglise Evangélique du Christ au Congo Kinshasa, later incorporated in Eglise du Christ au Zaire. | 7,195 |
| Salvation Army | | 67 |
| Witnesses | Témoins de Jehovah | 100 |
| | Total | 24,321 |

them were taken from closely controlled membership
lists.   Other  churches  such as DMN-Difuene gave an
impression of bureaucratic organization which inspec-
tion   showed   to   be merely part of the ritual of the
church, without efficient substance;   the   membership
figures   cited   by their representatives ("2,837 membres  flottants")  reflected  wishful  thinking  (cf.
Bernard   1970:212).    Others   such as DMNA were unin-
terested  in  bureaucratic  efficiency  and  did  not
pretend  to  know  how  large  they  were.   In these
instances the figures  in  the  table  represent  our
estimates  of  effective  membership, based on attendance counts.  The Protestant and  Catholic  Churches
suffered   the   consequences  of  being  prestigious
churches whose rolls included many  inactive  members
recruited through the system of confessional schools.
The official figures  given  in  the  table  are  too
large,  but  we  have  not  attempted to make our own
estimates of effective membership.   The   same  situation  may have characterised EJCSK, but the number is
smaller in this instance and it was obvious that this
church's  control  over  its  members was much closer
than than of the Catholics or Protestants.[4]

## The Regional factor

The leaders of nearly every church described  it
as  a universal church and were unresponsive to questions  tending  to  reveal  the  contrary.   All  the
churches in fact showed a clear regional affiliation.
Since there are no statistics  it  is  impossible  to
make  specific comparisons with the regional composi-
tion  of  the  general  population  of  Matadi.   The
history  of  politics  in  Matadi  from  1962 to 1964
shows, however, that the BaMboma and BaManianga  were
the  strongest  groups  in the city.  They controlled
the Mvuzi and Nzanza communes, respectively, and also
the Catholic and Protestant churches.

The term "BaMboma" applies to the inhabitants of
southern  Mayombe  between  Boma and Seke Banza.   The
dominance of this group among Catholics was attributable  to  the  strong  and  long-established Catholic
missions in the area.  On the south side of the Zaire
River,  the  people  of  Songololo Territory are also
called BaMboma but they are heavily Protestant.    It
is  not clear whether they were allied with the other
BaMboma in Matadi politics in the 1960's.

The Protestant Church (EECK)  was  formerly  the
Eglise  Evangélique  de Matadi et du Manianga (EEMM),
founded by  Swedish  missionaries but  merged  in 1970

Table 3.   The regional factor in church membership.

| | | | | | | | |
|---|---|---|---|---|---|---|---|
| EUDA | 1 | 2 | 3 | | | | |
| DMN-Difuene | 1 | 2 | 3 | | | | |
| DMN-Mbumba | | | 3 | | | | |
| DMN-Major | | | 3 | | | | |
| DMN-Nlandu | | 2 | | | | | |
| Catholic | 1 | 2 | | | 5 | | |
| DMN-Nsansi | | 2 | | | | | |
| EJCSK | | 2 | | 4 | | 6 | |
| DMN-Kinene | | | | 4 | | | |
| Witnesses | | | | 4 | 5 | | |
| Protestant | | | | 4 | 5 | 6 | |
| DMNA | | | | | 5 | | |
| Salvation Army | | | | | 5 | 6 | 7 |
| EC-Gonda | | | | | | | 7 |
| ENAF | | | | | | | 7 8 |

Numbers 1-8 designate regions, approximately from West to East, as follows:

1. Northern Mayombe      5. Eastern Manianga
2. Southern Mayombe      6. Ndibu
3. Western Manianga       7. Ntandu
4. Manteke                    8. Zombo

Table 4.
Regional origin of male leaders in three churches.

| | EJCSK (Nzanza) | EUDA | DMN-Difuene |
|---|---|---|---|
| Northern Mayombe | 0 | 6 | 7 |
| Western Manianga | 0 | 13 | 6 |
| Southern Mayombe | 4 | 11 | 5 |
| Manteke | 6 | 2 | 0 |
| Eastern Manianga | 1 | 3 | 3 |
| Ndibu | 10 | 1 | 1 |
| Ntandu | 0 | 0 | 0 |
| Zombo | 3 | 1 | 2 |
| | 24 | 35 | 24 |

into a new unified national Protestant church. The
Manianga connections of the mission explain the predominance of Manianga elements in the Matadi church.

The Salvation Army, which was strong in the
Ntandu region, had been established in Matadi only
since 1963. Half of its members were BaNtandu.

Table 3, based on general impressions, shows the
influence of the regional factor in each church.
Table 4 shows more precisely the influence of regionalism in the leadership of EUDA, DMN-Difuene, and the
Nzanza parish of EJCSK, leaders being identified as
those charged with specific responsibilities such as
catechist, youth advisor, and pastor.

All the indigenous churches except the Apostles
revealed in their ideology and their membership the
heritage of clandestine prophetic activity during the
colonial period. DMN-Kinene consisted of members of
a certain faction in the village of Kinkanza, near
Mbanza Manteke, most of them close relatives of the
late Kinene Jean, whose emergence as a prophet in
1953 was closely connected with the internal politics
of the Nlaza clan in Kinkanza (see Chapter One,
above). The nucleus of one DMN-Mbumba meeting was
composed of close relatives of the original Mbumba
Philippe, the prophet of Kinkenge in western Manianga. Kinkenge was one of the chief centers of
prophetic activity in the 1920's and 1930's.

In the 1950's, Kinkenge men in Matadi were among
the leaders of what became known, towards the end of
the colonial period, as the Church of the Holy Spirit
(Dibundu dia Mpeve a Nlongo). When this group began
to acquire property and a civil identity, disputes
arose, and in 1962 it split into two bodies called
the Eglise Prophétique Congolaise, consisting almost
exclusively of Manianga elements, and the Mission
Prophétique de Jésus Christ Ngounzisme du Congo, in
which BaManianga, BaYombe and BaMboma were represented. The former divided again into the present
DMN-Mbuma and DMN-Major (Nkamba Benjamin). In 1964
the Mission Prophétique began to divide into
DMN-Nlandu and DMN-Difuene, but in 1970 the separation was still incomplete as litigation continued
between the leaders of the two groups, each of whom
claimed the leadership of the entire Mission Prophétique and also ownership of the remaining properties
of the original united Church of the Holy Spirit.
The leadership of DMN-Nlandu was linked with Boma,
DMN-Difuene with Kinkenge, and regionalism was an
explicit issue between them from the beginning.

Regional influences were apparent in church ritual. DMN-A music, for example, is Manianga music, that of EC-Gonda reflects the cultural heritage of the BaNtandu. Regionalism in Kongo Central is not primarily a matter of ancient traditions, however, and certainly not of "tribal" divisions. The governing factor is the modern road system, which links western Manianga with Tshela and Seke-Banza, for example, and the BaZombo of Angola with the BaNtandu of Inkisi and Sona Bata, but the government's administrative divisions and those of the mission churches have also played a part. The history of the resulting conflicts closely parallels that of the Abako political party (Monnier 1971:369-85; Bernard 1970).

No adequate history of the evolution of prophetic churches in Lower Zaire has yet been written, and the available accounts are often little more than examples of the clichés of Kongo political rhetoric, let flow in this instance by the decree of December 24, 1959, permitting the existence of religious "sects." During the preceding decade certain younger leaders emerged to replace the older prophets, now in exile, with whom they remained to some extent in contact. After the surviving exiles returned, meetings were held in 1960 and 1961 in the attempt to organize a single prophetic church. The effort foundered on the rocks of personal ambition, competing definitions of the prophetic mission, and regionalism.

A mimeographed account by one Bayuvula Bennamis of a conference of prophets convened in Leopoldville (Kinshasa) in June 1961, allegedly by Bayuvula himself, gives the flavor of religious acrimony (Bayuvula 1963). Nowadays, he begins, prophets are not respected as they were in colonial times. There are too many witches who pass themselves off as prophets in order to be famous. What the prophets need is competent secretaries to organize a single church like the others, but unfortunately the old are jealous of the young and will not accept educated younger people. Bayuvula goes on to say that there were present at the meeting Mpadi Simon-Pierre [later head of ENAF], Luzodisa Joseph Batiaka-Kibenga [DMN-Major], Mavungu [Mawungu Samuel, DMN-Mbumba], Michel [representing the eastern Kongo movement, Dieudonné], and others. Several speakers maintained that the government itself could never be strong until the prophets were united, and that the government should conduct a test of candidates for the leadership of the new organization, in which the winner would be the one who most successfully performed the required miracles. "Those who will not agree to the formation of the new prophetic union are witches." A proposal to have such a union headed jointly by Mpadi and Mawungu was rejected when Mawungu and other Manianga men asserted that Manianga (Luozi) was the first to receive the Holy Spirit, and that therefore they could not be dominated by BaNdibu, BaNtandu, BaYombe and Bangala. Someone else demanded to know how a prophet with three or four wives (Mpadi) could presume to speak for the rest of them.

Meanwhile, the nascent EJCSK had been holding conferences of its own, asserting its universal role in the face of allegations that it was nothing but an agency of the Besi Ngombe, the people of the Ndibu region around Nkamba, dominated by the BMS at Ngombe Lutete. Mabwaka Mpaka in Manteke, renewing in 1960, after his return from exile, some of the glory of 1921, was persuaded to accede to EJCSK by the idea that he was given special responsibility for the Manteke region, though in an administrative sense he had none, and though his influence as a healer rapidly declined (JM Nos.15,16). His relative and fellow prophet in nearby Mbanza Nkazi, Kinene Jean (DMN-Kinene), refused the Nkamba offer.

A document prepared for a conference of EJCSK at Nkamba in 1959 put forward the centralized bureaucratic structures of the mission churches and the government as models to be imitated. There must be one headquarters, Nkamba, at which a register of all officers and members of the church must be kept. "We must follow numerical sequence" (tufueti kuenda bonso buena ndandani za numéros). Membership cards (bikalati) must be issued, showing the names of Kimbangu and Nkamba-Jerusalem (Dialungana 1959; MacGaffey 1969:131). At this time, Bamba Emmanuel (Eglise Congolaise, not represented in Matadi in 1970), Mpadi (ENAF), Nlandu Nathanael (DMN-Nlandu), Kimosi Jean (EJCDT, not represented in Matadi in 1970) and Gonda André (EC-Gonda, or ECUSE) were all still associated with Joseph Diangienda and the leadership at Nkamba, or at least not formally dissociated from it.

Mpadi Simon-Pierre, leader of the Khaki movement, was by far the best known prophet to survive the period of repression. The possibility of a relationship between EJCSK and Mpadi was sufficiently alive in May, 1960, that the church's newspaper *Kimbanguisme* (May 15, 1960) reported his return from exile; Mpadists in attendance wore a khaki uniform

marked with red crosses, while the prophet himself
wore an ankle-length red robe (pl. 12). Mpadi's
view of the matter, however, was that after imprison-
ing Kimbangu in 1921, the colonial authorities and
the Catholic clergy had seized the prophet's three
sons, two of whom were, in fact, educated in government schools; by teaching them white man's
witchcraft and giving them rosaries, talismans and
magical oils, the clergy had killed off the prophetic
succession (Mpadi, "Letter to Mavunza, May 14,
1940"). In 1939, according to Mpadi, the Almighty
Father, seeing that nobody was carrying on the prophetic work, came to Simon Kimbangu in prison in
Elizabethville and required him to write letters to
certain Besi Ngombe, telling them to assume the task.
The recipients burned the letters, refusing to obey
Kimbangu's instructions lest they suffer the same
fate as he. Thereafter the Holy Father had Kimbangu
write to certain inhabitants of Madimba and Kasangulu
(BaNtandu), telling them to form a Technical Commission, create a church, and nominate Mpadi, then
working for the Salvation Army as its head;
Kimbangu's letter, continues Mpadi, made no mention
of any member of his family (JM No.45). This version
of the spiritual history, backed by a mimeographed
flood of letters allegedly written by Kimbangu to
confidants, thus disqualifies Kimbangu's sons in particular and Besi Ngombe in general from leadership of
the true church, and legitimates the predominance of
Mpadi and the BaNtandu.

Regional loyalties founded schisms throughout
Kongo. In November, 1965, EJCSK leaders from Mayombe
demanded that their district should become a "Vicariat" of the church, with control over its own funds.
They accused Diangienda's appointed treasurer for the
district, a Ngombe man, of embezzlement, and said
that funds made available by the government to the
church to support its schools in Mayombe had been
retained at headquarters. They complained also that
Ndibu teachers had been appointed to local schools.
Both sides sought the support of government at various levels, amid charges of "politics" and "intention
to disturb the peace." EJCSK warned its adherents
that the Vicariat group were nothing but witches and
sellers of children; various mothers discovered
accordingly that the deaths of their children in
years past was to be laid at the door of the dissidents. In June 1966, the national minister of
justice, Madudu Philémon, himself a Manianga man with
separatist sympathies, recommended that the Vicariat

be created and the dissidents "be paid what they were owed," but in 1970 the schism persisted and the Yombe branch had become a separate church.

A few miles west of Nkamba, the village of Mbanza Ngoyo is in a cultural sense part of the Ngombe region, but it happens to fall within the ABFMS mission district administered from Mbanza Manteke (Nsona Mpangu). In 1921, Thomas Ntualani of Mbanza Ngoyo was one of many prophets inspired, it would seem, after the fashion of Kimbangu but, by their own account, on direct and independent contact with God. Ntualani visited Kimbangu at Nkamba, but (according to Ntualanist legend) the two prophets received a divine reproof for spending the night in the same place. The legends give great importance to the river that marks the boundary between the BMS and ABFMS districts, at which certain visions and miracles are supposed to have occurred. Kimbanguists call Mbanza Ngoyo "Nazareth," because Kimbangu's mother came from there. The Ntualanists said (in 1966) that God had intended Kimbangu and Ntualani, "brothers" of the same clan, to be brothers in the spirit, equal in rank. Ntualani died in prison. After his own return from exile in 1960, Ntualani's son Simon Kimosi (various spellings are in use, but his visiting card says "Kimosi Ntualani Simon, Prophète") was well received at Nkamba as "son of a prophet," until the EJCSK leadership insisted that there had been only one prophet and that therefore Kimosi was not the son of one. A sermon preached at Nkamba in 1965, obliquely aimed at the Ntualanists, dwelt on the text from the second book of Kings in which Elijah discomfits the "sons of the prophets" in favor of Elisha (JM No.44). Moreover EJCSK would not countenance the return of Ntualani's remains from Upper Congo as though they deserved respect equal to Kimbangu's. In 1963, therefore, Kimosi founded the Church of Jesus Christ by Two Witnesses (EJCDT), installing his father's remains in a mausoleum at Mbanza Ngoyo which imitated the one at Nkamba, and quoting 2 Corinthians 13:1 "This is the third time I am coming to you. In the mouth of two or three witnesses shall every word be established" (Mwene-Batende 1971). According to M.L. Martin (1975:58), EJCDT was banned in 1968, for political reasons.

Around all such schisms cluster charges of corruption, authoritarianism and misuse of funds. The churches were minor patronage organizations, offering resources and protection to their adherents in a competitive and highly politicized world, and mediating

between them and the government, the largest of the
patronage systems and itself also the source of most
of the repression against which one needed protection. Government educational subsidies made money
for salaries available to any religious organization
able to put together a school. Besides the welcome
flow of salaries, "our schools," staffed by "our
teachers" could be expected to see to it that "our
children" passed into higher education and better
jobs. On the other hand, constant obsequiousness
towards local authorites was advisable on the part of
both churches and their members. In the 1960's,
EJCSK regularly changed its local administrative
structure to match that of the government, and was
careful to invite administrative and military officials to festive occasions at the appropriate level.
In return, the government might grant favors, or even
support the church's leaders against dissident
members, on the grounds that Zaire had seen enough
chaos and that submission to constituted authority
was an absolute good. Naive members of EJCSK ima-
gined that their church membership card, imitating
the government's identity card, would get them past
police roadblocks, and that if necessary Diangienda
would intercede with the President himself.
        In completely new political conditions, the
churches thus reproduced some of the functions of the
old territorial cults, organizing benefits for the
inhabitants of a common territory in association with
a separately constituted and often violent system of
government. A sense of this function, and a recol-
lection of the life-giving virtues of nsi (country,
region), infused with a certain pathetic dignity the
competing myths of how the Holy Spirit, through the
person of this and that prophet, brought salvation
first, and primarily, to this or that region before
extending it "to all of Africa, and indeed the whole
world."

## The political factor

        The colonial experience contributed to the
diversity of churches a political factor, commonly
expressed by scholars as the difference between independent and foreign control. Until 1956 the
Protestant and Catholic Churches and the Islamic mosque were the only legitimate religious organizations
in Matadi. Both churches had their headquarters in
the downtown area, later known as the Urban Commune,
in which the principal commercial and industrial com-

plexes were situated, together with the private
residences of the European managerial class. The
African residential suburbs, later the Communes of
Nzanza and Mvuzi, housed not only a different population but a different institutional system.

By 1970 much had been done to change the
political role of missionaries and to transfer control of exogenous churches to local clergy, but the
buildings remained, as did the entire foreign complex
of mission schools, dispensaries and clerical bureaucracy. All these features, and more, are
ineradicably part of modern Zaire but were still felt
as foreign by most BaKongo, particularly since
foreign missionaries were still much in evidence,
though they rarely if ever penetrated the indigenous
sector of this plural society.

The Salvation Army and the Jehovah's Witnesses,
both established in Matadi after independence, are
both exogenous but were not seen as such to the same
extent as the others. Both were located in the African part of the city, and neither was set apart from
the community by its buildings or the life-style of
its clergy. Both were so organized as to make no
categorical distinction between foreigners and
natives. Witness doctrine, moreover, purported to
refute or amend the Christianity of the orthodox
foreign churches, and it was known that the sect had
been forbidden during the colonial period.

We should mention here that according to their
own doctrine the Witnesses are not a church but an
association, and their gatherings were not services
but study sessions. Nevertheless, prayers and hymns
were part of the program, the gatherings commonly
took place on Sunday mornings, and less-instructed
members spoke of "going to church." From our point of
view the Witnesses must be reckoned as a church
because they clearly belonged with the others in an
exclusive series; one was either a Witness or a
Catholic, for example, but never both.

Though they are independent of mission control,
the prophetic churches generally (ENAF excepted)
think of themselves as branches of Protestantism,
though they have adopted some items of Catholic ritual practice and though many of their adherents
individually are Catholic educated. The doctrinal
issues of the Reformation are not understood by most
BaKongo, whose differential evaluation of Protestantism is based not on theology but on political
history. Catholic missions arrived relatively late
in Lower Congo (about 1898), and found

English-speaking Protestant missions well entrenched.
BaKongo soon discovered that they could turn the
rivalry between the two to their own advantage.
Catholic missions were always, in fact and in popular
thinking, closely identified with the state, to which
the Protestant missions were seen as an alternative;
in the 1900's, individuals would argue that they were
bangelozo, "English speakers," and not subject to the
state.  All missionaries were regarded as dealing in
witchcraft (kindoki), but Catholics were clearly
identified as a better organized conspiracy.
Catholic, not Protestant, missionaries were said, in
the 1960's (and still in 1980), to have stolen the
powers of the ancestors, and to repair nocturnally to
Kongo cemeteries for nefarious rites.
    The political factor was less and less signifi-
cant as an indicator of what went on in church life
after 1960.  It coincided with no important ideological factors, and after independence the political
structure itself changed, as all churches in common
found themselves subject to restraint by the government.
    After 1960, "political" usually meant devious
and subversive, and EJCSK was careful to be loudly
"non-political,"[5] although to survive at all, let
alone prosper, an organization of any kind needed to
be actively and continuously political.  In 1966,
Emmanuel Bamba, a Kimbanguist leader who had left
EJCSK in 1961 to found his own Eglise Congolaise, was
arrested and later hanged by the government for con-
spiring to overthrow it;  his church was banned,
although it had had nothing to do with the conspiracy.  The violence of the government's reaction,
marking the end of a period of casual, musical-chairs
politics, was deeply shocking to the BaKongo;  in
that context many of them found tasteless the haste
and vehemence with which EJCSK dissociated itself
from Bamba (cf. M.-L. Martin 1975:127).  In 1973,
church leaders went out of their way to praise the
government for setting an example to the church in
the matter of salongo, or unpaid citizen labor on
Saturday-morning public works;  in fact, salongo was
a failure, and EJCSK itself had always operated the
only successful "volunteer" labor program in the
country.  Such boot-licking makes political sense
when the church's real power is slight.
    In April 1972, Mobutu decreed that the govern-
ment would recognize only the Catholic Church, the
Church of Christ in Zaire (united Protestant, ECZ)
and EJCSK, plus the Islamic Community of Zaire, the

Israeli Community and the Greek Orthodox Church. All
others were faced with stringent requirements that
none could meet. The Protestants, but not the Kimbanguists or the Catholics, were besieged by groups,
many of them reportedly "not even of the Protestant
persuasion," who were anxious to join. As a result,
the Church of Christ in Zaire, at its annual Synod in
1977, was faced with many of the organizational problems that had led to the multiplication of churches
in the first place: "tribalistic conflicts, power
struggles, refusal to hand over at the end of a man-
date, proliferation of sects." It voted to admit
several, including DMNA and EUDA, but subsequently
reversed itself.

In the same year Mobutu began to implement the
separation of church and state, declaring for example
that prayers would no longer be offered on public
occasions and restricting religious observances to
the private domain. In particular he forced the
Catholic Church to disqualify itself as a public body
entitled to comment on national policy; the President said in January 1975 that he had never had
trouble with the Protestants or the Kimbanguists, but
that the Catholics, "on orders from the Vatican,"
were always disputing the government's decisions.
Because the parochial school systems have always
been, for all the churches, the principal recruiting
device, the most consequential feature of the secu-
larization policy was that the government took over
the church school systems and substituted courses in
civics for religious education. It also nationalised
the Protestant (Kisangani) and Catholic (Kinshasa)
universities, partly for the sake of its own ideological supremacy and partly to break down the powerful
alumni networks, which channeled the products of
Catholic (and to a much lesser extent, Protestant)
schools into academic and bureaucratic jobs and fos-
tered a kind of religious tribalism among the elite.

In the absence of political parties other than
the government's MPR, the Catholic Church became the
prime organizational vehicle of opposition to Mobutu,
and thus it inherited, to a considerable extent, the
political role that Kimbanguism attempted to play in
colonial times. In that connexion, the church had
for years been concerned to develop a "Bantu theological perspective" in which its authenticity in terms
of African culture, and therefore its right to
represent popular interests, would be demonstrated
(Mudimbe 1981). EJCSK, on the other hand, had neither the wealth nor the personnel to articulate

substantial opposition, supposing it wanted to, and
in the preceding decade it had done much to cut
itself off from its popular roots. It continued to
associate itself with the party line, to an extent
that even some government officials (in 1980)
remarked as distasteful.

The de-institutionalization of the Catholic
Church, as one of the bishops called it, might have
been expected to improve the competitive position of
EJCSK. In fact, the reverse occurred. In secondary
education, nation-wide, the Kimbanguists enrolled a
mere 8 percent of the pupils, as opposed to 17 percent for the Protestants, 35 percent for the state,
and 42 percent for the Catholics. Catholic-trained
people already predominated in managerial roles, and
when religion was declared a private matter clergy
were free, like other citizens, to take jobs in
government and university. Their personal networks
still existed, though integrated in the MPR instead
of standing in opposition to it. The bishops argued
that Mobutu had done the Catholic Church a favor by
forcing it to depend less on its hierarchy and more
on informal popular support.

Mobutu's ban against the smaller and less easily
supervised churches may have been prompted by indications, among the BaLuba as well as the BaKongo, of
new movements in the customary sector that could
threaten the government, as in the past. In 1976,
church and state were reconciled. Mobutu restored
control of the denominational schools to their parent
churches, the sole agencies able to operate them
effectively. "Mobutuism," which had been developed
as a quasi-religious public doctrine connected with a
campaign for "cultural authenticity," declined simultaneously. By 1980 a number of new national and
foreign religious organizations had obtained recognition; DMNA was still struggling to do so.

## Education and employment.

The effects of education on church membership in
Matadi are complex and difficult to evaluate. The
available data do not permit any clear classification
of churches by educational or socio-economic criteria.

Catholics, Protestants, and Salvation Army
members were recruited almost exclusively through
confessional schools. The importance of schools in
recruiting explains the Kimbanguists' enormous
investment in education since 1960. Catholic or Pro-

testant education extending beyond the primary level tended to incorporate individuals economically, politically, and intellectually into the European institutional sector in which the Catholic and Protestant churches themselves were rooted. It also drew them into a greater variety of activities and responsibilities. A striking feature of many of the indigenous churches was the amount of time they demanded of their members. DMN-Nsansi, the extreme example, met every day for several hours, and every day one saw many of the same faces. Only the socially marginal could spare that much time.

Lists of church leaders, excluding women, the retired, and those employed by the church itself, confirm the participating observer's impressions of the social positions of different congregations (see Table 5). The Catholic, Protestant, Kimbanguist, and DMNA churches had many members who were poor and illiterate, as well as some who were educated and wealthy. Only the Witnesses made literacy virtually a requirement, since to belong was to participate in study sessions. The Apostles (EUDA) clearly represented the highest socio-economic level among the indigenous churches, of which DMN-Nsansi was more representative. Every congregation needed a nucleus of literate members who could read lessons and handle correspondence, and no healer, no matter how traditional his rituals, lacked among his clients a few well-placed individuals.

Table 5.
Occupations of the male leaders of selected churches.

|  | EUDA | EJCSK (Nzanza) | DMN-Nsansi | DMN-Difuene |
|---|---|---|---|---|
| Unemployed | 2 | 2 | 2 | 2 |
| Laborers | 1 | 4 | 3 | 11 |
| Semi-skilled | 13 | 9 | 7 | 0 |
| Traders | 0 | 1 | 0 | 0 |
| Clerks | 13 | 3 | 0 | 2 |
| Civil servants, teachers | 6 | 1 | 1 | 0 |
|  | 35 | 20 | 13 | 15 |

The same lists also indicate the influence of place of employment on the membership of the smaller churches. The overwhelming importance of the transportation authority, OTRACO (later ONATRA), among local employers may suffice to explain why eleven of

DMN-Difuene's leaders were OTRACO laborers, but also
makes it the more remarkable that seven Apostle
leaders worked for the Agence Maritime, six for the
state secondary school, and only 14 for OTRACO. More
than one quarter of the adult male population worked
for OTRACO, but the Agence Maritime and the school
employed only a few hundred individuals, most of them
in positions requiring a good education. Recruitment
to any of the smaller churches, except the Witnesses,
was usually a matter of healing: a man who felt he
needed spiritual healing for himself or a member of
his family would be likely to take the advice of colleagues at work, and of people from his home region.

## Means to salvation

None of the sociological factors differentiates
the churches other than statistically; there is no
church, for example, that is regionally or occupa-
tionally exclusive. Clearer contrasts, and a
structural classification, emerge when ideological
factors are considered.

All the churches offered the possibility of salvation to their members, "salvation" meaning a right
relationship to God resulting in redemption from
suffering. They clearly fell into two groups, the
"traditional" and the "spiritual," according to the
means whereby the members were assured of their relationship to God and hence of the possibility of
salvation.

Liturgical practice in the first group
emphasized traditions showing the history of man's
response to the possibility of salvation, the role of
mediators such as Moses, Christ and Kimbangu, and the
expected destiny of the world. The Bible was the
chief source of such traditions but the history of
Europe and Africa also provided material. The traditionalist churches were the Salvation Army, the
Catholics, Protestants, Kimbanguists, Witnesses, the
Black Church and the Apostles.

In the second group it was not important to
expound tradition. The Bible merely provided anec-
dotes and moral precepts as texts for homilies, and
history was ignored. The assurance of salvation was
provided by daily manifestations of the presence of
the spirit (mpeve) in the form of trembling, visions
and glossolalia on the part of the leaders or the
whole congregation. The spiritualist churches all
used, or had used, some version of the name Church of
the Holy Spirit (DMN) and in all of them the leaders,

or even all of the members, were commonly called prophets (bangunza), a term which is not regularly
applied to living members of any other church.

The distinction is clear, and logically based.
Given the signs of spiritual visitation one does not
need the guarantees of tradition, and vice versa.
The organizational consequences of the two modes are
quite different. Spirit possession puts every
believer in direct contact with God and is incompatible with strong church discipline. On the other
hand, the idea of tradition implies properly trained
and authenticated spokesmen, a hierarchy.[6]

The distinction is also immediately apparent to
the observer. On our first visit to the Apostles,
for example, we noted the absence of spiritual manifestations and were given a mimeographed biography
of the church's founder and a similar verbal biography of the founder of the Matadi parish. In
DMN-Nsansi, on the other hand, persistent efforts
failed to elicit any coherent history of the church
or its local congregation.

Kimbangu was himself an ecstatic. In confrontation with the administrator Morel he is described as
lifting his eyes to the heavens and speaking a new
tongue: "Tek Tektel Tek." His followers likewise
lifted their eyes and spoke this celestial language
(Raymaekers 1971:43). Though generalized access to
the Holy Spirit is incompatible with centralized control, EJCSK, grounded in a prophetic tradition, could
not deny spirit possession altogether, as the ABFMS
did. (The village of Mbanza Manteke was scandalized
one day in 1966 when a man presumed to speak in tongues at an ordinary regional pastors' conference,
though by then mission control of such matters was
already much relaxed.) In the mid 1960's, the prophetic function was restricted to Diangienda, as
successor to the prophet, and the "chief priests," or
sacrificateurs, his spiritual assistants. Several of
these priests were surviving assistants of Kimbangu
himself. One or two of them at a time would be sta-
tioned at headquarters in Kinshasa, the rest at
Nkamba, where (on feast days especially) long lines
of pilgrims would seek them out for a highly routin-
ized version of the prophetic functions of
divination, advice, and blessing (JM No.43, and fig.
4). Holding on to a bar which reproduced that used
by Kimbangu, the priests, with the ease of years of
practice, caused their shoulders to tremble while
they listened to clients' problems, before dispensing
holy water.

Edouard's vision:    bureaucracy versus charisma

Anyone who shows signs of possession in an ordinary EJCSK service is regarded as having some kind of
personal problem, and may be asked to leave.  On the
other hand, major revelations and ecstatic experiences can constitute a threat to the ecclesiastical
order, and must be contained.  Such a crisis arose at
Kemba after the death of Mabwaka Mpaka in 1965, when
it was announced that one of his hangers-on, an Angolan refugee called Edouard, had seen the late prophet
in a dream, complaining about the indadequacy of the
mortuary arrangements (JM No.15).  Edouard was marginal  even  to the EJCSK, and two months before he had
been expelled for sinful behavior.  Shortly after his
dream, I was told, he died, but on the third day he
rose again, unable to speak anything but English  and
Swahili, which nobody at Kemba understood.  Despite
this handicap, he was able to indicate what his
experiences had been during his absence.

By the time I arrived at Kemba, a small  village
near Mbanza Manteke, Edouard had almost entirely
recovered the use of his native tongue, but the story
he had to tell had worn somewhat thin by repetition.
The local EJCSK pastor took care to point out to me
that Edouard was simply the vehicle of a revelation,
not a teacher in his own right.  Edouard, on the
other hand, took advantage of a lull in a private
conversation with me to point out certain persons
walking about nearby, dressed, he said, in white
jackets like his own, but quite invisible to me.  In
other words, the issues of the significance of
Edouard's visions was clear from the start to the
people  at Kemba, and it restated the difficulties of
the compromise between the bureaucratic church and
Mabwaka's personal charisma.

In what Edouard said to me the original dream
and the three-day trance, now reduced to about
twenty-four hours, were not clearly distinguished.
He had gone to the forest to work, returning in
mid-afternoon. He was not ill, but after he had
opened the house (actually Mabwaka's kitchen) where
he lived, he began to feel cold. When he wanted to
go outside to greet someone, his feet felt heavy and
his body was tired, so he lay on the bed to sleep.
Then a bright light entered the house and beat upon
his eyes, even though they were shut.  Then in a
vision he saw, as a dead man sees (wamona monameso
bonso muntu fwidi), Mabwaka himself, as a black man,
but not ill any more.  The prophet asked Edouard what

he was doing in the kitchen; he replied that he was
keeping an eye on it, and offered to give back the
key. Mabwaka said, "I gave you the key for you to
use. I left it in your hands." Then the two of them
went to "South America," described as "the country of
our fathers." There Edouard recognized nobody he knew
except Diangienda, who said nothing. From America
they went to heaven where they saw the crucified
Christ, "at a traffic circle, a place where four
roads meet," and attended a church service.[7] There
they also saw four large placards with the names of
the elect written on them, before returning to sinful
earth where they saw people drinking, smoking, loung-
ing in bars, and picking up hairs from the ground
(toota nsuki).

    Back at Kemba, Mabwaka insisted that the "mis-
sion" (Mabwaka's establishment) not be allowed to go
to ruin. Imposing buildings were to be constructed,
including his own mausoleum, made of small (and
expensive) European-style bricks; "the family will
have to buy sacks of cement," and there was to be a
window giving a view of the coffin. Plantations were
to be maintained in the forest. Then Mabwaka departed, bidding his followers to be of good cheer: "I am
not dead. I am with you always." The detail about
picking up hairs is obscure; it was interpreted at
Kemba as a prohibition against protracted mourning on
Mabwaka's account.

    The trance, or fit, actually happened;
observers said Edouard foamed at the mouth and was
unconscious. Every detail of his vision, however, is
a cliché of popular culture. The prosaic key to
Mabwaka's kitchen is transformed into the symbolic
key of delegated authority, the key of the kingdom,
such as Kimbangu is said to have been given by Jesus.
(The modern prophet who calls himself Mbumba Philippe
distributes a photograph of himself holding a closet
key.) The word nsabi, "key" (Portuguese, chave) was
adopted long ago to indicate the locked box in which
a chief might keep his valuables, mostly magical
objects. To inherit the key was to acquire control
of the objects whose possession legitimated the position of chief. Even now, when there are no chiefs of
the traditional, magically endowed kind, succession
to office is discussed conventionally in terms of
"the key," and the idea of a locked container of
powerful and legitimating objects is very much alive
(JM No.17, par.13).

Pl.3: Festival, EJCSK, Kasangulu

Pl.4: Grave of Mabwaka Mpaka, Kemba, 1966

Mabwaka's description of the ideal "mission" whose construction Edouard was to supervise recalls his own hopes, or fantasies, as expressed to me in his lifetime. He had a blueprint of the great establishment he was to build some day to replace the meager mud huts of real life. Every prophetic enterprise looks forward to a new settlement, a great new community, an mbanza. Kongo social reformers of all kinds have the same idea, from those who write in scholarly journals of new plans for model cities and rural development, to the leaders of humble and short-lived local cooperatives, who dream of the day when their one truck shall have become a fleet, their one store a chain. Relgious and secular plans alike always include a school and a hospital; they differ in that the former also provide for churches, the latter for stores.

What happened to Edouard afterwards was described to me by the man who accompanied him to Nkamba. His account may not be historically correct in every detail but it certainly represents the popular view. It was clear that Edouard saw himself as the successor to Mabwaka and custodian of his tomb, just as Diangienda holds the key to Kimbangu's. Kemba might become a place of pilgrimage like Nkamba, and center of a vast economic and political enterprise. Precisely this sort of schism had presented the greatest threats to EJCSK since 1960, as in the case of the Ntualanist Church of the Two Witnesses (EJCDT). Did not Dialungana's most widely distributed pamphlet complain, "Now many have bestowed prophethood upon themselves, and chosen pools for themselves, and set themselves up as the equals of Simon Kimbangu; and they dissuade others from going to Jerusalem, for they also have their holy cities and their pools" (JM No.42). On the other hand, the authenticity of spiritual visions could not simply be denied.

Edouard was sent to Nkamba to have his spirit examined (mfimpulu a mpeve andi); a letter from the pastor at Kemba preceded him. On the way he met several people who had recently had dreams that they associated with his. At Kinanga near Kimpese a man had dreamed of Mabwaka's tomb, and in another village a woman had been told in a dream of her recently deceased mother's happy arrival in America. Before Edouard reached Nkamba, word was brought to him from the authorities there that Diangienda, who was in the United States at the time as a guest of the State

Department, had been able to welcome Mabwaka there
when he arrived, on the day after his death.

At Nkamba an examination of Edouard's spirit by
one of the sacrificateurs was arranged at the place
where blessings are normally dispensed, reputedly the
spot where Kimbangu set up his healing rail. A choir
was in attendance but the sacrificateur instructed
them not to sing; he said he wanted to hear Edouard
more easily, but clearly it would have been inconven-
ient if the singing had provoked Edouard or others to
ecstasy. When Edouard had finished his story the
sacrificateur thanked him and said he was the sixth
person already that year to have reported such an
experience, thus confirming the truth of what was
taught at Nkamba about spiritual visitations. After
consulting Dialungana, who did not appear on this
occasion, the sacrificateur informed Edouard that
although his vision had been genuine it did not signify a prophetic commission. It would be impossible
to build another shrine, but the people at Kemba
should consider themselves fortunate that the man
they had buried was like a king. Other basadisi
(helpers of the prophet, such as the sacrificateurs)
were expected to reside at Nkamba but Mabwaka had
been authorized to remain in the Manteke area because
of the exceptional prevalence there of witchcraft and
magic. Mabwaka was now dead, but his work would go
on. His message to Edouard was to be regarded as
personal advice to stop sleeping with other men's
wives and return to the fold. "After all," concluded
the sacrificateur kindly, underlining Edouard's marginality, "we do not think of you as an Angolan, but
just as one of ourselves."

## SALVATION AND HEALTH

The Salvation Army, the Catholics and the Protestants treated health as a natural rather than a
moral or religious problem. During the 1960's, the
same attitude was increasingly characteristic of
EJCSK. All the others promised health to their
members and tended to regard health as evidence of
salvation. In local definition, "health" and "sickness" include matters of psychological and material
comfort, as well as medical illness, and are closely
bound up with the concept of witchcraft, that is,
with interpersonal malevolence as a source of discomfort. Churches could be distinguished as offering
health now or later. Those offering health now were

further classifiable according to the ritual means
employed.

The churches that offered health to their
adherents did so in four basic ways that can be
related on the one hand to the common religious
assumptions of the BaKongo and on the other to the
internal and external organization of the churches.

1) Millenarianism. The Witnesses and the Black
Church offered their members the promise of a future
kingdom of God on earth in which sickness would not
exist. Witnesses advised their young relatives not
to take up careers in medicine because the kingdom
was imminent. The Black Church supplemented its millenarian promise with a service of herbal medicine
represented as the African equivalent of European
medical science. The millennium itself was closely
linked with the idea of pan-African independence, and
specifically to the independence of Angola, from
which most Mpadists came. Similar millenarian expectations were current among Kimbanguists in general in
1959-60, but since independence the millenarian element in EJCSK has been largely restricted to the name
of the church.

2) Fortification. The non-millenarian churches
and also, marginally, EJCSK, strengthened their
members against evil in this present world by appli-
cations of holy water, flags, batons, flapping
towels, and other symbolic agents of the spirit.
Such ministrations might follow a prophetic divination identifying a particular source of evil or might
offer simple general prophylaxis. Only in EC-Gonda
and DMN-Kinene was fortification apparently the chief
protective means.

3) Purification. The theory of witchcraft says
that a man who has evil in his heart will either
bring sickness upon himself or make himself vulner-
able to external spiritual attacks. For this reason,
and following the usual precepts of Christianity, all
the churches, and particularly the non-millennial
churches, urged their members to "cleanse their
hearts" (vedisa ntima). In DMNA and the Apostles
alone, tests of purification constituted a central
activity of the church. Every month, as a preparation for communion, members of the Apostles were
expected to confess publicly in small sectional meetings. The confessions were checked by an official of
the church who was directly "instructed by the spirit." In all the churches of the Manianga tradition,
purity is "weighed" by a rite called bascule (French;

in KiKongo, <u>ntezolo</u> a <u>mpeve</u>), but only in DMNA do
virtually all the members regularly participate in
the rite.

4) Accusation. A diviner (prophet) can be more
or less specific about the source of the evil
afflicting his client. If he goes so far as to name
individuals as witches, the client can be healed by
confronting the witch and inducing him to repent and
retract. Sometimes the witch accepts the accusation
and the prophet is thus the means to a reconciliation
between the parties. If the witch does not accept,
he either ignores the charge or may go so far in
reply as to bring a complaint of calumny aganst the
prophet in the courts. In 1970, the process of accusation and confrontation (<u>tadisa mambu</u>, <u>tengula</u>
<u>mambu</u>) was much in demand but extremely risky.

In rural areas, where the judges of the local
court were members of the community, an accused witch
who brought suit against a prophet was likely to lose
his case, if the prophet knew his business. In Matadi, the same was true of the communal courts applying
customary law, but since calumny tends to disturb the
peace an accused witch could also take his case to a
police court. The police magistrate, applying statute law and European standards, was likely to rule
that witchcraft does not exist, uphold the charge of
calumny, and punish the prophet or instruct him to
cease and desist. After 1960, when accusation had
flourished, and particularly after Mobutu seized
power in 1965, the prophets of the DMN group of
churches learned to be circumspect about accusation.
In 1970, DMNA admitted that accusation causes more
trouble than it is worth, and did not use the technique at all. The healer of DMN-Nsansi, the only
full-time professional among the Matadi prophets, was
also the only one bold enough to make frequent and
explicit accusations.

Among the traditionalist, non-prophetic
churches, accusations occurred only in the Black
Church, where they were infrequent and rarely led to
confrontation.

These three means to "healing now" presuppose
the model of a person as the content of a vessel;
fortification strengthens the vessel, purification
strengthens the content, and accusation is directed
externally against the witch. A fourth method of
relieving affliction is to attack the soul or content
of the witch by magical means (<u>min'kisi</u>). It is part
of the definition of a church (<u>dibundu</u>) in modern
Kongo thought, however, that true membership is

incompatible with the use of magic. In practice,
protective or fortifying devices are often distinguishable from magical charms only by the definition
given to them, not by their physical appearance and
use, but the intention and method of retribution,
together with the secrecy it entails, is used exclusively by magicians (nganga), and serves to
distinguish them from the prophets.

Varieties of healing practice are examined in
Chapter Six. The foregoing classification may be
summarized as follows:

1. No healing: Salvation Army, Protestant,
   Catholic, EJCSK.
2. Healing later (millennial): Black Church,
   Witnesses.
3. Healing now:
   a. Fortification: DMN-Kinene, EC-Gonda
   b. Purification: DMN-A, Apostles
   c. Accusation: all the other DMN churches.
4. Healing by magical attack.


## Organization of churches

The first two categories given above include
churches preoccupied with the idea of a kingdom of
God, to be located on earth or elsewhere. Given such
a goal, a church is in principle a permanent corporation whose membership ideally coincides with that of
the society. The obligations of membership entail
the church's supervision of most aspects of the
members' lives. This global concept is popularly
expressed in Zaire by the word mission, referring to
a comprehensive social organization with its own
schools, hospitals, laws, and bureaucracy, often with
commercial subdivisions as well. In popular opinion
and in the eyes of the government this has been the
only thoroughly respectable form of religious organization.

For the sake of respectability before the
police, if for no other reason, all Matadi churches
asserted from time to time, especially in formal
documents addressed to the government, that they corresponded in form to the global type of a church, and
pretended or aspired to a hierarchy of clerical
offices, a permanently enrolled membership, and other
apropriate attributes. In fact, such a form was both
beyond the means and inconsistent with the purposes
of most of them.

Pl.5: DMN-Nsansi: the bureaucratic function

Pl.6: DMN-Nsansi: the spiritual function

The predominant concern of the churches in the third category was not the transformation of the world but the day-to-day well-being of their adherents, that is, with healing. In such churches the typical local unit was not a permanent congregation guided by an appointed officer but a more or less transient population attracted to an individual of recognized competence, who worked with a staff appointed by himself. Since "healing" was in fact a matter of psychological and social manipulation, personal contact between leader and followers was essential. This need strengthened the regional factor in the membership of Matadi churches.

The assembled following of a healer is here called a "band." The term is borrowed from Kiernan, who so translates the Zulu ibandla (Kiernan 1977). The nearest equivalent in Matadi is the French word section, but an autonomous band, though similar in form and function, would not be called a section. The healing mode principally employed in it affected the size and internal organization of a band. Accusation, the most difficult mode, only worked when the healer knew intimately the social setting in which he intervened, and could count on the unanimity of his audience. One of them explained to me that a large group, in which opinion might well be divided or difficult to control, did not provide a suitable environment. Purification worked best in a group that was not only small but relatively closed and permanent, perhaps the nucleus rather than the whole membership of a given band. Purification meant more or less forced confession, followed by penitence, which established, maintained, and continuously revised within the group a dominance hierarchy which was also expressed, in part, by the allocation to members of various minor responsibilities.

All the healing churches offered fortification, that is, blessings of various kinds, which have no organizational requirements, internal or external. DMN-Kinene, which offered no other service, consisted entirely of a very small group of people held together chiefly by a common sense of grievance against the rest of Kinkanza village. EC-Gonda may not have offered any other healing service locally, but the prophet Gonda Andre himself did offer such services at his headquarters and on tour.

The two types of religious organization may be called the universal and the pragmatic.[8] Specialized in form and function, they were also distinguished by ritual patterns which may be charac-

terized, briefly though inaccurately, as European and
African.   The "congregation" of a "church" practiced
an essentially European liturgy which (except the
Catholic) conformed to the Protestant (Baptist) type:
hymns, prayers, Bible reading, sermon.   The liturgies
of healing practiced by bands were essentially African, though they had extensively appropriated
European Christian content, both Catholic and Protestant.   They are described and analyzed in Chapter
Six.

# Part Two

# *Plural Society*

# 3

# The Plural Context

The essential characteristic of the social context in which the various prophetisms described in
the previous chapter evolved is that of politically
determined institutional pluralism. To argue the
importance of such pluralism is to oppose the evolutionary perspective implicit in much contemporary
social science, especially when it treats of religious movements in colonial empires. To document the
content of pluralism in Zaire sociologically is to
substitute historical specificity for diffuse factors, such as oppression and deprivation, against
which prophets may be supposed to have been protesting.

## PLURALISM AND INDIRECT RULE

In Belgian Congo, Congolese undoubtedly had
reason to feel deprived, but an accounting of relative deprivation is not easy to reach. In the two
decades before 1921, social conditions had improved.
Rural settlements like Mbanza Manteke had been reorganized in healthier locations and the beginnings of
a public health system set up. The depredations of
the soldiery had been brought under control. A first
generation of children had been educated. Even
before the introduction (1910) of a poll tax, it had
become normal for men to enter wage employment. In
1908, the Free State became Belgian Congo, subject to
a more deliberate scrutiny than Leopold's empire had
been. On the other hand, raging epidemics of sleeping sickness continued; estimates of depopulation
during the three decades after 1890 run as high as
four fifths (Van Wing 1959:82,128-29). Reporting on

a trip through Lower Congo in late 1920, a missionary
commented on the number of wasted villages he had
seen.   "One  village had 40 graves, 20 of which were
quite fresh.   The  remaining  inhabitants  were  all
sick."   Sleeping  sickness and elephantiasis were the
principal scourges (Congo News Letter,   Jan.   1921).
The  catechism  of Kimbangu singles out the influenza
epidemic of 1918 as having something to do  with  the
origins  of  the movement, and describes it as "not by
the will of God," an expression  which  implies  that
the  epidemic  was  a  work  of witchcraft (JM No.39:
23).   Though colonial exactions  were  becoming  less
arbitrary  and  more  "paternalistic," even in 1930 a
missionary commented that "the  relationship  of  the
Congo  man  to the State resembles somewhat that of a
serf to his master" (Congo News Letter, Jan.1920).
        The project of civilizing the natives was furth-
er  advanced  in  Lower  Congo  than elsewhere in the
colony, thanks largely to intensive  mission  efforts
in which the Protestants (British, Americans, Swedes)
had been joined by several Catholic orders.   Manteke
men  educated during this period, many of them in the
households  of  Richards  and  other  missionaries,
remember  about  the nkisi cults little more than what
Richards told them.  The mission literature of  the
day  is full of "before and after" pictures contrasting semi-nudity with  service  uniforms  and  mother
hubbards.   Education and engagement in the industrial
economy created new though still narrow  channels  of
communication  with the rest of the world, whose political and economic currents affected the colony.   In
World  War I, Congolese became aware of "the Germans"
as a white power hostile to  the  Belgians,  but  the
idea  only  had important consequences much later, in
World War II.
        In the original "Pentecost of the Congo"   (1886)
the  participants  expected,  according  to my oldest
informants, that under the new dispensation of  power
represented  by  the  missionary, society would begin
anew.  Slavery  and  all  social  distinctions  would
disappear  along with witchcraft.  The inhabitants of
Manteke abandoned their old hamlets and built  a  new
community on high ground around the mission station.
        Although the missionaries  understood  what  was
happening  in  Manteke  as  conversion,  the  people
thought of it, in the  terms  provided  for  them  by
their  culture,  as initiation into a new cult which,
like other cults, would give them  access  to  powers
useful  in this world.  The missionary was the priest
(nganga)  of this cult.   The missionary  also  bought

slaves, that is, as he saw it, liberated slaves from
their masters (Axelson 1970:246-47). Even after the
government's official abolition of slavery, however,
the conceptual antinomy slave/free, which is a function of the system of matrilineal descent, remained
the only basis for social identity. The state did
not attempt to abolish descent and the body of customary law relating it to authority (kinkazi), exogamy,
rights in land, inheritance and succession; on the
contrary, under the policy of indirect rule, customary law was endorsed by the government. In
customary law the idea of individual autonomy before
the law, which is what the missionary and the state
meant by freedom, does not exist; everybody must
have his nkazi, the head of his descent group, to
speak for him (MacGaffey 1970b:213). The
missionary's acquisition of slaves therefore merely
prepared the way for his own metamorphosis into a
chief, according to indigenous rules.

Two developments frustrated this double process
of co-opting the resident missionary into local
society on indigenous terms, as priest and chief. In
the first twenty years of this century the missionaries began to withdraw from direct contact with local
populations, leaving Congolese personnel in charge as
catechists and teachers. The parallel withdrawal of
administrators, as the practice of indirect rule
developed during the same period, left
government-appointed chiefs in charge. Insofar as it
developed an internal administrative policy, the
Congo Free State (1885-1908) favored the eventual
assimilation of Congolese to the same civil status as
Europeans (Sohier 1966). In contrast, the policy of
indirect rule developed by Belgian Congo between 1908
and 1936 created a plural society divided into a
European sector, regulated by statutory (written)
law, and an African sector regulated by customary
law. Supposedly, customary law embodied ancestral
custom; in fact, it represented a transformation of
such custom in entirely new political conditions,
together with other new rules imposed by colonial
administrators in the name of custom. (The term
"customary," as used here, is adopted from the data
to be analyzed, and does not itself belong to the
analysis. For "statutory" I have substituted
"bureaucratic," since it better evokes the character
of this sector, but this too is not intended analytically.) The new policy, confirmed by the appointment
of Louis Franck as colonial minister in 1918, in
effect expected Congolese to solve their own politi-

cal problems in what Europeans regarded as the
traditional way.

In Belgian Congo there were as many African sectors as there were indigenous societies subject to
the colonial authority. Here I am concerned only
with the BaKongo of Lower Congo Province. In the
bureaucratic sector of the public domain, whites
occupied dominant positions, both personally and collectively, in all institutions, whereas blacks
occupied subordinate positions. In the customary
sector, by definition, whites were not engaged at
all; the "customary" behavior of Europeans scarcely
appeared as a category in colonial law and is not our
concern here.

In government and law, modified forms of customary institutional activity were carried on within
the framework of the colonial state with a considerable degree of autonomy. The management of land
ownership and usufruct, residence, descent, marriage
and public order at the level of misdemeanors
remained largely in the hands of Kongo elders;[1] the
corporate forms through which these affairs were managed were matrilineages. This autonomy was the real
basis for the persistence of a distinctively Kongo
ideology, although local institutions had been
deprived of much of the manpower that had formerly
sustained them, and the new "chiefs" had nothing in
common with those of the nineteenth century. The
people returned to the old criteria of status differentiation, many of them relapsing from
Christianity in the process, and began to besiege the
government's courts with arguments about land tenure,
all turning on questions of tradition and of
pedigree; arguments, that is, about who was a slave
and who was not. In Mbanza Manteke these arguments
had no economic importance, except that court fees
constituted an indirect tax, because it was still the
case that land was plentiful and anyone who was an
"owner," or child or grandchild of an owner, or
spouse of any of these, could obtain what he needed
without difficulty. It seemed rather that any quar-
rel turned to slavery on the ground that the
offending party "doesn't belong in this community
anyway." In the colonial state as a whole, the BaKongo, though subject to statute law and bureaucratic
organization in the governmental and legal functions
that the state attributed to itself, had no say in
government policy or in writing the law.

The situation with respect to religion, education and economy in the politico-jural domain
differed from that of government and law. The three
institutions were linked in precolonial society somewhat as follows. In the eighteenth and nineteenth
centuries people became chiefs by successfully participating in the system of trade traversing Kongo
territory, which brought slaves, ivory and other products to the coast in exchange for European
manufactures such as guns and cloth. Internally,
these items became symbols of chiefship and prestige
goods with which ritual debts were settled.
Chiefship itself was at least as much a ritual as a
political position; it was an expensive form of initiation into one of the many cults of the dead. A
parallel cult was that of territorial spirits
(bisimbi), a particular class of the dead, whose priest initiated the chief and made oracular
pronouncements on public affairs. Most adults were
initiated into at least one cult, the cults collectively serving functions of social control, economic
redistribution, and also education, in that through
them traditional knowledge was preserved and passed
on.

Colonial decrees abolished the public, corporate
cults of the dead, those centered on chiefs, territorial spirits and adolescent initiation, either
directly, by forbidding witchcraft trials, slave
trading and certain activities labeled "immoral," or
indirectly by destroying the trading system, in which
the greater part of the male population had engaged.
The newly created bureaucratic sector substituted new
corporate forms in which Congolese were recruited as
rank and file members exclusively. Once again, religion, education and economy were linked in a
particular way. The mission schools attracted young-
sters who as adults belonged to the church which had
educated them; on the strength of that education
they moved into the better paying and more prestigious occupations open to Congolese in the church,
the shools, the government, and the commercial and
industrial companies.

Almost simultaneously with its abolition of
slavery, the government conscripted all available
male labor, mainly for transportation and related
activities. Reforms introduced in the second and
third decades of this century, greatly reduced forced
labor requirements, but constrained the male population by taxation and other pressures to offer its

services in return for wages (JM No.13).  The terms
of  service were clearly distinctive:  labor legislation  distinguished    between   a   "work   contract"
applicable  to Congolese, which mobilized penal sanctions against    workers   who   contravened   obligations
formally or informally imposed upon them, and an "employment contract," applicable  to  Europeans,  which
provided no such sanctions (Young 1965:95-100).
      A corresponding   distinction   limited   Congolese
access  to  the  means  of  production.  No Congolese
could hold land in individual title, despite  several
half-hearted  legislative moves to that end from 1953
onwards (Young 1965:89-92), and the intrusion of Congolese  into  the  bureaucratic  (capitalist) economy
from bases in the customary sector was frustrated  by
a  judicial  policy that linked "customary" rights to
"traditional" functions.  Official policy  statements
regarding  the  future  disappearance of the barriers
between the two sectors are better read as reinforce-
ments  of  the structure than as contributions to its
downfall.  Colonial  ideology  described  the  native
community  as  in "the grip of clannish ties, victims
of empirical methods and ancestral shackles."  Policy
in the 1950's favored the development of an individualistic,  bourgeois  entrepreneurial  "middle  class"
supposed  to  serve both as a connecting link between
the rich and the proletariat and as a step towards "a
future  integration of both European and African middle classes." The use of class here is  a  deliberate
mystification, implying that the colonial state was a
nascent bourgeois democracy, structurally homogeneous
and  open.  In practice, licensing requirements frustrated would-be businessmen at every turn by  placing
upon  them  the  burden  of proving that they were no
longer motivated by "ancestral  mumbo-jumbo"  (Inforcongo 1959:401-09).
      From 1900  onwards,  most  men  worked  for  the
government  transportation  conglomerate,  on plantations, in government service, or as  household  help.
Lower  Congo, unlike some other parts of the country,
was not an area in which the  compulsory  cultivation
of  commercial  crops  on individual plots was highly
developed.  The most successful men became  teachers,
clergy,  and  medical  assistants.  The literacy rate
among men was certainly one of the highest in Africa,
thanks  to  excellent  mission  and state programs of
primary education, but secondary education, providing
training  necessary  for  even  lower  managerial and
technical positions, was not available to any  extent
before  the  mid-1950's.   Even  primary schools were

racially segregated;   this  segregation,  like  that
enforced  in residential areas from 1898 onwards, was
legitimated by reference to  pollution  beliefs  disguised   as   questions   of  public  hygiene  (Young
1965:93-94).
      By the mid-1950s, almost all BaKongo  were  pro-
fessed  Christians, Christianity being simultaneously
the publicly accepted source of  moral  norms  (to  a
greater   extent   than   in  other European colonies in
Africa)  and  the  principal  educational  channel:
people  became  Catholics or Protestants depending on
the school they had been able to attend.  Within  the
churches,  all controlled locally by missionaries and
ultimately by organizations  overseas  that  provided
theological canons, cultural ideals and capital, Congolese were restricted to subaltern roles, though  to
a  lesser degree than in the commercial companies and
government.  From the beginning, the Protestant  missions  maintained a sharp division between the social
situations of white and black personnel, justified by
references  to degrees of ability and "spirituality."
Black missionaries,  who  necessarily  violated  this
division,  were  tried out for a while but eventually
excluded as unsatisfactory.   BaKongo  who  had  been
educated  abroad  presented  a  still  more difficult
problem.  A Mpalabala man, Mvemba Stephen, brought to
a  prospective  mission  career excellent recommendations and a degree from  Shaw  University.   Richards
thought  perhaps  Mvemba could teach school at Mbanza
Manteke;  "he could live  in  a  semi-native  way  on
40-50  pounds a year."[2] The missionary at Mpalabala
felt he could use Mvemba as a  storekeeper  and  carpenter;   he could sleep in the store and be paid the
usual carpenter's wage of 4 pounds plus a  ration  of
rice, biscuits and meat or fish twice a week:

    Would Mvemba be agreeable to take this position
    I  wonder?   I  think that it is quite possible
    that he would but if so it would need some care
    to  disabuse  his  mind  with  reference to the
    footing which he would come out upon.  He would
    be  sure to expect to live in an American house
    furnished the same as he has been used  to  now
    for  years  and  to move in the same circle as
    missionaries at Matadi and neighborhood.  If he
    proved  himself  to  be the right man, he would
    after a time win all this as we  are  only  too
    anxious to get hold of really good men but just
    now he would be treated in the same way as [the
    carpenter  we  used  to  have].  If he agrees a

second class passage could be secured   for   him
to   Congo so that he might at once begin climbing down and not have to descend too many steps
of the ladder after his arrival out here.   From
the position of store-keeper he   might   advance
as   openings   occurred   in   the   transport, and
there are sure to be not a few as time goes on,
and should he prove to have a really missionary
spirit and develop helpfulness in the   work   he
would   possibly   make his way in that direction
also.   I mention this to show you that we   have
room   for   Stephen   Mvemba   (if you see well to
appoint him) provided that his   ideas   are   not
too   disproportionate   to his abilities and his
powers of usefulness (Charles Harvey,   Mpalabala,    February   7,   1895,   to Duncan;   ABFMS
archives, cited in Mahaniah 1975).

At this time, the basic salary of a married missionary,   $750, was 50 times that of the highest-paid
native evangelist.   Such a differential was necessary
simply   to   maintain   the   European in the life style
which defined him as such.
In the politico-jural domain, therefore, individuals participated   in   the   different   institutional
activities under quite different   ground-rules   which
segregated   them   by   color   and limited the range of
roles, opportunities and   responsibilities   available
to   them.   The   maintenance   and   operation   of this
segregation was itself part of the functional responsibility   of   corporate   units,   the   triumvirate of
church, state, and company to which Young refers, all
controlled by whites and serving the collective needs
of the European sector.
It was in the domestic domain, dominated by   the
activities   of   women,   that   the ritual and symbolic
contents of the indigenous   religion   survived   until
the public elements could be reconstituted by drawing
upon the Bible.   Colonial rule perpetuated with   little modification the precolonial mode of agricultural
production for subsistence, engaging primarily female
labor, as the customary sector of the plural economy.
Every woman produced what her household needed in the
way of vegetable foods, with a small surplus to sell.
Despite   certain   colonial   modifications,   customary
law, much of it expressed in the language of myth and
ritual, continued to regulate the family organization
and   the personal affairs of individuals with respect
to property and contracts.   With increasing   frequen-
cy,   children   were born in maternity clinics, but if

they were twins, initiates of the twin cult would
gather at the clinic to sing the prescribed songs,
thus keeping alive knowledge of the simbi spirits the
twins were supposed to incarnate. People came to
depend more and more on hospitals, but most European
physicians in Kongo can testify to the vitality of
the parallel practice of indigenous healers.
Funerals were conducted in traditional form, though
with some concessions to European hygiene, and served
to teach succeeding generations about the place of
the dead. Sickness and death were attributed to
witchcraft, and magicians could be sought out to provide protection against them. The indigenous
cosmology and religious vocabulary therefore remained
vital, although no collective response to witchcraft,
and the political and psychological problems it
represented, could be organized until the BaKongo
found in the Bible both the legitimating symbols that
such a response required and the figure of the prophet.

### THE ETHNOGRAPHY OF PLURALISM

Some critics of the model of social pluralism
seem to regard it as a forced and unnecessary analytical abstraction. In Zaire, pluralism is visible to
the eye in settlement plans, architecture, dress and
manners, and the individual moving across its boundaries experiences institutional contrasts
psychologically and physically. The new settlement
of Mbanza Manteke, begun in the late 1880's, reflected new social and political realities.

According to legend, the village was founded in
the remote past by immigrants from Mbanza Kongo, the
homeland of the BaKongo. They belonged to Nanga, a
matrilineal clan whose local representatives form an
exogamous group. Such local clan-sections are divided into "houses" (nzo), each of which collectively
owns land. The houses in turn are divided into
lineages, whose members share certain rights to mov-
able property. Relations between these units, and
the position of any individual in his lineage, are
given by a genealogy purporting to show descent in
the female line from a founding ancestor. Other
legends, all more or less controversial, also indicate that the founding clan was followed by other
settlers who were dependent upon the owners in one
way or an other: relatives by marriage, adult children of men of the clan, refugees, purchased slaves,
and others.

Sovereignty, that is, permanent rights over
land, of a political and social rather than directly
economic nature, is held by the house and the clan,
the estate of the clan consisting of the residual
rights of the constituent houses to the land of any
one of them should it die out. Persons, like land,
are owned by the house, not the lineage, and formerly
could be transferred between houses but not within
them. Compensation for homicide, for example, was
payable between houses of the same or different clans
but not between lineages of the same house.
Together, slaves, land and the persons added to the
matrilineal house by the normal processes of reproduction constitute the principal elements of its
estate.

A slave's living conditions and economic role do
not differ from a free man's; slavery is a form of
social dependence, not of forced or dependent labor.
Stratification is more an ideal than a fact. In
practice, there is a series of statuses between slave
and free, and movement up and down this scale may
happen to anyone. "Free" men are entitled, in time,
to become elders; slaves, in principle, may not. To
be an elder is to be recognized by other elders as
socially responsible for a group of dependents --
one's lineage or one's slaves -- in whatever contracts they may enter into. This status is accorded
by traditions of origin describing the direct descent
of free individuals from the founding ancestors or
alternatively, in the case of slaves, the interruption of the line of descent by a sale affecting
themselves or a matrilineal ascendant. Since traditions are validated not by written records but by the
testimony of the elders of related groups, who will
testify in their own best interest, the determination
of status is an intensely political matter. It is
the principal motive of village politics and a source
of considerable distress for the losers (MacGaffey
1970b: passim).

After the imposition of colonial rule, the village of Mbanza Manteke was moved out of the valley
where Richards had found it and settled in a healthier location on high ground around the mission
station he built. The Nzuzi house, last in the Nanga
clan, claimed ownership of Yongo, the tract on which
the mission itself was built. Members of this house
built pretentious mansions close to the mission
fence, and took it upon themselves to represent the
mission's clients (freed slaves, catechists from
elsewhere, and the like) in their dealings with the

village.  The Nsaka and Mfutu houses appropriated the
new government chiefship,  supposedly  a  traditional
institution  with  authority over a vast domain whose
limits were, in fact, simply those which the  mission
authorities  had  assigned to their station in Mbanza
Manteke.  Members of Nanga built  residences  in  the
fired  brick  introduced by the Europeans, with roofs
of iron, ornate windows, imitation upper storeys, and
redundant  gables.[3].   Client clans such as Ntumba,
Nkazi a Kongo, Mbenza and Nsundi built  behind  them,
usually  in  more  traditional  styles  and materials
suited to their  poverty  and  position.   Brush  was
cleared  on  orders of the public health authorities,
and latrines dug on the shoulders of the ridge.
     Mission houses,  some  of  which  survive,  were
built of planks, and raised on iron feet to frustrate
termites;  West Africans hired by the mission  taught
Manteke men how to saw planks.  The main building was
the church, by local standards a  vast  barn.   Other
buildings  housed  schools,  a printing press, and an
important hospital.  By the 1920's, these  activities
had  outgrown  the room on Yongo, and the entire complex was moved to a new and spacious station at Nsona
Mpangu, nearer the railroad.  The move also reflected
a shift in function;  missionaries increasingly  specialized  in secondary education, administration, and
skilled services;  more and more  they  left  primary
education,  evangelization,  pastoral  and elementary
medical care to BaKongo.  The remaining buildings  on
Yongo  housed  the  pastor  and  the local school and
congregation.
     Because of the importance  of  the  mission  the
government  made  Mbanza  Manteke  the administrative
center for the region.  In the 1950s,  two  complexes
of  buildings  were  put up under government sponsor-
ship.  The first was an administrative building and a
number  of houses for policemen and other public ser-
vants,  all  arranged,  like  the  school  buildings,
around a parade ground with a flagpole;  by 1965 this
complex was called "the commune".  The second  was  a
development  of  standardized  cement-block  houses,
built in rows in a plain style  like  the  government
buildings  rather than the pretentiously ornate brick
of older houses;  the new  houses  were  occupied  by
schoolteachers  and  government  officials,  all from
outside the village, or by Manteke people who for one
reason or another were alienated from the rest.  Both
of these complexes were adjacent to  what  was  still
called "the mission."

Aerial or ground photography in 1965 would therefore have shown a discontinuous settlement plan which could be shown by anthropological inquiry to reflect institutional discontinuities of which the people were well aware. The commune was thought of as "the" government rather than "our" government; in dealings with the villagers its personnel, themselves all from nearby villages, spoke French or sometimes Lingala, a language used by the national government. Their etiquette and their truth lay in bureaucratic norms; they marshalled the police and the populace in straight lines to address them, as did the pastor his flock and the schoolteachers their classes in the mission. Within the mission fence a youth could be arrested for practising drumming, on the ground that he had offended against the principles for which the departed missionaries had stood (MacGaffey 1970b: 276-84).

In the village proper, on the other hand, with its straggling collection of houses grouped by kin-ship ties, each house reflecting in its style, materials and mere location the social personality of its builder, the prevailing way of life was called "local custom" (fu kya nsi). Custom was marked by circular meetings in which men subtly laced their discourse with obscure proverbs spoken in a KiKongo marked by distinctive Manteke accents, and sealed their agreements formally by an exchange of cash tokens (mbungu). Here an elder would say, if asked who he was, that he was Nsundi (i.e., the local head of that clan), rather than that he was a salaried judge in the government's court. In the village, no one employed another for money. Here women avoided mentioning a son-in-law by name, or showing the soles of their feet to men with whom they might be talking. Here there were polygynous families, including that of the mayor, although by statute law the population was held to monogamy and it was the mayor's official duty to uphold the law.

As already noted, after 1900 most Manteke men spent their working lives away from the village pro-viding labor for European corporations connected with and dependent upon industrial forms of production and mechanized transportation. This complex intruded into the village in the form of the truck route link-ing the villages on the ridge with the Kinganga-Lufu valley and the Matadi-Kinshasa railroad and highway. Kinganga was until after 1960 a Portuguese trading post, and the valley also included the Catholic mis-sion at Konzo, the Protestant mission at Nsona

Mpangu, and the sisal plantation at Kitomesa, in all
of which some Manteke men found work within a purely
European institutional complex. Villagers thinking
about the landscape tend to dismiss the vehicular
roads. Their mental map links their settlements by
narrow footpaths which may be also the routes of
ancestral migrations; in theory, at least, four such
paths converge on each village (cf. Middleton
1970:39). Strangers are not supposed to know of
these routes, and witches are believed to try to
obstruct them.

In Matadi itself, where Manteke people are numerous, the European institutional complex is far more
elaborate, and the institutional cleavages characteristic of pluralism all the more conspicuous.
According to censuses, the population of Matadi rose
from about 54,000 in 1957 to 110,764 in September
1970. The total adult population in 1970 was 45,577,
of whom 10,317, mostly Angolan refugees, were not
Zairean citizens. The city comprised three communes
and an annex, a unit formed to administer newly settled areas on the southern edge of the town in which
refugees outnumbered the nationals. The following
description refers to 1970.

Matadi owes its existence to the port and rail-
head created at the end of the last century and managed in 1970 by the Office des Transports Congolais
(OTRACO, later called Office National des Transports,
ONATRA). The character of the three communes recorded this origin and reflected the resulting economic
structure. The downtown area, the Commune Urbaine,
housed the managerial elements of the principal
institutional sectors. In the multi-story buildings
on the main street leading from the town hall to the
port were the banks, the main post office, the Hotel
Metropole, the Catholic cathedral, the leading whole-
sale and retail suppliers of consumer goods, the
Agence Maritime and finally the offices of OTRACO
amid the marshaling yards and the docks. Further
uphill to the south, away from the Zaire River, were
the official residences of the managers, first the
iron-framed houses of the early colonial period, the
OTRACO compounds, and eventually the higher, cooler
and more attractive suburbs made accessible in modern
times by the automobile. In the residential area
stood also the Swedish Protestant mission (SMF), the
better schools of the city, the hospital, and (since
1966) the offices of the government of the province
of Kongo Central, now called Bas Zaire. In colonial
times the population of this commune was almost

entirely European; in 1970 it was mostly Zairean,
although many of the managers came from other provinces of the republic (MacGaffey 1971). One third
of the men living there were foreigners, mostly Belgians, Portuguese, and Pakistanis.

A ravine, which was also the <u>cloaca maxima</u>,
separated the Commune Urbaine, still popularly called
"the European commune," from the communes of Nzanza
and Mvuzi, formerly known as the <u>cité indigène</u>, in
which lived most of the skilled and unskilled workers
and the unemployed. Before independence (1960) the
<u>cité</u> was almost entirely a labor camp for workers
expected to return to their villages when they
retired or lost their jobs. In that period it was
very closely supervised by Belgian authorities. In
the 1960's Matadi became, like other towns, a refuge
for many who found the crumbs from the tables of
employed relatives more satisfying than the increasingly niggardly living rural villages afforded. It
also became the permanent home of a growing population of older people no longer interested in village
life and younger people who had never known it and
spoke only the urban dialect, KiLeta, rather than the
KiKongo of their parents.

Good official statistics on employment and unemployment are lacking. More than a quarter of the
adult male population worked for OTRACO, the largest
employer; at every change of shift in the docks the
bridges across the ravine resounded to hurrying feet.
In the <u>cité</u> itself the largest employers were the
communal governments. Other conspicuous enterprises
included the medical clinics (mostly private), the
schools, the bars, and innumerable little stores and
market stalls tended mostly by the owners or their
close relatives. The prices of all imported goods,
including rice, powdered milk and soap, were 10 percent higher than downtown. Most of the traders were
women, but men were the most important wholesalers.
The immediate hinterland of the city is rocky and
barren, but hundreds of women rented cultivable land
on the north bank of the river at some distance from
Matadi. Unskilled and semi-skilled workers in 1970
made from 10 to 15 zaires a month ($20-$30);
schoolteachers, approximately 15 zaires; government
clerks, 12; a graduate nurse, 20. Many
self-employed men made much more, and a number of
merchants were evidently wealthy. Men commonly had
more than one source of income, possibly including

rent from tenants, and their wives usually added to
the household income.

As in rural areas, the cleavage between bureaucratic and customary sectors was not spatially
perfect. The road network extended into the uptown
communes, for example, but few residents owned vehicles. They got about on foot and, though they might
use sections of the roads, for them the real ways of
the town were footpaths scrambling up rocky slopes,
through alleys and backyards: conventional and convenient routes that no outsider was likely to
discover for himself. Rectilinear islands of ugly
standardized housing, similar to the modern development in Manteke village, housed OTRACO workers amid
the individualistic jungle of private homes. The
missions and the state also maintained outposts in
the cite, chiefly offices and schools, but the spatial boundaries were respected. The Protestant
church compound was actually surrounded by a barbed
wire fence, erected no doubt for excellent reasons,
which reflected the European sense of property and
heedlessly interrupted more than one pedestrian
route. Behind the fence, the only one in the cité,
Kongo clergy lived in houses of European type and
occupied bureaucratic jobs formerly held by missionaries. They had lived all their lives in a
mission environment, and spoke KiKongo with a Swedish
accent.

From the point of view of Europeans in Kongo
there is only one social system. Though to some
extent they keep to themselves, everyday they meet
BaKongo and participate with them in the same institutions, apparently sharing the same assumptions and
values. They are aware of activities and ideas among
the local population which they do not understand,
but see them as marginal and residual. BaKongo
however must be to some extent adepts of two systems,
which they describe as kimundele (European) and
kindombe (black), and which demand different
techniques du corps (Mauss 1968:365-86). In kindombe
one points with the lower lip, not the finger, and
gives things with two hands, not one. Girls who go
to secondary schools wear the school uniform of
knee-length skirts but add a long wrap when they come
home, to hide their legs, lest they be taken for
whores; on the other hand, married women think little of revealing their breasts. If a door is a
European door, women enter first; if an African
door, men enter first. Examples could be multiplied.

Pl.7: Nzanza market, Matadi

Pl.8: Downtown Matadi

In the area of religious beliefs, differences
between the two systems are deliberately concealed;
knowing that Europeans do not understand, people will
sometimes say, especially if the topic is witchcraft,
"Ah, you don't know what goes on in our African
world" (mu kindombe kyeto). Sometimes they openly
discuss beliefs which they themselves may hold but
describe them as past: "It used to be thought
such-and-such." Sometimes they produce descriptions
and explanations which they know from experience will
satisfy European curiosity. They are not being
deceitful; the want to avoid a futile argument or
yet another blunt condemnation of their views, that
is, of their experience as they know it. Much of the
time, however, there is no question of deliberate
motive; the religious lexicon as it has evolved over
decades of colonial life now permits and even imposes
a dialogue of the deaf in which the words used mean
different things to the two parties, and each goes
away satisfied with the echo of his own voice
(JM:Intro.).

It is conventional in social science to ignore
the pluralism of a society such as I have been describing and to substitute a scale of linear progress
as a way of measuring the difference between village
and town. In this perspective, Mbanza Manteke is
traditional, downtown Matadi is modern, and the cite
is "transitional." Conventional though they are,
these terms lack both logical definition and empirical relevance. The port of Matadi was already in
existence before Manteke regrouped on Yongo, and the
new village conformed to imperatives orginating in
the town or beyond it, overseas. Statute law circumscribed the zone of customary law, but also modified
its content, by positive and negative sanctions that
induced chiefship, matriliny, land tenure and marriage payments to conform to European expectations in
these matters. In Matadi, likewise, the Nzanza market in its mud and filth is not a belated African
effort, hampered by traditional values, to catch up
with the downtown shopping area, where the streets
are paved and electrically lit; it is a recent product of decisions made downtown about commercial
licensing and capital investment. Much of what happens in the customary sector has traditional
precedents traceable through several centuries, but
the same is true of the bureaucratic sector. A village such as Mbanza Manteke must be recognized as a
fully contemporary phenomenon.

Finally, it must also be recognized that what I
have been calling the European or bureaucratic sector
is itself a local, that is, an African, phenomenon
and not a transplanted slice of Europe.[4] The Belgian colonial regime was quite unlike, and in many ways
carefully insulated from, metropolitan Belgium (Young
1965:20-28). It was, for example, utterly undemo-
cratic; even whites had no vote, and as labor were
relatively unorganized. The government was officially associated with both the ideological aims and the
practical activities of the Catholic Church, the
anti-clerical point of view achieving only an inter-
mittent presence in official policy (Markowitz 1973).
Top government personnel doubled as company direc-
tors, as they were to do again in independent Zaire.
Formally and informally the corporate units of the
European sector cooperated to maintain their joint
interests in the political domain, a policy charit-
ably described as paternalism. If secrecy,
authoritarianism, rigidity and the overwhelming
importance of large corporations were the distinctive
social marks of the European sector, culturally its
outstanding feature was the preponderance of the
petit bourgeois. The freedom, richness and complexity of European civilization, its great achievements
in art, literature, science, philosophy and ethics,
were strained to a thin gruel. The only book of any
importance that most literate Congolese found to
study was the Bible, outstanding in a ruck of evangelical and didactic tracts about hygiene, chicken
farming, daily prayers, and Horatio Alger for houseboys. Western art was represented by sentimental
madonnas and Western music by the lugubrious products
of the harmonium.
    After independence, the governing class that
emerged from the scramble of bank clerks, medical
assistants, ex-seminarists, schoolteachers and small
businessmen to take over the apparatus of the state
and to perpetuate, after a fashion, colonial policies, only superficially resembled the governing
class of the ideal-typical European nation state,
since the state remained dependent, economically and
politically, on Belgian, French, and American capital, supported (as in the Shaba crises of 1977 and
1978) by allied military forces. Unlike the bourgeoisie of Europe, this governing class lacked, at
first, the institutions necessary for its exclusive
reproduction, such as schools, relative endogamy, a
distinctive culture, and substantial private property. In the 1970s it moved some distance towards

overcoming these deficiencies as its members built mansions in the suburbs, acquired plantations and businesses, invested money abroad, and educated their children there.  Ultimately, however, their sources of wealth depended on the government and the nationalized enterprises, from which the new class drew salaries and other emoluments.  In this collective and individual dependence they resembled other African ruling groups before them, rather than a class in the European sense (Goody 1977).

# 4

# Success and Failure

In the plural social structure of Belgian Congo, Congolese, but not Europeans, learned two sets of rules (customary and bureaucratic), lived their lives in two different patterns of social interaction, and developed different identities or personalities in the two sectors. In the last chapter, I will argue that for many of them their experience was in fact schizophrenogenic. Successful men survived the experience. The prophets and their followers, not a representative sample of the population, were doubly unsuccessful, defeated in both the bureaucratic and the customary fields of their experience. Van Wing (1958:584) was at least partly right when he referred to Louis Franck, colonial minister from 1918 to 1924, and "the inevitable relationship between [Franck's] policy of respect for custom and Kimbanguism." Van Wing saw the policy as encouraging racism on both sides, but fundamentally what Franck did was to institutionalize social pluralism.

In the bureaucratic sector, literacy was a prime tool, and from the 1890's large numbers of BaKongo set themselves to acquire it, mostly in mission schools. Numerous missionary reports indicate that education was popularly regarded as the vwela (initiation camp) of the new cult, in which initiates acquired knowledge of the songs, rituals and taboos appropriate to the service of the spirit, from which in turn they would derive potency. Once literate, they found that they were restricted to subaltern positions in the mission hierarchy, as catechists and the like. From the letters they wrote to mission journals at the turn of the century we know that they were dissatisfied with their conditions of work, and with their inability to advance to real authority despite the universalism of the Gospel as preached.

The biography of Kimbangu states, immediately before the account of his first vision from God, that he and his elders wanted him to become a catechist. As the story of Ma Kinzembo makes dramatically plain, Kimbangu was born when the military occupation of the country was still not complete (JM No.39). He belonged to the first generation of BaKongo to grow up under colonial rule and to realize in his own life its peculiar frustrations. Thomas, a missionary, wrote in 1921 that Kimbangu had been for a short time a teacher in the mission school at Ngombe Lutete (BMS correspondence quoted by M.-L. Martin, 1975:44). Dialungana's history of the movement, probably seeking to minimize (as is usual in such histories) the extent of the prophet's indebtedness to existing sources of knowledge, declares that Kimbangu had never studied at a mission station but had learned to read and write a little from a village teacher (quoted in Chapter One). In any event, the sense of unfulfilled ambition is clear. Kimbangu was not a well-educated man, nor well-known to the missionaries; when R.L.Jennings of Ngombe Lutete heard about him, he had to look in his records to find out who he was. Kimbangu's first "helper" (according to the Catechism; the biography recruits him later) was Ntualani, a similarly marginal Christian whose mission identity card, which he brought with him when he transferred to the parish of Ngombe Lutete, says on it in English, the private language of the missionaries, "Thomas Ntualani is a member of this church. I don't know much about him." (signed) Thomas Hill.

Troubled in some way, either by disappointment within the mission or by the voice of Jesus, as the catechism says, Kimbangu tried working in Kinshasa for a while, where he devoted his literacy to inscribing shipping numbers on oil drums for one of the big commercial companies; even so he had money problems (Andersson 1958:50).

Others who had succeeded in becoming catechists were no more satisfied than he. In 1908, ABFMS missionaries reported an outbreak of "spiritualism" that had been going on for several years in Mbanza Nkazi, near Mbanza Manteke; church members were absenting themselves from mission services to attend all-night meetings led by two Manteke-trained catechists calling themselves <u>mim'bikudi</u> "seers" (Stuart 1969:316).

Morel found BMS catechists in abundance at Nkamba   in
1921.    Later, an administrative telegram referred to
a barricaded emplacement of prophets,   including   "13
catechists   from   the American mission at ba Mateke,"
who sang incessantly "no   more   government,   no   more
taxes,   no   more [government] chiefs, and Christ will
come to save us."[1]

Other   adherents   had   fallen   foul   of   mission
rules.   Ntualani   confessed   drinking palm wine.   In
the Manteke area, most of the prophets of 1921 and of
subsequent   years had been excommunicated by the mission for failing to live up to its rule of   monogamy;
other   evidence   suggests   that   individuals who fell
from grace by taking plural wives did so not so   much
from   moral weakness, as the mission assumed, as from
a decision to improve their prospects by adhering   to
custom   rather   than   written   law.   To an important
extent,   therefore,   leaders   of   dissident   religious
movements   were failures within the bureaucratic sector.   On   the   other   hand,   in   1921   and   in   the
pre-independence   years, those who had achieved relatively secure positions in the church did not   become
Kimbanguists.   It follows that, even though the dissidents were in a sense right,   in   that   their   cause
eventually   became   the cause of all Congolese, their
activities cannot be regarded as a simple function of
colonial oppression or the like.   Of the entire population subject to   colonial   rule,   only   the   losers
responded in this way.

In the   perspective   of   customary   society   the
position   of   individuals who became prophets or prophetic   adherents   is   defined   very   differently.
According   to its own ideology, as we have seen, customary society is stratified into freemen and slaves,
although   in   practice   the situation is more complex
than that, and the status   of   many   individuals and
lineages   is a matter of bitter and protracted debate
(MacGaffey 1970b).

In the region of Mbanza Manteke all of the   prophets   of   1921   and the majority of adherents to the
movement in the late 1950's were widely   regarded   as
of   slave   descent.[2]   Mabwaka   Mpaka,   for example,
belonged to a marginal lineage   incorporated   in   the
clan   Mfulama Nkanga.   As is common in such cases, he
lived with his   father's   rather   than   his   mother's
matrilineal   clan,   even   when   he   had   reached   an
advanced age.   His fathers would   welcome   him   as   a
client,   whereas   his mothers would constantly remind
him of his jural inferiority to themselves, his   owners.   From   his   fathers   in   the   village of Kemba he

obtained land on which to build his prophetic establishment called Kinzolani. Another example: in
1958, an entire lineage, reputedly of slave descent
within the Ndumbu clan of Kulu village, joined the
prophet movement as a political tactic in the course
of their perennial dispute with their alleged owners
as to whether they were slaves or not; the owners,
also of Ndumbu clan, included the village's government-appointed headman and his deputy (JM Nos.15,27).
    Despite its importance in Kongo eyes, Kimbangu's
pedigree is not mentioned as a factor in the vast
literature written about Kimbanguism by Europeans.
According to his son Diangienda, Kimbangu's clan was
Kisenga and his wife came from Nzinga.[3] In the
region of Nkamba, birthplace of Kimbangu and headquarters of the church headed by his sons, he is
widely believed to have been a slave from Manianga,
though only the EJCSK's religious rivals make the
charge explicitly and spontaneously. The social configuration is also the same as in Mabwaka's case:
Nkamba belongs to the prophet's father's clan, Mpanzu. The determination of slave status is always a
political issue, however, and never a simple matter
of ascertaining the facts.
    The two systems of status discrimination, custo-
mary and bureaucratic, were linked in practice. In
Manteke, the Nanga clan, no matter how miserable
their patrimony and dubious their pedigree, were
assured of a respectful hearing from their allies the
missionaries, to whom their headman was known as "old
King Makokila, chief of a large district" (MacGaffey
1970b:251), although to a passing Swedish soldier he
was "the old sinner" (Axelson 1970:235). As the mission's principal clients, Nanga became patrons to the
rest of the village, de facto "chiefs and free men"
(mfumu). In due course, when the policy of indirect
rule prescribed government recognition of chiefs,
Nanga obtained a right to that recognition almost
automatically. Even though nobody in the village
thinks of the government chiefship as traditional,
the position enabled its holder to influence judicial
decisions regarding questions of slave descent, which
he did as recently as 1966 (MacGaffey 1977a:252).
The only one of the elders of Nanga ever to have been
a Kimbanguist was also the only one whose slave background was generally recognized (MacGaffey 1970b:62).
    Nanga also did very well for themselves in the
bureaucratic sector. They held steady jobs at the
mission, their children were likely to be well educated, and in droves they left the village for the

best jobs commerce and government offered to Congolese. They could afford to buy good food, mosquito nets, medical care.

Kimbangu's work in 1921 defied the structure of authority supporting the distribution of resources outlined above, seeking to replace it with another. The movement was thus, in an analytical sense, political, although its direct object was the mission church. Its base was originally the rural population, even though nascent urban interests soon joined it. Inevitably also the government and the regime as a whole came to be directly or indirectly attacked; though Kimbangu himself by his own account (many years later) did not advocate non-payment of taxes, many of his followers did. Dialungana bitterly includes forced labor for the state among the sufferings from which God redeemed the black people through Kimbangu (JM No.42, par.3.2).

The prophetic movement, in the few short weeks of its autonomy, attempted to organize itself as an incipient church, whose charter (the Bible), structure (hierarchical, regional) and rules of membership paralleled those of a mission. This development was of a piece with the ambivalence of the prophets towards the missionaries, who were simultaneously the benevolent fathers (mase meto), bringing the gospel, and the enemy, depriving Africans of the "true" gospel to the benefit of Europeans. Congolese accounts of missionary behavior are filled with the idiom of witchcraft (the outer appearance, the contradictory inner meaning; predatory commerce in the guise of philanthropy), which is itself only the idiom of a beneficent and necessary magic in which one has lost confidence. The ambivalence of this attitude was evoked by, and parallels, that of the missionaries themselves, who joined to the gospel of brotherhood the gospel of white control. It is an oedipal ambivalence to which the metaphor of David and Goliath, evoked by Kimbangu, is entirely appropriate.

Spirit possession, sociologically, substitutes a superior for an inferior person in relation to an other. The prophet's biography shows him trembling and speaking in tongues in situations in which he would normally have been a loser. Confronting Morel, he "calls upon Jehovah," and thereafter speaks in heavenly language. The tactic worked; Morel was forced to give up his interrogation. The movement, as soon as it became a movement, defined itself and its internal hierarchy in terms of true as opposed to false prophets; false prophets may tremble, but only

because  they are possessed by an evil spirit, as the
true prophet in touch with God  is  able  to  reveal.
This  criterion  of  spirituality  is similar to that
invoked by missionaries in  rationalizing  their  own
use  of  power;   Steven  Mvemba was relegated to the
carpentry shop on account of his inferior spirituality.

The biography expresses the movement  of  events
in  February and March, 1921, as a struggle between a
failed and a successful catechist, Kimbangu and Mvwala.[3]  More  was going on, though, than a schismatic
struggle.  The story of how Kimbangu healed  a  chief
(<u>mfumu</u>  <u>mpu</u>)  is  really an account of how the chief,
epitome of the system of matrilineal descent and land
tenure, was subordinated by Kimbangu, and the rituals
supporting the chief's office declared to be  inferi-
or.   After the chief had been "raised" by the prophet
in the name of Christ, he happened to fall down, thus
violating  a taboo of his chiefship.  When he and his
followers immediately performed appropriate  gestures
to  ward  off  the consequences of this violation, he
was challenged by the prophet and  told  to  abandon
such  practices,  that  is, to give up his chiefship.
Reluctant to do so, he fell down  again,  and  became
ill once more (Raymaekers 1971:35.

When the prophet appointed  assistants,  one  of
them  promptly  suggested  that, "since we have taken
over the country,"  it  was  time  to  challenge  the
unjust administration of a local chief, and especially his allocation of land ("he takes  other  people's
forests  by  force").  In making this suggestion, the
assistant quoted John 15:1, "I am the true vine,  and
my Father is the husbandman," which he perhaps understood as indicating that he (his clan) was  the  true
owner  of  the  soil  that  his  "father",  i.e.  his
father's clan, possibly the clan that claimed him  as
a  slave,  was  occupying  as its own.  Be that as it
may, Kimbangu reacted sharply to the suggestion  that
someone  other  than  himself was "the vine," and the
following day he  arranged  a  test  of  spirituality
which  the  assistant  failed;   he  was  therefore
dismissed.  Kimbangu also took charge of  the  available  labor  of believers and unbelievers, responding
to insubordination with an access of  fury  and  the
threat  to  burn  offenders  alive--an  act  that  the
greatest nineteenth century chiefs would have boasted
of (Raymaekers 1971:33-34, 45-46).[4]

The social significance of  the  new  order  was
recognized  in  places  far  distant from Nkamba.  In
Kasangulu, in 1980, informants recalled, as a  factor

in a land dispute, that as a result of Kimbangu's new deal a slave lineage had been permitted, in 1921, to rejoin its erstwhile owners as equal members of the clan. What the prophets did was to proclaim a new society with a new tradition sufficient to erase old status distinctions in both sectors. Despite the nationalistic elements that were soon incorporated in the movement, they appealed primarily to losers, whether slaves or the unemployed.

By the end of World War II, Kongo society had changed; there had come into existence a substantial, recognized and self-conscious class of bureaucratic employees, educated by the missions for clerical jobs, who saw their future as a matter of advancement within the structure of the colonial institutions rather than replacing them with other institutions (Rubbens 1945). Most of them had been brought up in a mission rather than a village environment, and understood the structure of village life in terms of the colonial ethnography they had been taught in school (MacGaffey 1970b:290). On the other hand, for those who did not make it through the mission school system, life's prospects and experiences had increasingly become those of an industrial proletariat. In 1945, when strikes and riots broke out in Matadi and battle lines were drawn on either side of the ravine that divides the town, the clerical workers stood aside. Though the government of the day preferred, at its convenience, to see the riots as expressions of "xenophobia" (the colonial euphemism for black racial hostility) the issue was that most laborers earned no more than the minimum necessary to sustain a bachelor, and all were caught in a squeeze of rising prices. Conspicuous among the leaders of the rioters, and among the 900 persons arrested, were members of the still clandestine prophet movement (Jewsiewicki et al. 1972).

The prophets as teachers reinforced the indigenous cosmology according to which, as I have already mentioned, all whites were regarded as intruders from the land of the dead. In this perspective, further explained in Chapter Five, alienation and oppression were translated into the idiom of witchcraft and slavery. Exported raw materials, including ivory and rubber, were thought of as containers for the souls of enslaved Africans, and industrial accidents as the visible evidence of witchcraft transactions by which the slave trade was perpetuated. When political conditions deprived the ruling group of its institutional defences, latent

accusations of witchcraft were realized in a collective effort to rid the country of the oppressors.
The theory of witchcraft was put to revolutionary use
in this way in 1921, 1945, and 1960 (before independence), and after independence, though not among the
BaKongo themselves, in the Mulelist and other revolts
of 1964, directed against the class which by then had
taken over the management of the bureaucratic sector
(Fox et al. 1965). The ideology itself, that is to
say, is capable of describing the situation adequate-
ly and of mobilizing action to change it. Whether it
serves this function depends on conditions other than
ideological.

        During the 1950's, the social differences
represented by the different behavior of prophets and
clerical workers in the Matadi riots were formally
embodied in Kimbanguism and Abako, respectively.
Thus despite their overlapping memberships and rhe-
torics, the two organizations corresponded to
emergent class differences. After independence, as
Abako came to terms with other regional political
parties and dropped its interest in Kongo tradition,
it became simply the election campaign machinery of
the group in power in Kongo Central province (Monnier, 1971:303-end). All the organizational forms
implanted in the customary sector became subject once
again to the jealous supervision of the bureaucracy.
EJCSK, as we have seen, was forced to incorporate
itself on the model of a mission church, at some cost
in popular support. Meanwhile, the government progressively dismantled the distinctive institutions of
the customary sector. In 1973 it nationalized land,
thus depriving matrilineal descent of its main functional content. Individuals were encouraged to
acquire title to estates on condition that they
develop ranches, plantations and the like. The new
landowners belonged to the urban upperclass, who
alone had the neessary capital. The end of the era
of indirect rule thus entailed the eventual stratification of the BaKongo by class (MacGaffey 1982b).

        In post-revolutionary conditions the prophets,
in their capacity as healers, spoke to the condition
of the politically marginal by offering daily pallia-
tives for their distress.[5] These functions also
could be distinguished according to the sector in
which the afflictions seemed to originate, as long as
pluralism persisted. In the customary sector, the
link between healing and slavery is provided by
witchcraft, as follows: the afflictions for which
BaKongo seek the services of a healer, including both

diseases and misfortunes, are thought to be caused by
the illwill of others, and one of the commonest occasions of illwill is a political dispute about who   is
and  who is not a slave.  "Healing" consists in large
part of mediating such disputes. (See  "Therapy  and
its social context," in Chapter Six).

Besides many  whose  afflictions  originated  in
indigenous  institutions relating to descent, clients
of the prophets in their capacity as healers included
others  whose  afflictions were those of proletariat.
The local concept of disease  includes  such  misfortunes    as    theft,   debt,  unemployment,  scholastic
failure, and failure to make money.  Peasant life  is
an  unrelenting  drudgery  whose  stresses  were also
implicated in the world of witchcraft;    the   prophet
Kinene   kept   in a shed the hoes and other tools used
by victims of witchcraft  whose  dreams,  and  aching
bodies  the  next  morning,  told  them they had been
enslaved to  work  someone's  plantation  during  the
night.  The prophet's diagnosis in such cases pointed
once again to the illwill of relatives, neighbors, or
more rarely workmates, and his treatment offered psychological comfort through such  means  as  blessings
and ritual baths.

The observer is bound to comment on a discrepancy here.  In slavery disputes the idiom of witchcraft
at least identifies the actual parties  in  conflict,
and   may  induce some reconciliation between them.  In
the diagnosis and treatment  of  proletarian  afflictions,   however,   the   employers  and  managers  of
bureaucratic institutions within which tensions arise
are   protected   against   witchcraft acusations by the
police, in the first instance, and by the   fact   that
the  official  philosophy  of the entire bureaucratic
sector refuses to accept the legitimacy of the witchcraft  idiom.  After 1960, routine prophetic services
therefore  served  to  deflect  potential  aggression
against the ruling class and caused it to be absorbed
within the working class itself.[6]

In 1970, Zairean  society  still  displayed  the
pluralism  of  the  colonial  period,  a structure to
which the churches,  including  those  through  which
prophetic action was effected, necessarily conformed.

## EVOLUTION OF CHURCHES

In Chapter  Two,  the  universal  and  pragmatic
functions  of  churches were shown to assume distinct
organizational  forms,  called  "congregation"   and
"band,"  respectively.  The churches of Matadi may be

divided into three groups, exhibiting different combinations of these forms:

1. universal complex; bands absent or vestigial:
   Catholics, Witnesses, Salvation Army, EJCSK,
   EC-Gonda.

2. universal and pragmatic complex: Protestants,
   Apostles, Black Church, DMNA, DMN-Mbumba.

3. pragmatic complex: regular congregations and
   hierarchy vestigial or nominal: the remaining
   DMN churches.

This classification is also of historical
interest, since several of the churches, notably
EJCSK, changed their organizational form in the process of establishing and maintaining themselves, and
since the universal and pragmatic functions belong,
ideologically, to two different institutional
sectors: regular congregations are consciously "European" and bureaucratic; healing bands are
"African."
In 1960, most of the local Kongo churches
intended to function in both the bureaucratic and the
customary sectors of society, that is, to appear as a
"mission" in French-speaking society and as kingunza
in KiKongo-speaking, descent-based society. Official
church statutes attempted to express both aims, but
foundered on problems of translation. Language difficulties in turn simply reflected the
incompatibility of the two sectors, differing in ideology, organization, interpersonal norms, body
techniques, skills, equipment and goals. Some sort
of accommodation was possible at the level of organization and function, such that a church's corporate
framework and universal pretensions could take the
form required by the norms of the bureaucratic sector, while its pragmatic goals were accomplished in
customary form with a partially independent and less
stable organization, the "band." Compromises of this
sort tended to divide a church into two separate and
even antagonistic units, since in religious as in
other activities the bureaucratic sector was not simply parallel to but parasitic upon the customary
sector, being supported by a continuous extraction of
tithes, donations and "voluntary" labor.
Different churches responded differently to this
tension, and changed their response as time passed.
In 1970, the churches in Matadi exhibited various

combinations of the two complexes, although local
comment recognized only a difference in organizational level: bands were described as sections of a
church's regular congregation. DMN-Nsansi, nominally
one of 250 congregations of a church, was in fact an
autonomous band, loosely affiliated with some others,
in which bureaucratic features were present only as
camouflage, and universality was a theme restricted
to the prologue to the church's main act (see next
chapter). Its members and even its head assumed that
for regular worship, unconnected with afflictions,
one would attend a Catholic or Protestant church;
either would do. Operating almost entirely in the
customary sector, DMN-Nsansi had no regular membership or financial structure.

DMNA was not even bureaucratic to the extent of
camouflage; it neither initiated nor even replied to
government correspondence, and made a point of not
having membership dues, pastoral salaries, or public
healing services from which gift income could result.
DMN-Mbumba was divided into bands which also united
once a week as the local congregation of a church,
but many of its members individually belonged to the
Protestant Church (EECK). Other Protestants belonged
to semi-clandestine bands within EECK, whose rituals
were indistinguishable from those of DMN-Mbumba. The
Black Church (ENAF) did not permit its members to
belong to any other; few of the regular members of
this church appeared at the clinical sessions of the
band of this denomination. On the other hand, many
of the people who did appear at such a session in
ENAF (or DMN-Mbumba) on any given day were there only
to be healed and might not be aware of the doctrines
or even of the existence of the wider church.

The consolidation of EJCSK after 1960 forbade
the existence of autonomous bands and officially
assimilated healing functions into the regular organization of the church, but specialized healing groups
continually emerged within this framework. In 1970,
unofficial though not clandestine bands existed in
rural areas at least, though we found none in Matadi
itself. Apparently there were no bands, clandestine
or otherwise, in the Salvation Army, the Witnesses,
or the Catholic Church. Individual Catholics were as
numerous as Protestants among the clients of healers,
and all of the other churches had former Catholics
among their members. The Witnesses, although bureaucratic in form, and supported by foreign missionaries
and an international organization, turned their backs

to the state and to both medical science and education. The Salvation Army, having been almost
transformed into a prophetic movement by its followers between 1935 and 1940, had apparently shed all
its healing functions by 1960, although clandestine
bands persisted within it into the 1960's. In 1970
the functions of Apostles' bands (EUDA), as described
to us, resembled those of any DMN church, but we were
unable to gain admission and know nothing of the
rituals; regular services conformed closely to the
Protestant type (see Chapter Seven).
    Features of the history of DMN-Difuene and of
EJCSK illustrate in more detail the forces affecting
all the churches, and the relationship between organizational form and functional content.

## Education, politics and corporate identity

    Besides serving as a channel of recruitment,
school systems sometimes constituted the economic and
social base of the church itself. From the beginning, the modern Protestant and Catholic missions
assumed that education was a necessary preparation
for and accompaniment to spiritual conversion.
Africans were to be redeemed from ignorance, dirt and
idleness as much as from superstition; despite their
own efforts and protestations to the contrary, missionaries commonly confounded conformity to a
European life-style with redemption. By one means or
another, children were separated from the indigenous
social system and trained in a new world of trousers,
two-story buildings, tables and chairs, wage labor
and written documents. This new social system, the
mission, as an organization and as a visible physical
complex, set the colonial standard for religious
respectability and effectiveness. BaKongo reasonably
regarded admission into it as an initiation into
white man's magic, involving a more thoroughgoing
transformation of one's personal appearance, personality structure and power relations than anything
imposed by such indigenous cults as Nkimba. Such
opinions persisted in recent years (Andersson
1968:189).
    In 1921, the possibility of direct contact with
God, manifested by Kimbangu, supposedly made literacy, the ability to read the word of God, available to
all, without subordination to a priesthood and the
cost in souls that such an initiation was believed to
require. When the nascent EJCSK began to organize a

school system, many of its respected older members, the generation of 1921, believed that such a development was unnecessary, because literacy was a spiritual gift. The church's highly successful program of unpaid labor by its members built schools first, houses of worship second, and installed in them teachers and classes qualified for government subsidy. In Matadi as elsewhere, this complex, including the dispensary and housing for the principal staff, was generally known to members, in 1970, as "the mission."

Several other churches used the name "mission" as they attempted to take on similar form. In 1963, for example, one DMN branch, at the time calling itself Mission Prophétique Congolaise, announced that its purposes were prayer, confession, and healing "by prayer or by medication, as the Spirit may indicate." In addition it planned a list of social works in which the characteristic activities of prophecy, which do not readily lend themselves to description in French, and those of a mission, which were never realized, are ambiguously interwoven:

> Adjudication of the sick: because it may happen that the sickness involves antagonism among relatives, James 5:13-16 ("Is any among you afflicted? let him pray.") (La justice des maladifs: parce qu'il y a ceci parfois c'est une maladie qui est contre amis ou la famille.)

> Blessing to the world.

> ESP, Ecole Savant Prophète

> Ecole de la Sione

> A dispensary and two day-care centers; to be directed by a Congolese and a European, not yet appointed.

The Black Church declared in its "Manifesto" (JM No.45) that its doctrine could only be enumerated in the form of the following principles:

> Equality and absolute respect for all members.
> Non-interference in the affairs of another organization.
> Formal condemnation of demagogic confusion.
> Unique recognition of the Bible as a general, global code for every human excuse.

Such statutes, imitations of Belgian models appropriate to bureaucratically regulated corporations, are pathetically inappropriate to the real constitution and aims of prophetic groups. They are bids for a respectability measured by alien values, attempts to deflect anticipated criticism.

A prophet's commission is often brief and his congregation ephemeral. Relations with the government may well be critical, since whereas a slight official nod promises security, an official frown threatens destruction and personal risk. The DMN-Difuene file in Nzanza Commune in 1970 was impressively full of correspondence, though much of it consisted of such gratuitous items as a letter to the provincial governor announcing the death of the secretary-general of the church, together with a reply from some minor undersecretary assuring the church of his "émotions les plus émues". The church's letterhead, supported by a battery of rubber stamps, printed the words "République Démocratique du Congo, Province du Kongo Central" in large type, with the name of the church relatively small. Incessant appeals to the government for support against the illegal maneuvers of the opposition documented the church's long history of schism. This history is strongly reminiscent of the incessant splintering of Abako and other political parties into ever smaller divisions, and used much the same vocabulary ("aile Mpanzu") and the same repertoire of accusations.

Besides the realities of patronage, the tradition of segmentary dispersal from Mbanza Kongo underlay both the ecclesiastical and the political conflicts (MacGaffey 1970b:ch.1). Schismatic churches carefully traced their spiritual pedigree through a succession of prophets back to Kimbangu himself, embellishing the tradition with accounts of miracles and supporting it in the present with bureaucratic rituals. As in litigation between clans in recent decades, government documents, or imitations of them, were brandished like charms as assertions and repositories of power. The vacant pomp of formal correspondence replaced the resonance of semi-intelligible praise-names, as in the following extracts from a letter in which one ecclesiastical splinter dissociated itself from another. Such inflated rhetoric emanated from groups numbering in fact a few dozens only, although everyone carried some title such as conseiller technique, pasteur-visiteur, or président du conseil, by which he was customarily addressed.

A Messieurs les membres sortants de
l'Eglise Ngounzisme du Congo:
Panzu D.   et Landu N.

     Faisant suite par votre lettre du 11/9/67,
j'ai l'honneur de porter à votre connaissance
que, suivant la lettre no.  0026/BC/CF/SIEG.
/KV/66 de Monsieur le President Fondateur
Basolua Demithel, signé par les comités
Supérieurs du Saint-Siège, decident que [...]
     Lorsque Monsieur le Président-Fondateur a
reçu les documents du nouvelle règlement auprès
des autorités Central vous avez refise de
remplir ces documents, en disant par vos
membres de ne pas suivre les règlements du
Gouvernement parce-que sont des documents
politiques, et vous avez sortie dans notre
Eglise depuis le 26/8/66 par votre lettre no.
0020/MPM/SDG/PMD/LPH/MR/66 du 26/8/66 [...]

     The split between  DMN-Difuene  and  DMN-Nlandu,
last heirs to the undifferentiated Church of the Holy
Spirit and   the   property  allocated   to   it   by   the
government   on   a hilltop above Matadi, expressed the
eventual differentiation of functions  uneasily   combined    within    the    pre-existing   church.   We  have
already remarked, in Chapter   Two,   that   regionalism
was    a    factor   in   the  split, but so was the inherent
dilemma  facing  any church,  that  of   reconciling  two
incompatible  systems   of   social   relations   (Depage
1969-70).   According to Depage, a tension  existed   as
early as 1962 between two tendencies in the Boma DMN,
the Eglise Prophétique.  One group favored   the   idea
of   a "church" or "mission," and advocated hierarchical organization and European   Protestant   ritual   as
"signs  of modernity and means of entering into relations with the wider   society   and   the   governmental
bureaucracy."   The   second group preferred to exclude
the profane world and limit   centralization   for   the
sake of prophetic values and rituals.
     From the beginning, therefore, this  DMN   branch
revealed   in   microcosm the effects of the coincident
forces of   regionalism,   social   pluralism,   and   the
traditionalist-spiritualist    alternatives.    DMN-D
moved entirely into   the   bureaucratic   sector   as   a
matter   of   conscious   policy.  The final impulse was
provided by the legislation of   1965   on   non-profit
associations,   to   which   Difuene   wanted to conform,
whereas Nlandu said that he had seen   in   the   spirit
that  Mobutu was merely a temporary governor and that

Kasa-Vubu would return (a perennial Kongo fantasy,
that chiefship would return to its originators). In
1970, Difuene's staff carried membership cards as
"missionaries", and Difuene insisted that they were
in fact missionaries like any others. His campaign,
closely keyed to political realities and to control
of the school built on the property, made decreasing
reference to religion. Although Difuene continued,
personally, to regard himself as the true custodian
of the DMN tradition, he recognized the harsh reality
that the existence of his church depended on the tax
exemption to which non-profit associations were entitled. In an economy as close to subsistence as this,
a tax exemption is almost as good as a salary. The
statutes of DMN-D, as a non-profit association, listed its aims:

I.   Spiritual life.

   a.  To teach the divine word of our Savior
   Jesus Christ by the Holy Spirit, as did the
   Apostles of Jesus and his witnesses Simon
   Kimbangu and Mbumba Philippe.
   b.  Daily homage to the authorities and to
   the country.

II.  Material life.

   a.  Creation of churches, schools,
   dispensaries, hospitals, social clubs and
   educational centers.
   b.  Creation of orphanages.
   c.  Baptism by immersion.
   d.  Observe the marriage law.
   e.  Compose hymns.

   In 1969, Difuene managed to get the school
building registered in his name, giving him a distinct edge. The Nlandu group complained that they
had built the shool with their money. Fights broke
out. Difuene wrote a letter to the mayor of Matadi
(with copies to everyone in sight) reporting that,
after his rivals had been fined for assaulting him in
church, one of them had telephoned the army in the
middle of the night, saying that a riot had broken
out, and 100 people were already dead. In response,
a truck load of soldiers armed to the teeth had
arrived at the "mission," where they found nobody but
a few Difuenists, whom they proceeded to beat up.
"Mr. Mayor, there will be worse to come if you do

not have the telephonist arrested, he is a rebel bent on making trouble in our country!" And so on. By the end of 1970, the indefatigable Difuene had converted his ecclesiastical remnant entirely into an "educational institute," leaving his opponents with the ruins of the church building they had once shared. Here, on Sunday mornings, a few people persisted in the prophetic routines.

## EJCSK

In this chapter I have argued that the prophets and their adherents, in 1921 as in 1959 and 1970, came from the elements of the population that suffered most from the dual but related systems of status discrimination characteristic of Belgian Congo, and that prophetic activity both intended and to some extent succeeded in challenging this system with respect both to the mission churches and to customary society. Its limited success, however, depended on the play of forces in a much wider field, notably the development of capitalism and neo-colonialism. In post-revolutionary conditions the scope of the customary sector was rapidly reduced. Prophets generally were reduced to offering palliative services, often accompanied by bitter prayers regretting the "loss" of national independence. Churchmen (who were in some instances also prophets) struggled to create and maintain corporate existence in the bureaucratic sector. The squeeze of the times was readily apparent in the changing character of EJCSK.

Although EJCSK insists that it was "founded" in 1921, Kimbangu's movement was little different in character from the DMN-Nsansi of 1970, although enormously more successful. In Kimbanguist theology Kimbangu's success as a healer guarantees the promise of salvation. In 1959, healing was once again an important activity at Nkamba and elsewhere. In June 1960, the newspaper Kimbanguisme reported that 10,050 persons had been healed in the preceding two months: 4 people rose from the dead; 4,789 lame persons walked; 3,568 of the blind saw, and 902 lepers were cleansed. As the church took on bureaucratic organization and the form and functions of a "mission," spiritual healing steadily declined. The church built its own clinics in which, as in those of the mission churches, physical methods of diagnosis and treatment were practised under the supervision of the state (Desroche and Raymaekers 1976).

Rivals and critics held this change against the head of the church, Joseph Diangienda. They saw the routinization of charisma as his personal corruption and betrayal of the heritage of his father the prophet. According to the critics, perception of tithes, payment of salaries, and investment in buildings and vehicles meant that the leaders had sold out. They saw the exclusion of charismatic features as God's withdrawal of spiritual gifts from his disloyal followers. Said André Gonda rhetorically, of Diangienda, "Do we read in the Bible that Christ traveled in an automobile?" There were even some members of EJCSK who complained that they had to pay for such healing as the church offered, and who began to attend spiritualist bands in other churches whenever they had a serious "health problem." In 1965, in reply to a question, the professor of theology at the seminary at Nkamba explained that since there were two kinds of disease (those caused by God, i.e., natural causes, and those caused by witchcraft; a general Kongo belief), two systems of healing were necessary. He said that in 1921 the power of faith was so strong that Kimbangu could heal anything, but that since then, as a result of human weakness, faith was partly lacking; even Dialungana, who had a bandage on his leg as evidence of treatment at the local dispensary, was human, and his faith insufficient for perfect health. Diangienda said that cure was never automatic, and therefore must always be regarded as an act of God; if the church had the money, he would want it to open dispensaries everywhere.

The evolution of EJCSK was by no means simple, however, since it took place at two levels: the church's official statements and propaganda, and on the other hand its real organization and functioning. The church's organizational handbook (<u>Nsadulu yo Ntwadusulu ya Dibundu dia Kimbanguisme</u>, itself translated from a French original), was by no means a fantastic document like the statutes of some other churches, but in 1966 the Secretary-General, Luntadila, described it as an ideal rather than an actuality. It emphasized a hierarchical administrative structure, from the lowliest village catechist to the Supreme Head, Diangienda, and (as is to be expected) devoted much less attention to the church's political (decision-making) structure. At that time the various regions, predominantly rural, had their own treasuries, were largely self-supporting, and contributed little or nothing to the central funds of the church, which were raised directly by the head-

quarters staff, in Kinshasa and other major towns.
Special fund-raising festivals (nsinsani), often led
by Diangienda himself, provided most of the money,
which was then devoted to selected projects, especially schools and churches. During the 1960's,
Luntadila directed an increasingly elaborate, functionally specialized secretariat. Diangienda himself
handled an astonishing range of issues; the rank and
file of the church assumed that he knew all of them
personally, and counted on him to solve their difficulties. The church's principal deliberative body
for general policy questions was a council of 32 old
pastors, exiles of 1921 and the like, chosen by the
Supreme Head.

Residual charismatic elements clustered around
the principal features of the church's political
structure, signifying its capacity for creative
departures. These features were the head of the
church himself (mfumu a nlongo), his two brothers,
who with him were known as mvwala (pl. zi-), and the
"chief priests" or "sacrificateurs" (ngudi za nganga,
basadisi). Whereas the administrative structure was
centered on Kinshasa, the political structure centered on Nkamba, the church's spiritual home, and
especially on the mausoleum or "temple" (kinlongo,
"sacred place") of the prophet. And whereas the
administrative roles and functions, as the organizational handbook shows, were best described in French,
the political and spiritual elements, as Kimbanguists
understand them, are difficult to translate from
KiKongo. Such translation must refer to the cosmology and religious thought of the BaKongo which, though
they lie at the origin of Kimbanguism, have been concealed or superseded by the bureaucratic
organizational form of EJCSK.

# Part Three

# *Kongo Perspectives*

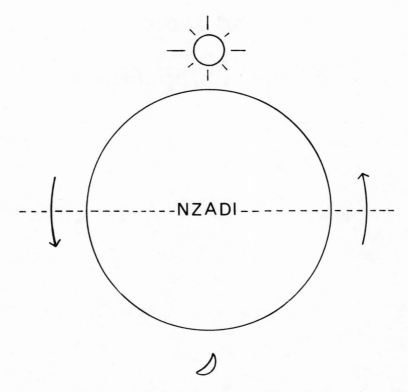

Fig.2: The reciprocating universe

# 5

# Cosmology and Religious Commissions

The first part of this study presented a history
of the movements and the origins of the prophetic
forms observable in the 1960's. The second part
showed that the society in which this evolution took
place consisted of two distinct and incompatible sets
of institutions within a single political framework,
and how the prophetic forms responded to the tensions
and opportunities of this context. The last part
shows how BaKongo, particularly the less fortunate
among them, interpreted and attempted to deal with
contemporary experience in terms of indigenous
knowledge, and how that knowledge, grounded in cosmology and ritual, defined both the role and the task
of the prophet, successor to the local priest of
former times.

As a prequisite to social action, all communities implicitly accept a certain cosmology, a certain
concept of the universe and the place of man within
it. A cosmology necessarily includes some organization of space and time; some contrasts among people,
animals and things; a distinction between life and
death; and a differentiation of gender. Any particular cosmology will also include discriminatory
principles less salient for the system as a whole,
such as a division of mankind into races or into
relatives and others, which may not be features of
another cosmology. Cosmological concepts are not
necessarily true or false. They vary in content from
one society to another and from time to time within
one society. They may be subject to debate and conscious reformulation.

I became aware of a distinct Kongo cosmology, or
at least some indications of one, in the first months
of my fieldwork in 1964, particularly when visiting

religious   settlements   of   the   Kimbanguist   Church
(EJCSK).   At Nkamba, "the New Jerusalem,"   for   example, it seemed that Kimbanguists derived some special
satisfaction   from   the   topography   of   the   place.
Nkamba is built on a small knob of land with water on
three sides and a ravine on   the   fourth.   From   the
main   entrance a stairway ascends to the mausoleum of
the prophet Kimbangu, situated on the   highest   point
of the hill, but the usual mode of access to the village is provided by a road   running   counterclockwise
around   the   hill   to   the top.   Newly   arrived bands of
pilgrims celebrate their arrival by   marching,   counterclockwise, around the village, singing hymns.

So far as I know there   is   no   rule   about   the
marching,   and   the construction of the road may have
been governed entirely by expediency.   Nkamba is simply   the   prophet's birthplace and was not chosen for
its topographical characteristics.   Nevertheless,   as
I   came   to know more settlements and heard villagers
mentioning features of the   landscape,   I   repeatedly
gained the sense of popular satisfaction arising from
perceived relations between land and water, hill   and
valley,   grass   and forest, inhabited and uninhabited
land, the graves of the dead and the   houses   of   the
living.   I   was studying government at the time, but
it gradually became apparent that the normative standards   of   political   action   presupposed   a   larger
normative and cognitive apparatus.   Unless one understood   what   picture   of   the   world   the   actor
entertained, much of his action was itself unintelligible.

Elements of cosmology were recorded at the   turn
of   the   century by such ethnographers as Bittremieux
and Laman.   Their accounts of rituals now   no   longer
practiced   indirectly provide additional but fragmentary information about the presumed structure of   the
universe.   Generations of foreign observers concurred
in the view that "the ideas of the natives"   were   "a
ruinous   heap"   (Phillips 1888:221).   "Take first the
wizard, the ndochi, as he is called.   No   theory   of
occult   art   or   magic, no diabolical attributes will
enable us to understand the native's   ideas   on   this
subject" (idem.).   "Kongos have no religion or system
of worship;   vague superstition takes   the   place   of
the   former,   and   the   arrangement of charms of the
latter.   There is no idolatory or attempt to communicate with a Divine Being" (Bentley 1887:503).   "There
is no coherence in their   beliefs,   and   their   ideas
about   cosmogony are very nebulous" (Weeks 1914:287).
"Their religion hesitated on the border of   magic ...

Nor did they have any really strong or really clear
convictions to put against the religions of the missionary" (Doutreloux 1967:10). More obliquely: "One
would seek in vain in Yombe culture and society for
large and coherent conceptions and structures such as
would give the human reality they incarnate the prestige accorded in Africa and elsewhere to other
civilizations" (ibid.:273).

Most of these writers were inclined to think of
culture as a collection of traits rather than as a
system or systems; individually little inclined to
speculative thought themselves, they believed, like
most Europeans in Africa, that the natives were incapable of abstract thinking. "The ideas are mostly of
the simpler forms, seldom passing the concretes of
actual experience, generalizations being, as a rule
beyond their power ... The fundamental act of the
intelligence, the intuition of likeness and unlike-
ness, is very circumscribed ... Analogies are
confined to the crudest forms, and a very simple figure of speech is apt to be unintelligible" (Phillips
1888:221). It is not hard to imagine some Nkongo
making exactly the same comment after meeting Phillips himself.

On the other hand, the same writers who denied
the coherence of Kongo thought were aware of the elusive presence of systematic order somewhere behind
the fragments of ritual and belief observable in
everyday life. Most of them supposed that a coherent
system existed at some time in the past, only to be
destroyed by European influences. "The magicians
employed as rain-makers, makers of charms, and doctors, perform certain rites that seem to be
propitiation of superior powers or ghosts; but
inquiry only confirms the view that they are shreds
and patches remaining from a time when they really
were such but from which the significance has departed, leaving the bare form" (Phillips 1888:223).
Doutreloux (1967:ch.6) says that traditional religion
survives only in the form of indistinct memories, but
he is aware of a common origin to Kongo magic, whose
vitality he stresses, and Kongo religion, whose inability to provide social and moral discipline he
deplores.

The BaKongo, however, are aware of order now,
not just in the indefinite past; they are evidently
quite sure of certain understandings that they do not
explain, the elusive common principles underlying
magic and religion to which Doutreloux alludes. Van
Wing (1959:381) describes the observer's experience:

For them, the world is full of natural forces,
superhuman and magical. They move at ease in
it. Thoughts and sentiments, words and deeds
are all in time arranged and harmonized within
it. The conception they have of it assumes the
appearance of a science, a form of knowledge in
which the contradictions and the gaps are
blurred to the point of being only more or less
obscure parts of a vast system.
    They install themselves in this system as
though in calm and assured possession of the
truth. Try to dislodge them by head-on argument and they will look at you as a specialist
looks at one whom he knows to be incapable of
understanding.

The continued vitality of organizing principles
is further indicated by the constant emergence of new
rituals in which the same themes and symbols inex-
haustibly recur.

## DIVIDED WORLDS

Fu-kiau, a self-taught ethnographer and Kongo
nationalist who writes, by preference, in KiKongo,
was the first writer to exhibit the principles of
Kongo cosmology as a system and to show how this cosmology is presumed in the performance of rituals from
the Munkukusa, Lemba, and other cults of the past and
the present (Fu-kiau 1969). I cite his work as a
confirmation of my own observations in a necessarily
difficult field, and from time to time draw upon
texts written by himself and his associates. At the
same time the two points of view, of native and
foreign observers, remain necessarily distinct
(Doutreloux 1971; MacGaffey 1972c). This chapter
describes the elements of Kongo cosmology at a relatively abstract level which is at the same time
sufficiently general to subsume regional variations,
variations expressed in particular cults, and changes
that have taken place during the last 100 years or
so.
    The Kongo universe is divided into two parts
such that the relations between the two are relations
of time, space, and cause. The people themselves
speak of the two parts most often as "this world"
(nza yayi) and "the land of the dead" (nsi a bafwa).
The worlds are separated by a body of water, tradi-
tionally called Kalunga, but most often referred to
in general as nlangu, "water," or m'bu, the ocean,

nzadi, "great river," or by various other words for water, pools, and rivers. The word nzadi, corrupted to Zaire, was applied by Europeans to the Zaire or Congo River exclusively, but it means any large body of water.

Several diagrams can be used to display relationships within the universe. For ease of exposition, I begin by describing the Kongo universe as a closed system. The simplest diagram, which usefully illuminates many cultural features, shows the worlds of the living and dead in mirror opposition within a static and repetitive universe (Fig. 2). Life is a cyclical or oscillatory movement between the worlds, resembling the path of the sun and the moon; between the worlds is Nzadi. Fu-kiau (1969:26,28,30) explains:

> The NKongo thought of the earth as a mountain over a body of water which is the land of the dead, called Mpemba. In Mpemba the sun rises and sets just as it does in the land of the living. Between these two parts, the lands of the dead and the living, the water is both a passage and a great barrier. The world, in Kongo thought, is like two mountains opposed at their bases and separated by the ocean.
> At the rising and setting of the sun the living and the dead exchange day and night.
> The setting of the sun signifies man's death and its rising his rebirth, or the continuity of his life. BaKongo believe and hold it true that man's life has no end, that it constitutes a cycle, and death is merely a transition in the process of change. In the following song from the Lemba rite we perceive this understanding of the continuity of life. Death is a way of changing one's body and location; he will continue in the cycle on earth.
>
> N'zungi!  n'zungi-nzila.
> N'zungi!  n'zungi-nzila.
> Banganga ban'e!  E,ee!
>
> Man turns in the path
> He [merely] turns in the path;
> The priests, the same.

Contrary to what many students have said, the sign of the cross was not introduced into this country and into the minds of its people

by foreigners. The cross was known to the
BaKongo before the arrival of Europeans, and
corresponds to the understanding in their minds
of their relationship to their world ...  [In
the Nkimba rite, a priest initiating his
charges] would use the sun in order to expound
his teaching about the earth and the life of
man, following the sun through its course about
the earth and thus pointing out the four stages
which make up the cycle of man's life:
(1) rising, beginning, birth, or regrowth
(2) ascendancy, maturity, responsibility
(3) setting, handing on, death, transformation
(4) midnight, existence in the other world,
eventual rebirth.

Thus in Kongo thought the path of the sun and of
the soul are analogous, both describing the periphery
of a divided universe. The analogical structure
includes points of transition or mediation between
the visible and invisible worlds:

| day | sunrise, sunset | night |
|-----|-----------------|-------|
| the living | birth, death | the dead |
| land | water | land |

The same analogy appears in the words of
Van Wing's informants: the sun endures, its passage
counts the years (ntangu mvu), whereas our lives are
but days (bilumbu beto bantu) (Van Wing 1959:297).
Hence benduka, "to decline, like the sun," is a
euphemism for death (Laman 1957:143); dead bodies
were buried with their heads towards the rising sun,
so that on rising the deceased might continue his
journey in the counter-clockwise direction (Weeks
1908:429; Cah.No.172). The analogy, which maps the
universe in space and time, also orders the moral and
sociological aspects of existence, according to
Fu-kiau's version of the cosmology. At Nkamba similar elements recur: the mountain, the water, the
counter-clockwise march, and the theme of relations
with the dead. In the statement of Van Wing's informants we notice in passing a preoccupation with the
contrast between the permanent and the transitory or
perishable aspects of the universe, given as the
essence of the difference between two related movements in time.
    The idea of the universe as a closed,
reciprocating system in two parts, as it is
represented by Fu-kiau, appears to have been more

complex in the nineteenth century, when it included a non-reversible time dimension and thus assumed a spiral form. At that time, a sense of the dead as moving, by a series of transformation in the after-life, through a hierarchy of increasingly remote but also more powerful and functionally less specific positions in the other world, apparently corresponded to the existence in the real world of hierarchies of titles which, although not specifically territorial, aggregated increasing numbers of local domains in their spheres of influence. Thus, in principle, the more remote the tutelary local spirit, the broader the zone of his cult and of the corresponding center of political power.

The most remote and most powerful of spirits was Nzambi Mpungu, the highest "nzambi," the paradigm of the series. Below him, partially localized, ranked great regional spirits (n'kisi nsi) such as Bunzi and Funza, sometimes confounded with Nzambi, and lesser bisimbi, some at least of which were thought of as very old ancestors. Any of these spirits, and also in certain contexts a human being, could be called nzambi. The hierarchy of spirits, thought of as something like a sequence of generations, was also a patrifilial sequence (father, sons, grandchildren), on the model of the ideal hierarchy of all local groups, in which each title holder stood in a paternal relationship to his subordinates. As Doutreloux precisely observes (1967:226): "From the Supreme Being to man, by way of the intermediary Spirits, extend the relations of Father to Son that structure the society of men."

In the twentieth century, the collapse of real political structures above the village level entailed the collapse of the spiritual hierarchy, so that the notion of ranked classes of spirits is now poorly articulated. Fu-kiau's version of the reciprocating model may be a modern development; he is aware of the spiral motif, but treats it as flat, a movement in two dimensions. However, it is likely that the universe was always ambiguous, both reciprocating and spiral, in different times, places and contexts, and that this variability corresponded to the instability of hierarchies and the presence in Kongo thought of two models of the ideal political system, egalitarian (kinkazi) and authoritarian (kimfumu) (MacGaffey 1970b, ch.10).

The origins of this cosmology must be sought in the social structure of the past, and are beyond the scope of the present study. It is sufficient to note here that the essential cosmological features of Fig. 2, a world separated by "water" from an "other world," reappear in countless contemporary descriptions of geographical relations. BaKongo are prepared to see any space which is the scene of morally significant action as divided into opposed halves, and to understand the action as a process of conflict, circulation, or reconciliation between the inhabitants of the two. They may endow not only the Zaire but any body of water with the significance of Nzadi. Lower Zaire is opposed to the rest of the country, Upper Zaire, but in other contexts this opposition is submerged in the unity of Africa, as opposed to Mputu, "Europe." "Africa" is this world, land of the living; "Europe" is the other world, land of the dead.

Neither Africa nor Europe means what European geography and history hold it to be (MacGaffey 1972b). Mputu is supposed to be a short form of Mputulukeezo, itself a corruption of "Portuguese," but it meant "agitated water" to H.M. Stanley's informants when he first visited the great cataracts between Kinshasa and Matadi. In that sense the word referred to the surf of the Atlantic Ocean (Kalunga), to the coast generally (whence came European goods), and to the seething rapids of Nzadi under which simbi spirits live. Modern Kongo and Teke informants describe the noise of rapids as the voices of the spirits. The superimposition of the cosmographic model on geography is almost explicit in Stanley's record when he notes of his informants, "They have a curious idea in their heads that I must have come from some place south of the BaKongo country, and floated down some great body of water" (Stanley 1879, II:414). Muene Mputo, reported Johnston (1884:148n) meant "chief of the sea" and not "King of Portugal."[1]

Laman (1953:3) mentions that BaKongo refer to Mputu Lukeeso as the abode of a primordial being called "Mbangu Bamba, the white one." This Mputu, he says, is the land of the whites, but not directly Europe; it is an aboriginal land where black and white once lived together. Laman's distinction does not do justice to the views of his informants, one of whom wrote (Cah.No.344):

People thought the whites were very strange in their eyes, and were much afraid of them. The knew the whites came from Mputu, and they thought they bought people to eat them, and that it was human flesh in those tin cans. They thought whites were not like people but were min'kisi, because they had white skins, and eyes that saw in another fashion, and their language was too strange to understand. Some people would watch where the whites defecated, and take their excrement as an ingredient to make charms with (longo mu vandila nkisi).

The association between Mputu, "Europe," and Mputu, the other world, is so close that it is difficult to find evidence that BaKongo, an educated minority excepted, make any clear distinction between them. Many of my informants did not know what distinction to draw, either in general or in particular instances where the problem was raised; certainly there was a real possibility in their minds that Europe and the land of the dead were identical. The problem is not posed to them in quite those terms because they have never formed an independent conception of Europe as a geographical entity which could then be contrasted with "the land of the dead" (nsi a bafwa). Several generations of intensive intercourse with Europeans and exposure to European propaganda have raised some doubts about the adequacy of indigenous cosmology without revealing just what is wrong with it. When shown a map indicating that it would be possible to walk dry-shod from Africa to Europe, a relatively well-educated businessman said (in 1966) "You see! I have always said we were all on the same shore" (simu dimosi).

BaKongo readily think of Mputu, like other countries, as divided into opposed halves, whether "Germans and Belgians" or "Americans and Belgians." My own informants seemed to divide Mputu into English-speakers and the rest, including Belgians, French, Swiss, Germans, Italians, and Japanese. English-speakers, renowned for their technology, apparently included the Russians, though not "communists." Little distinction was made between the British and the Americans; some believed that the two "clans" stood as father and son, occupying "the same settlement" (vata dimosi). Statements of this kind were made by fully literate men who spoke fairly good French and read newspapers from time to time. America itself is known to be divided into two parts, North and South, regarded as divisions of one country. Many people assume that South America is populated by blacks and that KiKongo is spoken there (MacGaffey 1968).

Understanding these oppositions and the analogies constructed between them, we can readily
interpret such sayings as the following, from
Mayombe: "Kuyila! it's getting dark! cry the
witches in the morning [i.e. their "day" is coming
to an end]." Ti buisi buyilanga ko, k'anu tufuanga
ko; buisi bulengede kuila, k'anu Bamindele bafuanga
kuau ko! "As long as night has not fallen we
[blacks] do not die. When the night has fallen, the
Europeans do not die." (Bittremieux 1922-7, s.v.
yila). Likewise the belief in the village of Kemba,
in 1965, that the Angolan named Edouard, after "returning from the land of the dead," spoke English and
Swahili (a language of Upper Zaire, to which Mabwaka
and other prophets were exiled in colonial times),
becomes intelligible; these are the languages of the
dead (ndinga za nsi a bafwa), as he told me, the
languages of the inhabitants of other worlds.
Edouard's account of his travels mentions "South
America" as the land of the dead on the way to
heaven.

In the three communities in which I resided for
some time (Mbanza Manteke, Kasangulu, Matadi) I was
widely regarded as a Nkongo returned from the dead.
Factors contributing to this idea apparently included
the following. I lived among BaKongo, participating
in their activities, and not in any of the European
enclaves. I contributed gifts at funerals and other
occasions when such gifts serve to affirm social
relationships. I ate freely at other people's
tables. I spoke a KiKongo which (although nowhere
near as good as that of longtime missionary residents) was much better than Europeans usually
speak.[2] I carried (for my own convenience) a
shoulder bag (n'kutu) which, though rarely seen nowadays, is one of the traditional symbols of an elder
(Troesch 1961), and was intensely interested in and
well informed about religious and political matters
that are the private concerns of the elders. I could
find my way from village to village by footpaths that
are thought of as knowable only by local people.
(Mabwaka Mpaka, the prophet, explained that the map I
used, and which I had in fact bought from the National Geographic Insititute in Kinshasa, had been
provided for me by the ancestors in America.) All
these features were remarked on more or less widely.
People attributed my difficulties with the language
to my long sojourn in America, and my interest in
tradition to my desire to recapture my personal heritage. On occasion, the fact that I could recognize

certain deceased worthies from their photographs
(which I had seen before) was taken to show that I
knew them in America, their present home.

A very few of those who knew me best did not
share the general view, regarded it as ridiculous,
and helped me in my inquiries into it. Their immo-
derate laughter when the subject came up perhaps
expressed a degree of personal embarrassment. They
included my servant, who had attended secondary
school for one year and who attributed the views of
the majority to their lack of education; his education, however, had not seriously modified his beliefs
about related matters. A lady whose household I
joined in Matadi took pains to introduce me to groups
of her friends as "a real white man" (nkatika vrai
mundele); the expression, and the doubtful looks
that would greet it, showed that it was easier to
think of me as a transformed African than as a regular European. Likewise it was easier to suppose that
I had settled in Manteke and become friendly with the
head of the Nsundi clan there because I was originally of Nsundi descent than to accept that these events
were largely fortuitous; there is little room for
accident in Kongo thought.

From the Kongo point of view whites are of two
types, those who are so by origin and those who,
though of African origin, have become white. I have
been asked, "Were your ancestors black or white?" and
also, "Is it true that you are black?" The division
at issue here corresponds in some respects to the
distinction between two kinds of bisimbi (local spirits), those who were once people and those that have
existed from the beginning. White men who were originally black are Africans (BaKongo) who died and
crossed Kalunga, "the great plain that the eye may
traverse but not the feet." Natural deaths as well as
those attributed to witchcraft serve to effect this
transfer, but the main narrative focus is on the
latter, that is, on premature deaths caused by
witches who have sold their friends' and neighbors'
souls for profit. This "commerce" (zandu) is a
secret or "nocturnal" transaction, but its effects
are visible by "daylight," that is, in the ordinary
world. Not only are individuals seen to die but on
rare occasions the new abode in which they appear as
dependents of their new owner is a village not many
miles away. Normally, therefore, transactions are
carried out over long distances, it is supposed, so
that the original relatives of the victims will not
have the opportunity to recover them. "A deceased

person may show himself in any country at all.    On
journeys  to Matadi and the coast the bearers may see
someone  who  has  lived  in  their  village" (Laman
1962:17).
     In this aspect, therefore, witchcraft  is  simi-
lar,  as  a  European  would  say,  to slave trading
(MacGaffey 1970b:219). It is not  clear,  however,
that  BaKongo  make  any distinction between the two.
Repeated contemporary references to nineteenth century trade, the slave trade in particular, show that it
is regarded as a trade in souls.  Some of the techniques  used  are  identical.  Informants  recall, and
written sources confirm, that slave-catchers used  to
leave  food  so that hapless travelers, finding it and
picking it up, might be seized  for  debt  and  sold;
modern  witches  are  supposed  to leave money in the
road for the same purpose.  Similar stories are  told
of more recent exports, such as the urena fibers cul-
tivated  in  Manianga  under  Belgian  encouragement.
When  producers  brought their bundles to be weighed,
some bundles proved surprisingly heavier than others,
because they contained "people" whose sale to Belgian
traders was carried on under cover of the fiber business.    "We   hear,"  wrote A.M. Lutangu in  1917
(Cah. 209), "that in the  sale  of  persons  they are
weighed  in  a balance like porters' loads." The Free
State's interest in rubber and ivory is explained  by
the  need  to  provide containers for the souls being
exported--witchcraft is always a matter of  "shutting
people   up"   (kanga)  in  magical  containers  like
"charms" (min'kisi).  A text of the Ntualanist Church
(EJCDT), shown to me in 1966 but supposedly recording
a prophecy of Ntualani in 1921,  says  "Pray  to  our
brethren who were sold in the ivory and rubber to the
land of the Americans.  The Lord will send them  back
to  this  country  to teach skills and give knowledge
superior to that of the whites."[4] An  editorial  in
the  Abako  newspaper  Kongo  dia  Ngunga  (1 October
1960), written in  French,  demanded  "the  immediate
return  of  the  entire Kongo generation exploited in
1350 (sic) ...  The Kongo people vigorously  protests
against  this human traffic and formally condemns it.
It demands that all those powers that have  exploited
the Kongo people, transforming them into merchandise,
should return this human body which was  conveyed  in
(transmis en)  a  chemical  product." Here it is clear
that modern anti-imperialist arguments against  the
export  of  raw materials from Africa have influenced
the writer's language, but produit chimique also connotes magical medicines.

It is also clear that the nineteenth century slave trade is not distinguished as an historical phenomenon from subsequent phases of relations between Europe and Africa, including those of the present day. In the twentieth century the principal traders are supposed to have been the missionaries, with whom local witches cooperated: "The sole work of the witch is to cause sickness and death, which is done by drawing off the soul of the victim. That soul or spirit is then sold to white men who hide them in their travelling trunks, water-tanks, salmon tins, etc., until they are able to dispatch them to Europe, or to the bottom of the sea" (Claridge 1922:147; also Van Wing 1959:273). The prophet Simon Mpadi and his followers describe at length the methods used by Catholic missionaries:

The Catholics have a kingdom of the blacks, under the earth, the grave. When a black man dies, the whites keep him chained under the earth. Their nurse gives him an injection which makes him crawl on all fours, like an animal. On Fridays, the priests bring them food consisting of a spoonful of rice and sugar, and ripe bananas. Jesus Christ denounced the activity of the white priests and was therefore put to death. Matthew 23:8-36[5]; 27:13, 14, 20-24.[6] After that, God in his mercy sought another way to relieve the black souls of their captivity in subterranean villages; see chapter 11:3-12.[7] Thus the prison constructed by the priests was destroyed, 18 March 1921 [the manifestation of Kimbangu]. (Mpadist letter dated 15 March 1969.)

BaKongo usually describe Protestants as less active in the traffic than Catholics, or simply as their reluctant abettors. They attribute the difference to the close association between Catholic missions and the colonial government, and to the special position of "America" in Mputu. (Most Protestant missionaries are English speaking.) Slaves were exported to America rather than Europe, and the Americans are the type of ex-Africans who may some day return to Kongo, endowed with all the technology for which America is famous, to rescue their suffering brothers. "Tell your friends (mpangi zaku) when you go home," as an old man said to me in Kinshasa in 1966, "that we're waiting for them; this is nobody's

country but theirs."[8] The Belgian fear, frequently
expressed, that the Americans would try to take over
their colony, reinforced this expectation during
colonial times.

During my fieldwork I was repeatedly asked questions about America which I subsequently saw were
founded on a particular myth which must therefore be
very widespread. It was only in 1970 that I heard
the myth itself, from a man who though he was a professional magician was not steeped in traditional
lore; he had been brought up in Matadi, and spoke
only the hybrid KiLeta dialect of the town. The
island in the story, as in other fragmentary versions
I heard, is evidently compounded from (1) the idea of
a separate country (nsi) divided by water from the
rest of Mputu, whether "Europe" or North America"
(2) rumors about Haiti (3) rumors about Manhattan
(JM No.5). The idea of the American forest with no
food in it seems to fascinate BaKongo.

## The slave trade

This form of commerce (zandu) was not
created by black people but by Mpelo [the
Catholic missionary]. In that commerce, from
the time of our ancestors it was our custom to
sell people, but they did not die entirely.
They were sold to the Portuguese, who afterwards stuffed them into ships for
transportation to Belgium. When they arrived
there the Belgians collected them together and
sent out a notice to all the nations, asking,
"What shall we do with these people? for they
are worthless." Some said they should just be
killed, but others disagreed. Then Misioni
[the Protestant missionary] stood up and said,
"No, it is not proper to kill them; they
should be sent to an island with water on every
side, where they will die of hunger, and that
will be the end of them." Everbody agreed with
these words, so they signed an agreement, and
put the people in ships and cast them away on
an island, where there was a forest with no
food in it, and the sea on every side.
But truly God does not sleep, for we are
one flesh and blood, only the skin color is
different. So God gave them civilization
(ntemo), and skyscrapers sprang up, and food
appeared, and every needful thing.

When the Belgians came to see what had
happened to the people they had abandoned they
found nothing but skyscrapers (zibilidingi),
with no room any more to plant food. And so it
is to this day. You can find palmnuts, and
everything that we make use of here. Perhaps
not every foodstuff that we find in Kongo is
there, because their time is not yet come.

So Mpelo considered the matter and decided
that that was the wrong thing to do. "This
time, when we buy someone, we had better finish
him off for good." When a man dies he has no
means of knowing that he is going to Belgium.
All these people who are sold end up in Europe.
But only God can transform a man. Lots of people when they have been traded have the idea
that now they are going to be rich, they will
have their own magic (magie). But when someone
has gone to Europe, that's where his name is;
as for a way to return here, there is none, he
wants the white man's ways.

Now this business of being a white man:
from the beginning, God who made heaven and
earth arranged it that whoever had a black skin
should be black, from the beginning to the end;
or if you are a white man, so you are from the
beginning to the end, and there's no way of
changing it. That's our pedigree. Many things
are understood, and many we cannot understand.

Later, according to the history our ancestors left us, Mpelo, seeing how things were,
sent a message to the [colonial] Government
saying, "The medicines the people use (and
which are a source of power to them) have not
been taken away. It is time to take them."[9]
So now they have in Belgium a whole house [the
Royal Museum of Central Africa, Tervuren] full
of our things, although they have no idea how
to use them.

Modern Matadi is full of stories about the slave
trade. Many of its inhabitants are sailors who
repeatedly visit Antwerp, London, New York, Philadelphia and the Gulf ports and who, though they rarely
see more of these places than the quayside, might be
expected to disabuse their compatriots of ancient
errors; on the contrary, they are often cited as
authorities and sources of information, and if they
should be accused of witchcraft their employment is

likely to be mentioned as giving them exceptional
opportunities to sell their victims abroad. Anybody
connected with the port has special trading opportunities, and it is still said that when any of the
European staff is about to go on leave a number of
fatal accidents can be expected as he collects souls
with which to do a little business while he is at
home. On the other hand, some of the accidents are
"voluntary," according to popular report;
individuals make contracts with Europeans, selling
themselves in order to be taken to Europe, where they
expect to make good, become wealthy, and in fact
become white men. At the Lukala cement factory
senior employees with four and six years of secondary
education have refused invitations to eat in the
homes of white supervisors, lest they be captured and
translated by something put in their food, and it is
"common knowledge" that most of the white personnel
there are not real whites at all but "locally made:"
they are black supervisors who have contracted to
become white in order to exploit their countrymen
more effectively. They effect their passage to Mputu
and eventual return in their new skins through a deep
pool or well in the neighborhood into which candidates for transmigration throw themselves, and from
which they emerge in their new skins; "you never see
them arriving by ordinary transportation." Whether
anybody really committed suicide with this intention
is less important than the prevalence of the idea
that people do.

After my return to Kongo in 1970 I would be followed across the Matadi markets by a murmured wave of
explanations: "He's black" (ndombe kena). My wife,
whose KiKongo is not as good as mine nor her pursuit
of customary lore as zealous, was not so regarded,
but as part of the fruit of my success in America;
she was taken for a madami (white lady) I had managed
to marry. "He died and was sold" (fwa kafwa, tekwa
katekwa) was the summary explanation; in more detail
the story was that my "uncle" (a wealthy man, my very
good friend) had sold me to America to raise capital
for his tavern. A relative of his had in fact died
some years before by falling from the top of a palm
tree, a mode of death that attracts special attention
and is likely to be regarded as a result of witchcraft. After changing my skin and making good I had
been able to return to Zaire and was now about to
bring charges against him. People would ask me about
their deceased relatives, supposedly transferred to
America; I found these inquiries difficult to answer

sympathetically, and excused myself by explaining
that such large numbers of migrants arrived in America all the time that it was hard to keep track of
them (cf. Claridge 1922:58). Still more difficult
was the plea of the tearful woman at the end of her
tether, beset by illness, poverty, and the problem of
raising her children unaided, who wanted to know when
"your followers" (nkangu aku) would arrive, all problems end, and all tears be wiped away.

It should be apparent that the Kongo definition
of "white" and "black" has little in common with
European ideas of race. Less obvious, but equally
important here, is the fact that the European ideas
themselves have little that is scientific about them
and are no more (and no less) rational than Kongo
thought. Both are products of their particular cultures, transformations of experience according to
rules of thought that precede it, though they are
generally regarded by the natives as absolute realities attested to by volumes of empirical evidence and
daily experience (MacGaffey 1978).

Many experiences which a European might see as
contradicting indigenous cosmology in fact tend to
confirm it, or are seen as doing so. The hypothesis
that Europeans are visitors from the land of the dead
offers an elegant explanation for the following range
of facts and near facts of which BaKongo are aware.
Mputu, like the land of the dead, is cold. Like
ghosts, its inhabitants, in Kongo as at home, eat
sweet bananas but refrain from eating red pepper.
(ndungu).[10] They are under some kind of obligation
to sleep at noon, presumably because for them noon is
midnight. Europeans command marvelous skills, and
above all they are white-skinned and speak totally
foreign languages in which their esoteric knowledge
is communicated. For health reasons, apparently,
many of them repair periodically to the ocean to
bathe, that is, to the water between the worlds, in
the same way that, formerly, the initiates of various
cults and, nowadays, the Kimbanguists renew their
forces by plunging into pools and streams designated
as points of contact with the other world. It is
supposed that, like Kimbanguists from Nkamba, Europeans bring back little bottles of seawater as
talismans and all-purpose medication.

Not only the Kongo answer to the problem of how
to situate white people in the universe but the problem itself is alien to the occidental mind. The
referential content of the English word "death" partly coincides with that of lufwa, but the latter is

not defined by contrast with "being" or "life." Lufwa
is an alternative form of being, distinguished from
the present by its invisibility. In Van Wing's
superb phrase (1959:250), "The dead are the living
par excellence." BaKongo say muntu mu meso kaka
kafwanga, "one dies only to sight." Indigenous meta-
phors for the ability to communicate with the dead
include "having opened eyes," "four eyes" (two for
this world, two for the other), and "night vision."
In the past, individuals set off deliberately for the
land of the dead (Europe) over land or by sea, to
join lost relatives or to solve the mystery by personal exploration; such action would be absurd,
indeed inconceivable, if lufwa meant what "death"
means.[11]

     It is also important to notice that the answer
to the problem is not derived from the evidence that
BaKongo adduce in support of it, from mere erroneous
interpretation of the empirical world. They think of
early morning mist as the cooking fires of the dead
(bafwa balambanga) because the belief that, in a
cyclical universe, the hour of the evening meal among
the dead coincides with the dawn of the living,
predicts the resemblance of cloud to smoke (cf.
Mauss 1968:115-20). Because Europeans are the dead,
they are expected to take siestas at noon, their midnight, and lo! so they do.

     Mputu, like the land of the dead, is located not
only in Europe but also, as the BaKongo say, somewhere in Kongo, in three senses: it is night as
opposed to day, it is the scene of the inward causes
of visible events, and it is the European institutions actually established in Kongo by conquest and
occupation. Certain aspects of modern prophetic
activity to be considered in later chapters make use
of these associations.

## RELIGIOUS COMMISSIONS

     The principal religious functions presuppose the
cosmology outlined above. They are fulfilled by four
occasional or ad hoc roles, "commissions," which are
central to all ritual activity and in fact to the
social structure as a whole. The four roles are
those of chief, witch, prophet, and magician, all of
whom are said to possess "four eyes" or "night
knowledge," the ability to move about in the other
world and to deploy powers derived from it in this
world of the living.

A commission is a type of corporation that resembles an office in having its own identity, recruitment rules, distinctive scope and standardized procedures. It differs from an office in that it is filled intermittently as need arises and thus has no regular succession (Smith 1974). The position of headman (nkazi) in a Kongo clan is an office whose functioning is continuously necessary to the clan's dealings with others. Chiefship, on the other hand, was usually a commission during the nineteenth century, that is, it was filled only in circumstances of public affliction, identified by a diviner. During the same period the position of priest of local spirits, whose modern successor is the prophet, was probably also contingently filled, although good information on this point is lacking. The other two central roles, those of witch and magician, are also contingent. Strictly speaking, they are not commissions, because they are not part of government; that is, they are not charged with the regulation of public affairs. All four roles, however, have much in common, and it is convenient to refer to them all as commissions (MacGaffey 1970a).

Under colonial rule, chiefs (mfumu) in the sense understood by BaKongo, ceased to exist, but the idea of what a chief should be remained alive. Chiefs, initiated to particular titles, supposedly wield the same power as witches and magicians (kindoki), with the difference that a chief wields it on behalf of the community, whereas a witch (ndoki) uses it to benefit himself or satisfy personal grudges. The difference is not an empirical one, but a matter of political judgment. The issue is only settled, if at all, by carrying out a testing procedure, such as divination.[12] The magician (nganga), operator of one or more charms (n'kisi), is primarily a healer, though part of his business is to defend his client against witchcraft, legitimately using destructive means otherwise similar to those of the witch himself.[13] Moreover, like the witch, the magician seeks his personal profit; since Kongo thought regards the rewards available as limited, anyone who makes conspicuous profits is considered to have made them at other people's expense, by witchcraft. "Although witches recognize one another, no witch can ever admit to himself that he is one. Non-witches just use their eyes. If they see a woman who always seems to have money, they know she operates a money kundu (witchcraft substance)" (JM No.9:12).

A modern writer, anxious to discriminate between
the legitimate violence of a healer and the illegiti-
mate violence of witches, emphasized that when a
magician sends a curse he does so in the name of the
client, not on his own responsibility (JM No.8:8). A
modern magician, interviewed for a Kinshasa newspaper
(Salongo, 9 April 1963), made the distinctions that
such healers usually bring out during an
investigator's first interview:

> In principle, a good healer does not kill. On
> the contrary, it is his responsibility to pro-
> tect the human species against ill luck and the
> hatred of malignant sorcerers (ndoki). He must
> therefore think to heal them. Hence the old
> misunderstanding between nganga buka (sorciers
> guérisseurs) and ndoki (sorciers maléfiques).

The healer went on to say, "I am sometimes
accused of being demanding in the matter of prices."
He thus obliquely referred to the accepted definition
of nganga as one who heals for a fee and comes under
suspicion thereby. Later he described some of his
clients. One well-dressed man, an inspector of reve-
nue, was seriously ill; in the course of a domestic
dispute his two wives had obtained "fétiches" from a
witch (ndoki), which were driving him mad. Some
clients were students who had taken "doses surna-
turelles" to become more intelligent. Others were
victims of their families, who had sold them to the
devil. One had been bewitched by his uncle, a cabdriver; thanks to the healer's counter-attack on
behalf of the nephew, the cabdriver had suffered a
horrible accident. The nephew was recovering from
the witchcraft; although he had failed his exams he
had learned the names of some healing plants and was
thinking of becoming a healer himself. These typical
incidents reveal the latent aggressiveness of "healing" and provide modern examples of afflictions,
which may lead some of the victims, as in the past,
to an active role in the cult of the affliction as
part of their cure.

The complete set of religious roles, that is, of
all types of persons who have kindoki (witchcraft
power), is thus organized, in popular opinion,
according to the premise that extraordinary power is
used to kill or to bring life (distinction of
effects), in either the public or the private
interest (distinction of ends). The sociological
importance of these discriminations is that they pro-

vide normative guides to action and principles of
legitimation. The set is a summary of the distinctions people make in responding to what seem to them
to be uses of power derived from the dead;  it is not
a description of what in fact happens:

|  | Ends: | |
|  | PUBLIC | PRIVATE |
| DEATH | chief, elder | witch |

Effects:

| LIFE | prophet<br>(ngunza) | magician<br>(nganga) |

    The powers of life and death are largely imagi-
nary.  Recognition of their supposed use is a
function of judgments blaming or crediting individuals for the balance of contentment resulting from
natural and social events. The terms for ordinary
people who lack witchcraft power (kindoki and kundu)
are derogatory. People who have power of any kind
obtain it directly or indirectly from the other
world; they are relatively successful: they live
longer, and have more children and more wealth (both
mbongo). At what point such success conflicts with
the public interest is a matter of judgment.
    The contrast between particularistic (private)
and universalistic (public) intents and values (the
distinction of ends) is associated in Kongo thought
with a contrast between a social order based on
self-seeking exchange and one based on an authoritative hierarchy. Charms (n'kisi) are bought and sold,
and represent that which is exchanged in any
profit-seeking contractual relationship. As such
they are closely associated with food, especially
meat, and with witchcraft substance (kundu), which
originates as the flesh of victims that witches trade
among themselves in a sinister perversion of normal
social relationships. The danger of all magic is
that it may force the user to accept flesh debts. It
is better to seek benefits by submitting oneself to a
benevolent public authority, chosen by a high-ranking
local spirit (simbi). The priest or public diviner
is such an authority, responsible for maintaining the
general conditions of public well-being. His function should ideally be associated with that of the
chief, whose power of death-dealing enables him to
destroy witches and criminals.

In the twentieth century, Kongo society was deprived by colonial rule of its self-reproductive autonomy. The organizational sphere of chiefship was destroyed, and its functions assumed by the state. Under the policy of indirect rule, which nominally favored the perpetuation of indigenous social organization, a kind of ghost or shadow of Kongo society emerged in which slavery, that is, reallocations of persons between descent groups, reappeared under cover of colonially-sponsored litigation. Although chiefs were abolished, descent groups continued to exercise important responsibilities with respect to their own boundaries, internal organization, and material resources (land, inheritable wealth, labor of women). The system of lineage headships and interlineal committees (kinkazi), largely unrecognized by colonial authorities, continued in effect. Ideological attribution to elders of "witchcraft for looking after the clan" (kindoki kya ndundila kanda), which the same elders might also be suspected of misusing, reflected the political functions of lineage headship. Clan elders thus remained as the only representatives in the customary sector of the idea that government should be founded on controlled mystical violence.

Under colonial control the nature of witchcraft changed, in the sense that the content of the process of accusation and restitution changed. To be a witch in the twentieth century no longer meant the likelihood of execution or enslavement. On the other hand, it became possible, in certain contexts, to accuse someone of being a "witchdoctor" and thus an obstacle to the march of progress. Magicians therefore abandoned the spectacular costumes, dances and formidable sculptures of the past, and adopted discreet identities as "herbalists." Their functions as healers, mediators, counselors and entertainers persisted, however, and even took on new importance as the BaKongo became subject to new pressures. Colonial authorities, who quite rightly saw in "politico-fetishistic" movements a threat to their control, prevented the ideological expression and management of collective local interests, formerly carried out by simbi priests. Eventually the prophet took over the function of priest-diviner and adapted it to new circumstances, with political as well as religious consequences.

In discussing religious commissions, we are dealing with norms and signs, not with descriptions of behavior. For example, some prophets provide

their clients with cords to wear on their wrists;
such a cord, though indistinguishable to the eye from
another that the prophet would condemn as a charm,
and thus as evidence of selfish concerns, is said to
be something far more abstract, a barrier (nkaku)
against witchcraft. Both prophet and magician, if
they work full time, or nearly so, must be supported;
though the prophet charges no fee, his grateful
clients bring him gifts of foodstuffs, useful items
and even money, all sharply distinguished in their
own minds from payments (MacGaffey 1970b:115). One
Matadi prophet cut the distinction still finer by
asking his clients to pay for the large numbers of
candles kept burning during his rituals; the candles
he actually bought cost much less than the money he
took in for the purpose. Nevertheless, to be a prophet is to claim that one heals altruistically, and
to have that claim accepted by a certain following.
Ideological discriminations are thus constantly
present in action.
      The same distinctions of ends and effects that
distinguish the religious commissions also organize
the inhabitants of the other world, known collectively as "the dead" (bafwa). Chiefs and elders give
cultic attention to (lineal) ancestors, priests serve
local (communal) spirits, magicians control charms
for individual (private) ends, and witches are
believed to derive their powers from malicious ghosts
(minkuyu) who were witches in their lifetime or from
sinister charms incorporating the souls of victims of
witchcraft.[14]
      Ancestors ( bakulu), identified sociologically
by kinship with the living, are thought to be like
the elders they recently were: very conscious of
their due and likely to punish disrespect. This punitive tendency is considered justifiable, and
descendants hope that if they behave themselves their
ancestors will exercise this capacity for violence on
their behalf against enemies. When the purgative
ritual Munkukusa was practiced (ca. 1952), only the
graves of pagan ancestors were resorted to;
Christian ancestors were thought likely to be soft on
witches (JM No.26:1,2). In contrast, local spirits
(bisimbi) are primarily benevolent; their business
is to set limits to (kakidila) the inevitability of
death. The contrast is evident in the attitude of a
man who, in the old days, might have wanted to found
a new village. He would use divinatory methods to
determine both the absence of ancestors from the spot
(lest their resentment ruin his enterprise) and the

presence of <u>bisimbi</u>, without whom nothing could
prosper.

Though primarily benevolent, <u>bisimbi</u> are capable, according to the stories <u>told</u> of them, of
gratuitous malice. Likewise, the ancestors, despite
their punitive self-righteousness, can be surprisingly generous, notifying a descendant in dreams that
they have hidden treasure for him in a certain place,
for example. Surveying Laman's information about
charms, M.C. Dupré remarks (1975) on the same relationship between two classes of charms, those
belonging to the class of water charms (<u>min'kisi</u> <u>mya</u>
<u>mamba</u>, <u>mya</u> <u>nlangu</u>), on the one hand, and on the other
hand charms belonging to and drawing many of their
ingredients from the earth or the sky (<u>mya</u> <u>nseke</u>, <u>mya</u>
<u>zulu</u>). Water charms, dominated by Funza, emphasize
the benevolence of nature, while retaining its
malevolence as a subordinate theme. In earth and sky
charms, the same themes appear in reversed order of
dominance; the predominantly destructive nature of
these charms is employed to combat witchcraft. Thus
according to Dupré the antagonism linking water
charms to sky charms recurs within each class, defining with maximum clarity the ambivalence of the
universe, which the mind can only conceive as divided
into opposed values.

The cosmology incorporates psychological and
philosophical reflections and perceptions. The world
of the ancestors and of witchcraft is a world of
social tensions between rival generations and competing neighbors, of hidden hostilities and
unacknowledged motives. One reason why BaKongo
believe in witchcraft and sometimes admit to being
witches is that they know how jealous and competitive
they are and how much time they spend in reaching
covert agreements in the hope of outsmarting others.
Despite their idealization of chiefly authority,
BaKongo have always been individualistic
entrepreneurs eager to make a profit. <u>Kitemo</u>, the
rotating credit association, is both a favorite device in real life and the form of organization
attributed to witches. In communities where men and
women have known each other all their lives and where
interpersonal disputes are constantly subject to formal and informal public regulation, diviners and
elders are psychologically shrewd and profoundly
experienced. The idiom in which they express themselves is unlike that of European psychology, but no
more metaphorical and no less effective. It is true
because it works.

On the philosophical side, the cosmology incorporates reflections on the transitory nature of human
life as compared with the permanent features of
experience, including landscape, weather, harvest,
hunting luck, disease, childbearing, and the corporate units of society. Kongo religious activities
can be seen as so many efforts to ameliorate and sta-
bilize daily life by linking it with permanent
factors. Diseases, for example, are hypostatized as
spiritual patrons who will prove beneficient in the
long run if only they are properly supplicated. The
appropriate supplication or treatment is always
represented as traditional, that is, as guaranteed by
the succession of magicians through whom the local
population keeps in touch with the original expert
who "brought up" the charm.[15]

In modern times, as the next chapter shows, prophets succeeded to the priestly functions of healing
and divination in what purports to be the public as
distinct from private interest. The prophet is
deemed to heal because, unlike the magician, he is
commanded to by God and is thought to derive no personal benefit from his work. Trance, glossolalia and
similar pneumatic appearances metaphorically express
the prophet's subordination to the Holy Spirit, in
whose name and with whose power he supposedly acts.

# 6

# *Healing*

The group of organizations calling themselves
churches is divided, as we have seen in Chapter Two,
into those that offer "healing now" and those that,
for various reasons, do not. In local theory,
"disease" (<u>mayeela</u>) is a broad category of afflictions of all sorts, or conditions perceived as such:
diseases, misfortunes, failure of expectations, and
startling experiences. This conception of disease is
more realistic on the whole than the popular American
view that illness is either a "real" chemical, physical, or biological condition to be manipulated by
appropriate techniques, or a "psycho-somatic" condition of "mental" or social origin (Moerman 1979).
The Kongo conception is consistent with more sophisticated views that admit the influence of personality
and social relations on such questions as the subjective perception of discomfort; response to
medication; menstrual regularity and ability to conceive; vulnerability to infections and physical
accidents. Conversely, the American predisposition
to divide events into physical and mental is constantly being challenged by the discovery of physical
factors underlying or contributing to anti-social
behaviors, learning ability, schizophrenia and stress
responses.

Kongo thought, like that of the Azande
(Evans-Pritchard 1937), attempts to answer the "why
me?" questions. Acknowledging the direct physical
causes of injury and (nowadays) infection, BaKongo
still want to know why afflictions are distributed as
they are, and rarely admit chance as an explanation.
This attitude pushes them to examine the social environment of the "sick" person and to identify sources

of tension in social relations. Some of their causal
allegations, couched in the idiom of witchcraft, are
fantastic, others shrewdly realistic. Successful
healers are those whose combination of psychological
insight and social skill generates effective therapy.
Most physical and psychological problems "heal themselves," and every medical profession offers
extensive rationalizations to cover the gap between
its claims and its actual achievements (cf. Turner
1967:356).

The idiom of witchcraft also has the merit of
situating the healer himself in the patient's social
nexus and does not pretend to reduce the
physician-patient relationship to an extra-social,
technical one. BaKongo frequently speak of two kinds
of disease, those caused by Nzambi and those caused
by mpeve zambi, "evil spirits" (Ward 1890:43). Any
disease may be "caused by Nzambi," meaning in effect
that it cannot be blamed on anyone and may not be
amenable to therapy. Evil influences formerly
included the autonomous action of ancestors, local
spirits or charms, but are now usually limited to
witchcraft or the injudicious use of magic. This
change means that therapy is usually a matter of
adjusting interpersonal tensions directly, rather
than re-asserting the internal discipline of a
lineage (ancestors), local group (local spirits) or
specialized association (charms). To a considerable
extent, however, the churches, some more than others,
have assumed the moral and social functions of local
and lineal groups, in the name of the Holy Spirit.
Recognition of the need for vermifuges or antibiotics
does not preclude inquiry into the alleged cause of
the disease; the two courses of action are in principle complementary, but individuals will give more
weight to one than to the other. An inquiry conducted in the late 1960's showed that 65 percent of the
clients at the divinatory séances of Mama Ndona at
Lukala were also receiving treatment at the nearby
Kimpese mission hospital (Masamba 1976:22).[1]

Since physical and social problems are conceived
from the start as a single field of action, BaKongo
resort not only to healers but to arbitration by the
courts or family conferences. As conflict-resolving
institutions, the healing churches resemble judicial
institutions rather than other religious organizations. Public demand thus expects modern
institutions to serve the multiple functions of the
chiefs and diviners of the past, for whom the activity of government (luyaalu) included public health,

criminal justice, rainmaking, leadership, and the
regulation of markets.

Modern judicial institutions include family
councils of elders, police courts, and magistrates'
courts of first and second instance. Committees of
elders, operating entirely within the customary sector as part of the system of social regulation I have
called kinkazi (MacGaffey 1970b:213), are capable of
satisfying multifunctional demands because they are
continuous with the milieu that generates the
demands; the witchcraft complex is part of their
terms of reference, and blessings as well as fines
result from their decisions. The police courts, on
the other hand, operate by written law of European
inspiration, wich recognizes witchcraft only as a
false accusation contrary to public order, applies
European criteria of evidence, and provides no blessings. Whereas prophets as arbitrators often summon
or are summoned by elders, they have no common understanding with the police, with whom their relations
are marked by distrust on both sides. (This official
hostility notwithstanding, individual police officers
often consult prophets, and a prophet is happy to be
able to mention a policeman or soldier as one of his
clients.) The magistrates' courts are hybrids,
pseudo-customary institutions set up by written law.
Those of first instance, staffed by local elders, may
be sympathetic to local considerations, but are subject to bureaucratic review; the appeal courts,
operating at the level of the territory (rather than
the "sector" or "chiefdom," known in present-day
Zaire as "local collectivity"), are more remote from
local concerns and more likely to apply European criteria of evidence and judgment (MacGaffey
1970b:284-86).

As medical institutions, the healing churches
compete with both doctors and magicians.
European-trained physicians regard both prophets and
magicians with distrust, arguing that parallel practice impedes their own therapies and is often
positively harmful. They themselves are usually
insensitive to the ways in which linguistic and cultural barriers and the depersonalizing procedures of
a hospital corrupt diagnosis and impede therapy. By
1970, no serious attempt had been made to establish
cooperation between the bureaucratic and the customary practice of medicine, to make use in the
hospitals of the social knowledge possessed by indigenous healers covertly doing the rounds of the same
wards.

Magicians and prophets, on the other hand,
recognize the virtues of x-rays, surgery and
anti-biotics, and often insist that their clients
seek out or return to doctors. Some of them give
technical lectures about anemia or tuberculosis.
They also administer herbal remedies, some of which
have genuine medicinal properties. Their principal
concern is to treat the moral causes believed to
underly the visible pathology, but the relation
between the two constituents of disease is complex;
BaKongo sometimes argue that what looks like a
disease to a European doctor is an illusion created
by witchcraft, that witchcraft can frustrate diagnosis and cloud the eye of the x-ray machine, or that
spiritual revelation is superior to any mechanical
device or book-learning.

From the point of view of the public, European
medicine demonstrates no obvious superiority to African healing techniques. If they and their families
are able and willing to provide the resources necessary for a visit to a good hospital (usually
mission-run), if their problems are relatively simple, clinically and psychologically, and if in fact
they are treated by a competent physician, people
will probably find the results gratifying. In practice, the sources of "European" medical help included
state hospitals and clinics, private clinics registered and supposedly supervised by the state, and a
variety of independent operators, usually ex-hospital
dishwashers using stolen hypodermics. In 1970, one
state hospital known to me was run by an incompetent
physician whose chief concerns were seducing nurses
and peddling government medical supplies for personal
benefit. The private and state clinics were generally staffed by men of good will and little training,
with limited resources, whose diagnoses and prescrip-
tions, even in simple and routine matters, were often
erratic (I speak from experience). The independent
entrepreneurs ranged from traveling drug peddlers to
a man I saw giving a penicillin injection after wip-
ing the needle on a piece of cotton which for
convenience he held down on the bare ground with his
big toe.

Against this competition, the magicians and prophets hold their own among the poorest and least
educated elements of the population, virtually all of
whom believe in the efficacy of magic, the reality of
witchcraft, and the possibility of raising the dead.
Of the handful of BaKongo I have ever known of whom I

could be sure that they did not share popular
beliefs, and who themselves knew that they did not,
one secure and prosperous individual sent his family
to the clinic whenever they needed attention. His
wife laughed at the prophets I was studying, but
rushed to consult one when a child of hers did not
recover fast enough from an injury. His oldest
daughter, a candidate for nursing school, consulted a
magician for persistent pains in her joints.

   More representative was a man I shall call Kingani, whose history reveals almost all of the usual
means of conflict resolution employed in Kongo in the
1960's. It will be useful to list them:

1.  Appeal to the elders under customary law.
2.  Litigation in the magistrates' courts.
3.  Resort to a magician; purchase of imported
    magic.
4.  Resort to prophets.
5.  Informal appeals to relatives and the public.
6.  Hiring military personnel, illegally, to use
    violence against one's opponent.
7.  Fingering one's opponent as "an enemy of the
    revolution."
8.  Personal violence (extremely rare, and in this
    case unintended).

Not included in this list, and of minor importance,
are appeals to the dead and the use of surgery as an
ordeal.

## Kingani's troubles

   Kingani, who belongs to the Nlaza clan in the
village of Kinkanza, was about forty years old in
1970, a muscular but not particularly intelligent
man. He had received a Protestant primary education
and became a marine mechanic working in the port of
Matadi. In 1951 he married a woman by whom he had in
due course eight children. During the 1950's he did
very well as a mechanic, attracting the attention and
favor of his European employer. Kingani says he is
naturally gifted as a mechanic and, unlike Europeans,
who always have to consult the book, he can tell what
is wrong with an engine by listening to it. By 1970,
however, he had reverted to the lowest grade of
mechanic, earning about $25 a month, little over the
legal minimum. He had divorced his wife, was having
trouble marrying another, and was deep in chronic
disputes with his relatives.

The story of Kingani's problems begins in 1957,
and as usual with such stories there are two sides to
it.  Kingani was making a good wage and  intended  to
invest  his  money in the village, as did most people
in his position at that time.  Matadi was little more
than a labor camp for the port;  political and managerial   opportunities   did   not   exist   there   for
Congolese, who could see themselves as successful and
prestigious only in the context of  village  society,
in  which  traditional  institutions  were  preserved
somewhat  artificially  by  the  colonial  policy  of
respect  for  customary  law.  In customary society a
man's position was fixed in principle by descent, but
principle  could  be  bent to accommodate exceptional
personal wealth or ability.
     Kingani thought he was exceptional.  Besides the
money  he  was making there was the fact that his own
maternal grandfather, an acknowledged expert on  clan
traditions and other forms of esoteric knowledge, had
specially chosen and trained him, so Kingani said, to
be  his  sucessor;  "siswa yasiswa, I was left in the
place." To live up to this designation Kingani  proposed  to  build  a  large  house  in Kinkanza and he
invested some of his money in a stock of white  linen
sheets  with which he made an ostentatious display at
a Nlaza funeral, draping the entire funeral enclosure
with  them.  Not  surprisingly,  these  pretentions
annoyed his maternal uncles and other elders, to whom
Kingani  was  merely a young man who owed them deference.  "So  I  gave  up  my  plan  to  build  in  the
village," says Kingani, "because  I  saw that they
would kill me if I did." The killing he feared  would
be effected mysteriously, by witchcraft.  So he built
his large house in Matadi instead.  He still  regards
himself as a chief in exile, and tends to treat every
conversation as a public meeting, addressing  to  any
available ear interminable speeches in the traditional manner, interwoven with an astonishing  number  of
proverbs  and  archaic  phrases.  This might be very
entertaining, but his  tone  constantly  tends  to  a
whine of self-justification, and his audience is soon
bored.
     At about the time he built his  house  his  mar-
riage  began to go to pieces.  Of his eight children,
the second, fourth, and sixth eventually died--not at
all  an unusually high proportion.  He began to think
that the resentment of  his  elders  had  caused  the
deaths,  by witchcraft, but his elders in turn blamed
him.They said that as a sailor, that is, as  one  who
occasionally  traveled down the Zaire River as far as

the mouth, he had every opportunity to sell his children "overseas," that is, to profit by exchanging them in witchcraft transactions. He also quarreled with his wife, who admitted in court in 1968 to being responsible for the bickering. By the time the divorce was pronounced they had appeared before the court three times and also, under customary law, the elders had tried several times to arbitrate their difference. On each occasion, Kingani was found to be in the right, he says.

After his divorce Kingani went to pieces. He sold all the furnishings of his house and spent his money on beer and women, to the great annoyance of his family, particularly his father and other elders of his father's clan, Mfulama Nkanga. When he began to collect himself and to think of marrying again, he saved about $100 towards the marriage payment and entrusted this sum to a maternal uncle who lives in Matadi and who appears hereafter as the villain of this piece. According to Kingani, this uncle, Kimfunya, concluded that by customary law he could dispose as he liked of his nephew's earnings, and did so. Kingani regarded this behavior as a continuation of the vengeful attitude maintained by his elders since 1957. The rest of the story consists of his efforts to resolve his dispute with his uncle Kimfunya in Matadi and his father, Kimpala, who lives in Kinkanza. Kingani considered that they were responsible for his lack of success as a mechanic, for various incidental afflictions, and for further failures in his auxiliary occupation, that of middleman between the sculptors of African curios and the sailors on foreign ships in the port, from whom watches, umbrellas, radios, nylon shirts and other valued goods can be obtained at low cost. He also believed that his father and his uncle were determined to sabotage his second marriage.

In his negotiations with his elders Kingani used the resources of the kinship system, particularly the good offices of a man called Nzazi who belongs, like Kingani's father, to the clan Mfulama Nkanga. On this account, Kingani calls Nzazi "father," although the two men are much the same age, and he expects Nzazi to speak on his behalf to Kimfunya, the uncle. Nzazi is a wealthy and widely respected man who is regarded as the leader and spokesman of Mfulama Nkanga members in Matadi. Kimfunya, however, belongs to Nlaza, and would pay no attention to Nzazi, a much younger man than himself, were it not for the fact that he also is a child of Mfulama Nkanga and must

therefore, by conventional etiquette, treat Nzazi
with respect as his "father," although no genealogical link of any kind can be traced between them.
Nzazi carries messages between Kingani and his uncle
and acts as witness and moderator in their negotiations. He says it is true that the uncle hired
off-duty soldiers to beat up Kingani; this maneuver
is a common one in Mobutu's Zaire, and I have known a
village burned down by gendarmes at the instigation
of its local enemies. The military are immune to all
forms of civilian control, and its members do what
they please provided only that they do it discreetly.
A similar meaninglessness characterizes the relations
of the population with the government's political
security organization, and the uncle exploited that
too, by informing the authorities that Kingani was a
threat to the regime. Kingani's name was therefore
put on a list of people in Matadi against whom
repressive action should be taken, but it happened
that another relative of his employed at a higher
level in the political bureaucracy saw his name on
the list and erased it.

On the other hand, Kimfunya has grievances of
his own, the chief being that Kingani circulates
through Matadi telling everyone who will listen that
his uncle is a witch. At one point, also, Kingani
struck his uncle or in some way caused him an injury;
the nephew agreed to pay Kimfunya's medical expenses,
but the fault remained.

In the late 1950's, Kingani had taken a
night-school course in the writing of French. He
employed his newly-developed skill in writing to
Paris for items of European magic such as "the penta-
cle of Dom Bernardin" and "L'Oeuvre d'Henri
Durville," which Kingani calls "prières." His fathers
were annoyed and took him, in 1960, to the Kinkanza
prophet Kinene Jean, who exonerated him, saying that
prières were not nefarious magic but the same sort of
recitations that prophets use. Nevertheless,
Kingani's fathers confiscated the prières, and so his
enemies among his relatives were able to go on "eating" his children, he says. In Matadi he endeavored
to protect his house against his uncle's nocturnal
attacks by placing charms above the doors and windows, under the bed, and in other strategic
locations. When he got religion in 1970, however, he
abandoned all charms, replacing them with crosses.
The fact that from the beginning of his troubles Kingani was interested in charms shows that he felt the
need for additional weapons, whose effectiveness lay

in the fact that he let it be known that he had them.
Conversely, his elders were justified in thinking
that Kingani was trying to make trouble.

In 1970 Kingani began to consort with a woman
whom he proposed to marry. A contract was drawn up
with her relatives and in June she formally moved to
his house, although Kingani had only made preliminary
payments and was still collecting the principal. By
this time she was already pregnant, but Kingani found
himself to be suffering from impotence and on this
acount he consulted a magician ( nganga) who diagnosed
his uncle's witchcraft as the cause of the trouble.
Nothing came of the diagnosis and whatever treatment
the magician offered to go with it, and in July Kingani renounced all kinds of magic, as well as
drinking and womanizing.

Simultaneously he began to attend the divinatory
seances of a prophet (ngunza), who was himself in the
process of marrying a clan relative of one of Nzazi's
wives. By the time Kingani took his seat in front of
him the prophet knew a good deal about the problem.
Denouncing Kimpala and Kimfunya as the cause of the
trouble, the prophet issued writs summoning them
before him.

On the appointed day Kingani's father Kimpala
appeared, having traveled from Kinkanza. As monoto-
nously talkative as Kingani himself, Kimpala agreed
that he had harbored resentment against his son on
account of the latter's misguided conduct and he
therefore confessed witchcraft guilt. All that was
now past and he sincerely desired his son's happi-
ness. The prophet therefore put Kimpala through the
public ritual of cleansing and reconciliation. The
following day Kingani held a private ceremony of
reconciliation at his own house, and of this ceremony
I am formally the witness; as a nominal member of
the Nsundi clan I am his "grandfather." He made a
speech detailing the circumstances, sang a hymn, and
presented his father with a secondhand overcoat
obtained from the ships and also a large quantity of
sugar to make doubly sure that his father's heart was
sweetly inclined towards him.

Unfortunately for Kingani's prospects, his uncle
had refused to heed the prophetic summons. Kingani
did his best to compensate by performing a ceremony
of reconciliation with one of his own sons who was
named Kimfunya after the uncle and is therefore entitled to understudy him in social relations. For the
ceremony, father and son removed their shoes. Father

recited a long statement of intent while standing facing his son and holding his hands. Then he spat lightly into the palms of the hands three times, and performed dumuna in which, still holding son's hands, he caused him to jump upwards three times. The son then crawled three times between father's legs in order to be "reborn."

Kingani wrote letters to his uncle and to his elders in the village telling them what he had done. His motives were, as usual, mixed. In part he was expressing his good faith, in part he was putting them on the spot for not participating in the recon- ciliation. He hoped that failure to heed the prophet's summons would be regarded one day by a court of law as evidence of witchcraft.

His efforts were in vain. After returning to the prophet, who provided him with a new finding that his uncle and relatives in the village were still doing him harm, he expressed his impatience with the prophet's efforts to solve the problem. He was suffering from his uncle's nocturnal attacks, one of which he described. He woke up one night to the sound of feet walking across the roof. Convinced that his uncle was trying to get in and afraid that the signs over the doors and windows might not be strong enough, he rushed out of the house, stark naked, with salt in one hand and pepper in the other. That's the only way to confront witches, he explained; you have to show your virility (kibakala). He was just in time to see his uncle disappearing across the roof in the shape of a cat, which jumped to the ground at the back of the house, resumed human form, and made off.

A few days later, Kingani cheered up. He had discovered a new prophet, an Angolan, whose rituals were new and more promising. The choir sang loudly while the new prophet examined Kingani's head and chest. After "listening" a while to his prophetic baton, the prophet stopped the choir and abruptly announced, "Your uncle!" This diagnosis, which sur- prised no one, was elaborated somewhat, and the prophet chided Kingani for not taking sufficiently active measures to protect himself. "Look at her!" he said, pointing to Kingani's pregnant concubine, "the child's the wrong way up! Her case is practi- cally hopeless already."

Kingani was sent to the prophetic dispensary for medicated incisions around his hips to restore his prowess, and told to bring the uncle, Kimfunya, and

also Nzazi, as "father," so that the prophet could
thrash the matter out. The concubine began to suggest that if Kingani's uncle was going to kill her
baby and perhaps herself in order to spite his
nephew, perhaps she should not marry him after all,
and so play safe.

Nzazi, who had amiably carried messages to the
uncle on Kingani's behalf, refused to go along with
the new plan. He had no use whatever for prophets
and clearly saw the real sources of Kingani's trouble. Kingani despaired; all seemed lost. He spoke
bitterly of giving up his prospective wife, selling
his house, leaving his job. He was at the mercy of
witches.

Kingani's difficulties were originally provoked,
perhaps, by aspects of his temperament which can be
described as paranoid and perhaps also as
manic-depressive. Whatever their putative origin, it
is clear that Kingani was reacting against real
threats, not imaginary ones, even though his description and evaluation of them in terms of witchcraft
may be regarded as fantastic. "Many paranoid persons
properly realize that they are being isolated and
excluded by concerted interaction, or that they are
being manipulated. However, they are at a loss to
estimate accurately or realistically the dimensions
and form of the coalition arrayed against them" (Lemert 1962:14). Kingani's history illustrates Lemert's
account of the paranoid relationship, in which, from
the point of view of others, the individual shows:

1. A disregard for the values and norms of the primary group, revealed by giving priority to
   verbally definable values over those which are
   implicit, a lack of loyalty in return for confidences, and victimizing and intimidating persons
   in positions of weakness.
2. A disregard for the implicit structure of groups,
   revealed by presuming to privileges not accorded
   him, and the threat or actual resort to formal
   means of achieving his goals.

Others respond to the individual so perceived by
subtly excluding him. He is progressively isolated,
because he is unable to communicate with them, and
comes to see them, quite reasonably, as united in a
conspiracy against him. In KiKongo, "conspiracy" is
manenga (also table ronde) a form of witchcraft
revealed in dreams when groups of people are seen
conversing together. As Lemert writes (1962:14-15):

The need for communication and the identity
which goes with it does a good deal to explain
the preference of paranoid persons for formal,
legalistic, written communications, and the
care with which many of them preserve records
of their contracts with others. In some ways
the resort to litigation is best interpreted as
the effort of the individual to compel selected
others to interact directly with him as equals,
to engineer a situation in which evasion is
impossible.

I did not see Kingani again for a couple of
weeks. When I did, he was transformed. Sweating
heavily, he was carrying a large bundle of woodcarv-
ings obtained from across the river, which he
proposed to sell on the ships at enormous profit.
His concubine, he said, had seen his former wife gos-
siping in the market with a woman from another house
of Kingani's clan, had heard her name mentioned, and
proposed to take the two of them to court to find out
"what they meant by it." No more talk of selling the
house or giving up work; he had resumed the offen-
sive.

## A SPIRITUALIST CHURCH

In 1970, the prophetic style was probably best
represented by Makanzu, founder and pastor of the
Matadi congregation of the church headed by Nsansi
Felix (DMN-Nsansi). The pattern of Makanzu's activities could be seen as the most naive of popular
responses to the multiple pressures which generated
and modified the independent churches, the one least
marked by special considerations and policies. It
was also, for the same reason, one of the least
stable.
Makanzu, a man of about thirty-five, was a professional sailor, one of many in Matadi who are
members of the mariners' union. He founded the
congregation while on leave in September 1969. In
November 1970 he was about to take to the sea again,
partly to fulfill professional obligations, partly
because his religious activities had given rise to so
many difficulties that a long interlude seemed advisable. Members of other churches who knew him said
that he had been active in prophet circles in Matadi
in 1956 and that he had at one time set himself up as
a bibliomancer; somehow, said my informant, the
Bible always fell open at the Book of Daniel.

Makanzu's family came from the Catholic parish of
Kyonzo, north of Matadi. He told me that he had
wanted to be a priest and had attended junior seminary, but his parents objected. Parts of his account
of his life were evidently fantastic.

## The services

The premises of Makanzu's church were extensions
of his house: on one side an office, and on the
other a tin-roofed enclosure with a cement floor.[2]
Seating spaces were provided for the prophet and his
assistants, the choir and musicians, and the congregation. The only noteworthy furniture was a square
concrete podium, approached by three steps on every
side, the top of which carried the prophetic symbol,
an S inscribed on a Greek cross. This podium was
called kinlongo, a word which usually means temple
but which an elder of the church translated as
"altar." The choir consisted mostly of women and
boys; various percussion instruments were played,
but the long dance drum, ngoma, was missing.

Services were usually held every day from about
3 p.m. to 6 p.m. On Sundays there was no prophesy-
ing (bikula mambu), but the names of those whose
problems would be dealt with the following week were
announced. In the mornings the prophet made house
calls.

The congregation of about 150 usually included a
number of individuals and families waiting their
turn, which might not come for several days, and a
number of people with nothing better to do, for whom
a prophetic séance was entertainment, a combination
of theater, hymn-sing, and advice column, with the
possibility of scandalous revelations and dramatic
confrontations. The staff included the pastor who
conducted the regular service, the choir leaders and
principal musicians, the uniformed ushers, the prophet's assistants or acolytes, and the secretary.

The weekday service was always in two parts. It
began with a regular Protestant service: hymns,
prayers, sermon on a Biblical text. This part gave
everybody time to assemble. It announced that the
occasion was religious and respectably so. It grati-
fied individuals, such as the pastor and others, on
whom it conferred functions and titles. And it
warmed the scene for the entry of the prophet.

The shift to the second phase was marked by a
change in the music, from well-known hymns found in
the Protestant hymnbook to popular Kimbanguist hymns

sung in the local (central Kongo) style. The melo-
dies and harmonies were much the same, but the
singing was more enthusiastic and the words, although
still Protestant and evangelical in style, referred
specifically to prophetic activities (cf. Kiernan
1977). A series of hymns introduced Makanzu himself
and commented on his opening rituals, which in style
though not in content were as obviously Catholic as
those of the first phase were Protestant.[3] The prophet entered in solemn procession with six or seven
acolytes, most of whom were women dressed in white as
nuns. He wore a white cassock and carried his prophetic staff, studded with brass nails. After
walking three times around the kinlongo the prophet
slowly mounted it and began to pray silently. The
hymn changed: "On the hill the Apostle of God is
praying." The prophet began to tremble and to speak
in tongues. His acolytes might also tremble and
utter ecstatic cries. Sometimes a sort of spiritual
dialogue took place between them and the prophet,
while choir, orchestra and congregation maintained
maximum volume. The prophet was given one of a
number of bottles of water assembled at one corner of
the podium and invoked a blessing on it. In a spectacular performance he trembled violently and the
bottle seemed to leap in his hands, splashing water
about. After more prayers and blessings the prophet
poured a little of the water from a cup into the
mouth of each acolyte ("All who have received water
to drink shall be saved"). The prophet rinsed his
hands and dried them on a napkin, which was folded
and placed on top of the cup. He might then address
the congregation, or proceed directly to divination.
Surrounded by his acolytes, he sat next to the secretary's table at the head of the room. A client was
brought to sit on a bench in front of him: "Hear,
hear, the time for prophecy has come."
    The prophet read his Bible. He began to speak
in tongues and to tremble; an assistant held the
chair firm. The monotone voice of the spirit sounded
much like Latin, mixed with French phrases and Biblical names. A discreet signal silenced the choir
while the monologue continued, changing suddenly to
intelligible KiKongo spoken at high speed and interrupted by passages of gibberish. The prophet recited
the client's symptoms in detail, pausing occasionally
to ask if the acount were correct. He repeated himself frequently, and might interrupt himself to lead
a pertinent hymn. (A summary impression of a séance
is included in JM No.22). He searched for the source

Pl.9: Sunday morning trance, EC-Gonda, Kasangulu

Pl.10: The descent of the Spirit.
Drawing by Kazi Thomas

of the trouble: the work of God or of the devil? if
the latter, is the witch in father's or mother's
clan? Having identified it, the prophet came to himself and spoke in his normal voice, discussing the
diagnosis with his client and recommending treatment.
The client, and other people present, might be possessed, but most remained calm and some were even
hostile to the proceedings, having been brought there
unwillingly by relatives. The secretary kept a
record of what was said, which the client was
required to sign (without having read it).

Special rituals were performed when the prophet
had successfully resolved a problem. If an affliction had been attributed to a witch and the witch
admitted his fault, he was first purified (hymn: "Eh
Mr Makanzu he walks softly, softly"). As a penitent,
he was supposed to carry around the church a heavy
iron bar which was struck to announce his sins. Then
"the witch water" was fetched in an enamel basin
whose surface was divided into four quadrants by a
wooden crucifix floating in it and a red ribbon laid
across it. The acolytes, some of them trembling,
prayed around the basin and blessed the water ("Holy
Spirit, descend we pray"). The prophet also blessed
it, dipping two fingers of his right hand in each of
the four quadrants ("Witches will be burned ..."). 
The witch's face was painted blue and he was given a
comic "witch's hat" to wear. He was paraded around
to cheers and jeers and stood upon the kinlongo
before coming to wash his hands in the basin. When I
saw this done, the witch was a cheerful old man,
something of a clown, who turned the whole affair
into a warmly good-humored occasion, with the help of
the prophet, who warned everyone that they might be
in the old man's place.

So far, the rite seems to be an invention of
this church, but it continued with a common Kongo
ceremony for the reconciliation of parents and children. The witch prayed, spat in the sick person's
hand (saliva conveys a blessing), and jumped him several times in the air (dumuna). The sick person (who
in this instance was the witch's son) was passed
three times between the witch's legs from behind in a
symbolic rebirth; his face was then washed by the
prophet with water from the basin. Finally, all the
parties were "put under the flag" of the church,
which was held over their heads by the acolytes while
prayers were recited. This procedure is common in
DMN churches as a means of protecting those who have

been ill, are about to go on a journey, or something
of the sort.

To some extent the successful prophet keeps his
congregation in good heart by inventing or exploiting
special occasions of alarm or rejoicing. Makanzu
also invented spectacular rituals when opportunity
served. He required a husband and wife who had been
deeply involved in a witchcraft partnership to symbolize the end of it by standing on the kinlongo
holding between them a live chicken which they then
tore apart as each "went his separate way." Each was
then blindfolded with a red cloth.

Makanzu thought of himself as a Catholic, and
thought of all the rituals he performed using water
as Catholic rituals. The others, such as the "rebirth" and the divided chicken were traditional, and
not specifically religious. He complained that the
Catholic clergy did not exercise their powers as priests to heal and manifest the Spirit, and that until
recently they had prayed in Latin, suggesting that
they were keeping something secret from the people
(both of these are common Kongo themes). Members of
his church continued to belong to whatever church
they were baptized in; he himself would go for communion, he said, to either a Catholic or a Protestant
church. Like most Zairois, he attached no importance
to theological differences between the two, though he
said all prophets had to enter the way of Protestantism.

Magic?

In various ways, Makanzu constantly made it
clear that he would have nothing to do with magic and
the activity of magicians, nganga za n'kisi. A
client observed to be wearing a cord of some kind
around his neck or wrist (presumably a charm (n'kisi)
was always told to remove it as contrary to the will
of God. If the client were known to have repaired to
a magician or to have used charms, the prophet would
blame part of his troubles on the fact. In the sermons he addressed to his flock from time to time, the
chief purpose of which was always to define his own
activity, the prophet emphasized that everything he
did was directed by the Holy Spirit, and that he
charged no fee. Occasionally he prescribed a herbal
remedy, always pointing out that it was merely a herbal remedy, not n'kisi.

Nevertheless, almost everything Makanzu did
closely resembled the activities of the nineteenth

century diviner, variously known as nganga manga, nganga ngombo, or by the name of any of a large number of charms, such as Ntadi, used to "sniff out" (fyela). Makanzu even described himself as m'fyedi, "diviner." The similarities include the following:

1. Ecstatic assistants, the "acolytes," formerly known as min'tombo.
2. The presence of a participating public.
3. The use of songs to "bring down the spirit," whose words descriptively summarize the proceedings.
4. Divination proceeding by a series of rhetorical questions which the diviner answers: does the trouble come from God (is it "natural") or from man (witchcraft)? If from man, from father's side of the family or from mother's (ku mase evo ku ngudi)? And so on.
5. Treatment by means of blessings, potions and ablutions.

The structure of Makanzu's regular divinatory séance (the second or post-Protestant phase) closely follows the practice of a diviner (nganga ngombo) described by Bahelele (1964). Initially the diviner blessed (sakumuna) his equipment instead of Makanzu's bottles of water. The opening songs and responses established his role as diviner: E sweka, "Hidden!" E solula, "Reveal it!" E wawe, mu luvemba yatela ngombo, mono nganga, waw'e, "Listen, by chalk I divine, I am nganga." Thereafter, the diviner pursued the usual series of questions leading to the identification of a witch. Makanzu built up the excitement by interpolating increasingly specific divinatory statements as interruptions to loud music performed by his assistants, in exactly the same way that diviners did (Cah.341; see also Buakasa 1968:168-69; Cavazzi 1968,II:181-83). A priest of nkita spirits, as described by Bittremieux, goes into ecstasy at the urging of her clientele and the increasing volume of the music, and utters an incomprehensible monologue in the language of magic which she breaks off, just like Makanzu, in order to announce her questions recto tono (Bittremieux 1936:159).

Sometimes the prophet's debt to indigenous religion is only revealed by close observation. The lustration with witch water, described above, can be regarded as what Mankanzu said it was, an attempt to copy Catholic practice. The bowl of water divided in four is none the less obviously the yanga or diyowa

of bygone cults (e.g. Bittremieux 1936:160-61).
While blessing this water Makanzu raised his hand in
the air before dipping his two fingers in it, but in
some repetitions of the blessing he first touched his
hand to the floor instead. Asked why, he explained
that the gesture referred to Christ's harrowing of
hell: having brought down power from heaven (<u>ku</u>
<u>zulu</u>), Christ also went to the dead to bring up power
from below (<u>ku nsi</u>). The distinction unconsciously
imposed upon the Biblical text by Makanzu is that
which divides the other world into upper and lower
parts, land <u>bisimbi</u> and water <u>bisimbi</u>, or God above
and the dead below.

Gestures implying the use of power from above
and from below are often contrasted in the rituals of
spiritualist churches. Applying holy water to the
sites of affliction in a client's body (usually the
legs, belly, or chest) a healer may use the sole of
his foot instead of his hand. The gesture, called
<u>dyata mu binkoso</u>, "walking on joints," is supposed to
convey the generalized power of the dead (<u>ngolo za</u>
<u>nsi</u>, powers from below) (JM No.48, par.9 and note).
The choice of hand or foot is said to be dictated by
the Holy Spirit, for whom the healer, whether in
trance or not, is simply a medium; one healer said,
however, that the use of the foot was required when
the client was a woman with chest troubles, since it
was not seemly for a male or female healer to be laying hands on her bosom. Therapeutic "treading on
joints" is found in disused <u>n'kisi</u> cults and in the
<u>nkita</u> cult in its modern form (Buakasa 1968:159);
its inverse or polluting form is the ritual insult
<u>dyata va mbula</u>, "treading on the forehead."

It is important nevertheless to notice the
differences between Makanzu's practice and the generality of <u>n'kisi</u> cults, ancient and modern. They
include: (1) his use of plain water instead of medicated palmwine or a concoction of ingredients from
the charm (<u>miemo</u>, <u>bilongo</u>); in this connection the
whiteness of the enamel basin and the prescribed
clear glass for bottles of holy water is important.
(2) His use of plain white ritual clothing, with at
most a few touches of red or an embroidered sign, and
no body paint. (3) His insistence on not using any
charms or other equipment, with the exception of his
staff and the flag of the church. Whiteness was
classically used in the <u>n'kisi</u> cult as a sign of the
dead, of clarity of vision, and of vindication (as in
clearing someone of debt or suspicion), but was only
one element in a dense complex of colors, textures

and verbal associations. In prophetic practice,
whiteness is a powerful moral and philosophical
statement of purity, clarity, transparency, and sin-
cerity; it symbolizes the prophet's commitment to
openness and publicity, as opposed to the murky
secretiveness of self-serving magic.[4] As one prophet said, "The Holy Spirit in a man is like water in
a glass, hiding nothing."

The resort to whiteness is partly an accommodation to censorship--holy water and white robes are
acceptably Christian, body paint would declare its
indigenous origin--but it is not simply protective
coloration for covert paganism; a distinction is
being made, within the implicit structure of indigenous religion, between cults associated with the
pursuit of personal advantage and those that assert
the priority of public interests and values.[5]

## Therapy and its social context

Makanzu's secretaries kept typewritten records
of his cases, running to several hundreds when I saw
them. My sample of 86 was selected unsystematically
under the constraints of the time available and the
legibility and intelligibility of the texts, which as
records left much to be desired. Makanzu kept them
partly to supplement his memory and partly out of a
belief that a record of what he said would protect
him in case of litigation or other troublesome challenge.

Of the 86 clients, 28 were men, 50 women, four
married couples, and four unspecified. The records
indicated the symptoms, usually vague and various; a
specific illness such as diabetes or tuberculosis was
mentioned in seven cases. The remaining indications
can be grouped in five categories with frequencies as
follows, according to the number of cases in which
they were mentioned:

| | |
|---|---|
| parasites | 19 |
| menstrual and reproductive troubles | 26 |
| money shortage, failure of ambitions | 15 |
| nightmares | 15 |
| miscellaneous discomforts | 54 |

The parasites are mostly intestinal worms, which
probably infest 60 percent of the population.
"Failure of ambitions," in the case of men, usually
means unemployment or failure to be promoted; in the
case of women, it usually means failure to find a

husband. (In another church, a prostitute came to
the prophet complaining that she had no customers.)
Reproductive troubles are extremely common as a
result of exhaustion, poor diet and hygiene, widespread syphilis, and probably sheer anxiety; the infant
mortality rate is about 40 percent.

Makanzu usually offered multiple diagnoses and a
combination of remedies. The client always suspected
witchcraft, but was frequently told that no witchcraft was present or that the actual resentment of
the suspected witch had not reached the witchcraft
level. Some difficulties were attributed to natural
causes ("Nzambi"), some to the client's own bad
habits or witchcraft. Failure of ambitions was usually blamed on the resentment of father's clan; when
the client was a soldier from up-country, the prophet
always asserted that the man's father had not wanted
him to join the army.

The commonest causes of trouble were family
resentments of one sort or another, usually that
mother's or father's relatives disapproved of the
client's marriage or felt that they were not getting
their due. In 17 instances, the records specifically
mention that the client had been hurt by the effect
of slavery disputes in the clan; in such cases, two
or more lineages arguing about who is a slave and who
is not are believed to bewitch one another.

Family disagreements and slavery disputes are
both matters of village politics, in which
town-dwellers are involved because most of them come
from villages to which most of them may well return,
but also because village elders, retired from wage
work and resident on their ancestral lands, control
the administration of marriage, divorce and inheritance under customary law. As such, they are
frequent visitors to town, and often expect their
dependents to appear in the village. In Kinshasa,
but to a much lesser extent in Matadi, townsmen may
abandon their village ties entirely and meet the
demands of customary law and its bureaucratic supervisors by recruiting among their friends what may be
called a nkazi of opportunity, or nonce elder, to
fulfill the formalities. Working men and women in
town usually submit to the control of their village
elders, however, out of loyalty to all that the village represents and also because the elders are in
fact useful in negotiating one's affairs--a marital
dispute, for example.

Economic relations parallel these social relations. In the villages, food is cheap and relatively

abundant; in town it is much more expensive and
often scarce. Townspeople, on the other hand, earn
wages and can relatively easily buy imported goods
such as sugar, clothes, watches, radios and pressure
lamps. Cooperation guided by kinship norms enables
both parties to bypass the commercial network to
their mutual advantage. On top of this reciprocity,
however, social obligations induce a flow of goods
from younger, working people in town to their elders
in the village. At weddings and funerals, tokens of
esteem register the closeness of the relationship and
build up implicit credit upon which one may draw on a
like occasion or in time of need. Although the
receipts at such events are redistributed by the
recipients, a larger share goes to the elders, for
whom the continual sequence of rites of passage thus
functions as a social security system. In addition,
cadets casually visiting on holiday are expected to
honor their elders with gifts or luxuries such as
bread and sugar which at the same time symbolize the
giver's cash employment and urban environment.

The chief beneficiary of these presentations is
father, the origin of the child's substance and of
his capacity to succeed in the world. In modern
times father bears most of the expense of raising and
educating the child to fit him for good employment.
Father is entitled to a return for his outlay, and
entitled to feel aggrieved if his due is ignored.
Strong feelings of this kind can take effect as
witchcraft, causing the child to fall ill or to fail
in his enterprises.

Life is hard for both villagers and townspeople;
real wages fell by two thirds between 1960 and 1966,
and in Manteke people were noticeably worse off in
1970 than in 1965. Elders suffering the drudgery of
rural life and envious of the electricity, piped
water and other amenities of the city tend to feel
that their children owe them something. Younger people facing unemployment (about 40 per cent) or meagre
wages and struggling to produce and raise healthy
children in a disease-ridden environment are inclined
to blame parental ill will for their difficulties.
The town is thus constantly looking over its shoulder
to the village. Most accusations of witchcraft are
directed against famille ku vata, "relatives in the
village;" hardly any against neighbors or work mates
(LaFontaine 1970:249).

Makanzu's diagnoses in 86 cases mention causes
roughly classifiable as follows:

| | |
|---|---|
| None mentioned | 7 |
| Natural causes | 8 |
| Family | 29 |
| Clan (slavery) | 17 |
| Self | 10 |
| Twin cult violations | 9 |
| Other | 6 |

The category "self" includes those in which the client himself is blamed for his problems. In four of them the client had acquired charms not just to heal a sickness but to benefit himself, perversely; in two, the client had bewitched himself or herself. The category "other" includes one theft and three cases of gratuitous witchcraft, that is, cases in which the client's problems were blamed on mere spite unmotivated by some sense of social debt.

In 27 cases Makanzu told the client to seek medical help; in 31 he offered reassurance, either verbal ("be confident, there is nothing wrong") or in the form of prayers, special blessings, or courses of ritual ablutions ("bathe six times"). For family and clan problems he would either send the client to his village to negotiate or summon the relatives in question. The latter course the prophet undertook only if he knew what he was getting into, meaning that he knew something about the village in question (6 cases only). He referred twin cult violations to the adepts of that cult for treatment. The several kinds of prescription were not exclusive. "Bathing six times" meant that the client came to the prophet's assistants for ritual ablutions on six successive days; addressing his congregation, the prophet used to emphasize that the assistant would be of the same sex as the client and that propriety (luzitu) would be observed: a minimal garment would be worn. For the theft he said, "The government won't let me identify thieves, but privately I will tell you that Alphonse did it."

## Selections from Makanzu's casebook

1. A man complained that his money disappeared and he had no luck at work. The prophet told him that although he wanted to blame his wife his troubles were his own fault, he did not know how to look after money.
2. A woman complained of insanity (kilau), saying that she was in great distress, her body trembled with fear, she shrieked and gabbled, and dared

not go out lest somebody kill her. The prophet revealed that to advance her trading business she had entered into a compact with her husband and bought charms for which she was to pay five souls. She had a long history of involvement with magicians, one of whom gave her a cord to wear that was supposed to bring her luck but which was in fact not just a cord but a device dangerous to her (bungwa bakuvana); this matter had already been exposed (bikuduswa) by a prophet in Kinshasa when one of her children fell ill. Another magician gave her something "for luck" which was in fact witchcraft meat. Makanzu told her to confess her sins and try to follow the path of God, lest she go completely mad.

3. A couple complained that their child had no strength in his legs. They had tried medicines (bilongo) and charms (min'kisi) to no avail, and were afraid he would be a cripple like some other members of the family (polio?). The mother suffered from things bumping around in her heart and stomach. The prophet found that her clan wanted her to return to the village and were keeping her child's legs there to force her to do so.

4. A woman suffered from heartburn, headaches, dizziness, and had trouble climbing hills. She had had trouble giving birth and her children were never well. She had been infested with worms all her life. The prophet explained that her uncles were at odds because some of them felt cheated of their share of her marriage money ("they ate nothing"). There were slavery problems, and some of her relatives had given her worms in her youth so that she would be unable to marry. Her husband was fed up, but his words were daylight words only (did not amount to witchcraft). She was told to go to a doctor, to bathe 9 times, and to purify her house to get rid of "evil spirits" (generalized witchcraft).

5. A woman who had suffered a series of miscarriages was told that though she did not know it her lineage were slaves whom the elders of the clan kept as though they were chickens in a coop, to kill off or to sell. Her brother had struggled to find out their true pedigree (lusansu) so that they could redeem themselves and be free, but although he had the ability to argue the case in daylight he was not old enough to have the nocturnal ability (ngangu za mpimpa) to fend off witchcraft.

6. A woman complained of stomach ache, poor vision and "some live thing gripping her throat." Her money kept disappearing. In a dream, one of her mothers offered her human flesh which she did not accept. Since then she had had trouble, and had been accused of eating a classmate who died suddenly. Makanzu explained that she had worms and rheumatism, that her lineage were in slavery, and that her child was stealing the money. She should receive spiritual ablutions and see a doctor.

7. A girl complained of trouble in her chest, fast heartbeat, generalized pain and feebleness, fever, bad dreams, and a burning cough with spots of blood. She had been to white and black doctors and spent her money to no avail. X-rays showed nothing. The prophet explained that she had tuberculosis and should go back to the doctor. Although the devil was keeping the disease from showing on the film, no witchcraft was involved; she had picked up a contagious disease (maladi ma nsambukila),

8. A woman said her child was continually vomiting. Makanzu told her that her suspicion that her clan was at fault was incorrect. Her husband had a drinking companion who had put something in his beer after an argument about a woman. The prophet recommended prayers and a visit to the doctor. (The "poison" was deemed to have attacked the husband indirectly by harming his child, though the child did not himself drink it.)

9. A man said he suffered from general ill-health and bad luck; also, there had been several deaths in his village. At one time he was out of work, and used to dream of building a house in the village, but did not want to. The prophet said that his relatives accused him of having many charms (bintombe-ntombe bingi, from tomba, "to seek"), in violation of a clan taboo (kandu) against their use. There was also a slavery dispute.

10. A woman complained of sore arms and legs, stomach pains, and lack of success in finding a husband. Men asked for her, but her elders did not conclude any contract. She copulated with young men in her dreams. The prophet explained that her elders had married her by witchcraft to a nocturnal partner to whom she bore children, so that in

the daylight world she could have none.
Moreover, she had been given worms by the witchcraft guilt of her mother's parents, who had
refused to marry her off; the mother's justifiable resentment had perpetuated her own troubles
in her daughter, who was recommended to bathe 16
times, take medicine for worms, and see a doctor
if that did not work.

These cases show that the total course of a
"disease" is a complex social process. J.M. Janzen
has investigated a number of such histories in
detail. He points to the importance of what he calls
the therapy managing group, the people who decide
what action to take (Janzen 1978). A prophet is more
likely to recognize the existence of such a group
than a European physician. Any therapist's (or magistrate's) encounter with an individual is likely to
be only one of a number of such encounters, widely
scattered in space and time. The manipulation
attempted by the therapist is only one of several
manipulative strategies at work, not all of them well
meant. A woman who brings a list of ailments to a
prophet may be hoping that the prophet will identify
her husband as a witch so that she will have one more
argument to beat the poor man with. The illness of
children may provide their elders with an opportunity
to level charges of witchcraft against another
lineage with whom they are engaged in litigation over
land.
　　The prophet's own manipulative endeavors depend
on his experience and intuition and on his authority.
The last is a function of his style, including his
repertoire of dramatic gestures, exotic clothing,
solemn or spirit-guided speech, and the support of
the core members of his congregation. When a client
did not recognize the ancestors whom Makanzu named as
central to the slavery problem in his clan, the
congregation jeered. When the shrew who hoped to
have her husband denounced as a witch was told that
she herself was the witch, but refused to admit it,
the crowd sang "When Mr Makanzu teaches, people will
not listen." The prophet himself lectured her severe-
ly: "I am the ferry to help you over the Zaire of
your disagreements. You say I failed to discover
your husband was a witch because he had hidden his
witchcraft in a charm (mpungu). Yet I can tell,
under your clothes, that you have syphilis. I could
say, though I did not, with whom you have committed

adultery. The eye of God looks down upon earth and
sees every bird that flies; what charm will suffice
to hide anything from him?"

I feel sure, though I have no direct evidence,
that Makanzu's congregation also passed on information to him informally. The waiting-list procedure
meant that people with trouble in mind would probably
sit for several days in a crowd that included a
number of relatives and acquaintances of
long-standing who stood in the same kind of relationship to the prophet. Most of the clients and the
congregation were BaMboma, from the Boma or Manteke
side of the river, people who came from the same villages and schools and had ridden the same trucks to
and from Matadi for years, and could be expected to
discuss their problems while they waited.
Presumably, the waiting was essential to the
prophet's eventual diagnosis. About once a month he
found it necessary to harangue the congregation on
the need to observe the kind of bureaucratic ideals
that the real local bureaucracy rarely obeyed; "the
Holy Spirit," he would say, "comes to no private
arrangements, has no friends in the office. Stay in
line!" (mpeve a nlongo kasadilanga mu ki-arrangement
ko, vo mu ki-connaissance. Suivez ordre!)

To judge Makanzu as a failed Catholic priest is
largely irrelevant. The nearest equivalent in the
United States is not the priest but the social worker, helping clients to raise children, look after
their health, find work, manage their quarrels.
Since Makanzu belonged entirely to the same class as
his clients and shared their life, he was in some
ways a superior social worker. We might complain
that his medical advice was inadequate, that he perpetuated ignorance or even exaggerated some of the
tensions he purported to relieve, but in the Zaire of
1970 he was not only the best source of advice and
help for the poorest and most ignorant of a
hard-pressed people, he and healers like him were the
only source. The social services left by the Belgians had degenerated to a mere appendix of the
bureaucratic patronage system, and official concern
with the actual conditions of the people went, in
Matadi or Manteke, no further than propaganda.

## The prophet and the police

When Makanzu set up as a healer in Matadi in
1969, he took to the provincial Department of Justice
an undated document, the "statutes" of the "Eglise de

Mpeve a Nlongo" (Church of the Holy Spirit) and a
letter from its founder and head announcing the opening of a regional section of the church in Matadi and
appointing Makanzu regional pastor. The purpose of
the statutes was to claim official recognition and
civil personality (corporate identity) under the law,
but after the recognition accorded to EJCSK in 1959
the government developed no clear policy with regard
to the multitude of would-be churches. During the
1960's, some of them with the right connexions in
provincial and even national government were able to
obtain some sort of government paper, but the effective legal value of anything of the kind was doubtful
in an era of uncertain constitutionality and abrupt
political realignments, in which patronage counted
for more than rights (Bernard 1970:212).

This particular Church of the Holy Spirit
(DMN-Nsansi) was never more than a few loosely constituted centers such as the one in Matadi, linked by
personal acquaintanceships, but its statute said that
it had been founded in 1956 "to evangelize religion,
extending also to educational and medical work."[6]
After sending in his letter of introduction from the
founder, Makanzu was summoned to the Matadi city
hall. He was in jail at the time, serving 30 days
for not having paid a girl he had slept with ("les
parents en ont été contrariés"), but he explained
that he was appealing the judgment. He also expanded
on the aims of his enterprise, as follows:

> Help for the sick by prayers. Divine worship
> by songs and prayers. We also do divination.
> This is how we proceed. The sick person freely
> presents himself, during office hours, and asks
> about his sufferings. Using water from a basin
> on which we have laid hands, we wash the inval-
> id, or else she is washed by another person of
> the same sex. Afterwards there is a blessing
> consisting of another laying-on of hands and an
> invocation addressed to Almighty God. Invalids
> recover, even those who are at death's door.
> As all these prayers and healings do not give
> rise to the receipt of any fees, it may be that
> a dozen patients arrive each day.

Having recorded this statement, the magistrate noted:
"It results from the inquiry that miraculous cures
are produced after divination. This may well be
either a threat to the peace or an impediment to the
public health services" [emphasis added].

Makanzu was then sent on to the provincial medical officer, who replied that he had nothing to do with religion, only with people applying for license to open private medical clinics. Having failed to classify Makanzu's activities according to the institutions it recognized, the bureaucracy allowed him to operate under the meager cover of the documents he already had.

In 1970 Makanzu got into trouble as a result of a visit he was invited to make to a village in Mayombe, where he was already well known and where the local authorities supported his action in identifying a witch. A man called Simon was to be healed of "fast heart-beat, congested chest, coughing", for which a magician called Albert had treated him. Makanzu's diagnosis read:

> One healer (n'sadi) gave you an object to hold until you got better, but it did not help. You called in a magician, who gave you a chicken and other things. This chicken, however, is really a dead man, appointed as a guard over you. It is put in your house to kill anyone who approaches you. The name of the man who is bewitching you is Albert. In daylight, he comes to you and gives you things he says will cure you, such as a stone. This stone is no ordinary stone but a witchcraft bullet. Once upon a time he quarreled with you about money. Moreover, there is a silk-cotton (m'fuma) tree in the village, where witches congregate. This tree, already pointed out by another prophet, should be cut down under my supervision. Everybody says you are a witch, striving for advantage in your employment and using charms to obtain more money. It is true that you have charms in your house, but you merely paid money for them, you do not hand over people. The witch, on the other hand, has twelve powers (douze malins) and steals people's money by magic. He has charms in his house, and has boxed you in to a four-cornered stone; you will never be healed unless you escape from it.

Albert's real crime, perhaps, and certainly his vulnerability, was that he was not a local man but a long-resident stranger from Manianga. Having no chance of redress in the local courts, he took Makanzu to court in Matadi, where he explained that since 1925 he had himself been a healer:

I know certain native preparations (<u>produits
indigènes</u>), and I have caused many women to
give birth and even cured the insane. But this
prophet, who often comes to the village, well,
one evening the headman had everyone turn out
at his prophetic altar, and the prophet, not
knowing I was there in the dark, said to Simon
that he was ill because a certain Mr Albert had
it in for him. "He is the reason for your
suffering, and he's a master witch." At that
everybody yelled, and this man, showing he
thinks himself better than the government, gave
the order to arrest me. Fortunately an official was there who calmed the situation.
<u>The Court</u>: Why did you not dispute the
accusation on the spot?
<u>Albert</u>: I was afraid.
<u>The Court</u>: Did you expect him to kill you?
<u>Albert</u>: I have known this man since he was a
child, but now that he's become a prophet I was
too surprised to reply.

Makanzu, in reply, emphasized that he carried on
his work under the supervision of the local authorities. In fact, some members of the locally dominant
faction, allies of Simon, were using the official
positions they held to sanction and cover entirely
unofficial political maneuvers which, in customary
terms, were sanctioned and legitimated as divination.
The communal court in Matadi decided that it was not
competent to decide the case but the resourceful
Albert took it to the police magistrate in the city,
who promptly fined Makanzu for defamation (public
accusation of witchcraft) and confined him to his
house for a month. The following day, Makanzu's
congregation was despondent. How could anyone be
healed if it was forbidden to confront witches? The
parallel between this repression of prophetic activity and that which occurred in Belgian Congo was
mentioned, and the conflict could not be solved: the
government is God on earth, yet here it is contradicting the Spirit. If we have to start praying in
the forest again (as in colonial times), we'll be
back where we were. Tentatively, the congregation
resolved to continue, proposing that if a witch were
identified they would all sign a letter to the
government telling it what he had done, and how they
suffered in consequence. Throughout this discussion
the prophet himself said nothing.

# 7

# A Sequence of
# Intentional Responses

The previous chapter exposed some of the vicis-
situdes of healing in a plural society, resulting
from the institutional incompatibility of the two
sectors. In describing the plural structure of Belgian Congo, and the position of prophets in each of
its sectors, I relied on the ordinary categories of
social science, such as "institution," "political,"
"religious," and the like. These categories sort the
data in a satisfactory way, and it is hard to think
what a sociological analysis would be like that did
not use them and the investigative questions associated with them. Nevertheless these categories, which
we endow with universal analytical value, are derived
from the institutional structure of our own society;
"religion," "government" and "economics" are derived
from church, state and market, supposedly independent
activities.

Application of such schemes to a society differently structured raises problems such as we have
already encountered. Kimfumu, for example, as
"chiefship," is political, but as "an affliction
cult" it is religious. Much that goes on in the
areas designated by the terms kingunza and kinganga
(the activities of prophet and magician, respectively) we would wish to classify as religion, politics,
medicine, law, or art. Kongo categories, that is to
say, seem heterogeneous to us. To treat "medicine,"
"art," or "government" as analytically distinguishable "aspects" of various kinds of Kongo behavior is
to effect a translation, by analogy with our own
institutions, that makes Kongo behavior intelligible.
This translation is important and necessary, but it
minimizes the role of the actor's own cognitive

processes, since it treats the categories of his intentional thought as mysterious complexities to be dissolved. In this chapter we will explore the function of these categories in the thought of three different charismatic leaders.

Simon Kimbangu, born in 1889, was a member of the first generation of the colonized, a victim, as Bernard remarks, but not a rebel (Bernard 1970). He called on God to help black people, but launched no general campaign against the whites. Simon Mpadi, on the other hand, was born in 1909 and brought up in a society in which the autonomy of the past was only a memory. He had experienced the full repressive weight of the colonial system, including the persecution of the prophets of 1921; in the 1960s, the brutality of those days was still vividly recollected. In 1939, Belgian Congo had not recovered from the depression. The administrative structure of indirect rule, begun in 1920, had recently been completed by decrees providing for the creation of artificial chiefdoms (sectors), urban communities for the developing proletariat (extra-customary centers), and the system of customary courts of first instance (native tribunals). The problem of what to do with the growing middle class of evolués was being raised (Rubbens 1945). In other words, the encapsulation of indigenous society within a colonial capitalist state was beginning to produce an internal class differentiation, and to effect an assimiliation of African and European that the principle of indirect rule could neither prevent nor contain. Whereas Kimbangu had accepted, in effect, the principal assertions and demands of the European regime, two decades later Mpadi rejected them.

To these two responses discussed by Bernard we may add that of the Apostles (EUDA), whose history coincides with that of independent Zaire. Many members of EUDA were men who had succeeded, individually, where Kimbangu and Mpadi, before becoming prophets, had failed. The three responses, belonging to distinct phases of socio-political evolution, can be compared with reference to the paradigmatic set of religious commissions (chief, priest, witch, magician) which is the framework of subjective representations, and which in turn presupposes the cosmology outlined in Chapter Five. To pursue this comparison, the Black Church and the Apostles, hitherto mentioned only in passing, will have to be described in more detail.

## KIMBANGUIST THEOLOGY

To the missionary, all indigenous cult leaders were witchdoctors, and witchdoctors were virtually indistinguishable from witches (cf. French sorcier). In KiKongo, this condemnation was expressed in terms of ngang'a n'kisi and ndoki (for which I have been using the English words "magician" and "witch"), and the BaKongo readily assimilated it to their own condemnation of occult activities carried on for private and therefore anti-social benefit. In the Pentecost of the Congo (1886) and similar capitulations, they accepted, as their forefathers had frequently done, a reconstitution of public moral discipline, the domain of the chief and the priest, without essentially changing their cosmology or their sense of the powers of life and death. Bula Matadi (the colonial government) was the new chief, the missionary was the new priest; witchcraft and magic were renounced.

In the twentieth century Congolese increasingly felt that their commitment had been betrayed; the new chiefship did not offer its dependents the expected rewards and the new priesthood did not heal. The political factor identified Protestantism as a variety of Christianity having authority and yet opposed to the state. In the Protestant Bible, as they read it, BaKongo found a picture of an oppressed people whom Yahwe would redeem if they obeyed him and detailed descriptions of the kind of spirit possession and healing they had always considered necessary to combat witchcraft.

Accepting all the Protestant taboos against smoking, alcohol, dancing, and the use of magic, Kimbangu added divination and healing and was called ngunza, "prophet." The internalization by Kimbanguists of the missionary assessment of the sinfulness of Africans is striking; together with resentment against missionary "deceitfulness," one frequently hears the theme that colonial experiences themselves were a punishment for sin. Descriptions of Kimbangu's miraculous visit to his disciples in Lowa after his death, recounted by the disciples themselves, portray a punitive prophet who paradoxically collaborates with the government: "On account of their general sinfulness, all the disciples were

allotted seven years of exile in addition to the original 33 years agreed between the prophets and the
government" (JM No.18; MacGaffey 1982a).

The word ngunza is ambiguous; its meaning can
be approached through either African or European conceptions and institutions.  Mentioned in Jennings'
correspondence for the first time on 1 June 1921, the
term ngunza comes from W. Holman Bentley's translation of the Bible, written in São Salvador dialect
and used by the Baptist Missionary Society.[1] Originally it meant, according to Bentley's dictionary
(1887), "one who speaks on behalf of a chief; a herald, preacher, prophet." The word is otherwise rare
and ill-documented.  Its use thus points unmistakably
to the Protestant Bible, and that aspect of its meaning indicates the intention of Kimbangu and
Kimbanguists to create a reformed Protestant ministry.  On the other hand, the word can be thought of
as held against the mission church, which included no
ngunza, and as summarizing all the elements of the
new ministry that distinguished it.  The new elements, all related by Kimbanguists to Biblical texts,
are central to the old Kongo religion.  Besides healing, they include the complex of revealed power
accessible through a chosen individual and subsequently through his grave, which serves as a point of
contact with the other world.  The paradigmatic word
for the complex is nlongo, "sacred" (JM, p.26).

Diangienda's title as head of EJCSK, Mfumu a
Nlongo, is officially translated "chef suprème," but
the word nlongo calls for something much stronger,
such as "sacred head." Diangienda, though not called
ngunza, is the prophet's successor and, through his
custody of the mausoleum, the means of access to his
father's coffin.  This role, classically, is that of
mwana wa mbuta, the son of his father, custodian of
father's grave[2].  Diangienda continues the patrifilial succession of spiritual mediators extending from
God to man through Christ and Kimbangu.  This succession is known in Kimbanguist theology, modeled on
ordinary Protestant teaching, as the order of Melchizedek, but the Biblical expression covers a
conception with much older local roots, the "spiritual hierarchy" relating man to Nzambi (see Chapter
Five).  Comparing this hierarchy with the mediating
structures of prophetism, an associate of Fu-kiau,
Diantezila (1970:8), drew the diagram reproduced here
as fig.3 and wrote, "Beneath these appearances may be
discovered many things that could be useful for the

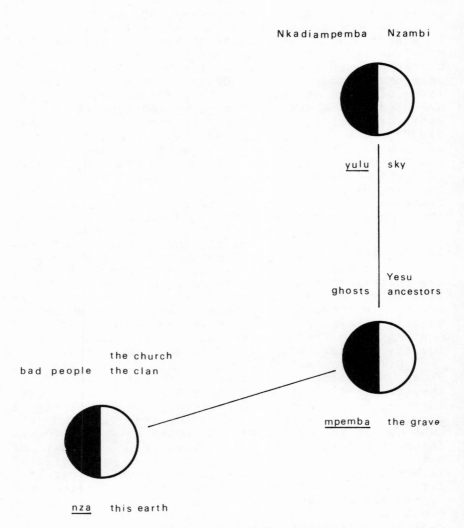

Nkadiampemba   Nzambi

yulu | sky

ghosts | Yesu
       | ancestors

the church
bad people  the clan

mpemba   the grave

nza   this earth

Fig.3: Cults ancient and modern

vitality of Christianity in this country because they
are the foundation of indigenous belief."
     <u>Mvwala</u>, a term by which Diangienda, together
with his brothers, is also known, means a successor
and delegate in the sense of this hierarchy;
<u>Kimbanguisme</u>, 3 Feb. 1962, translated it as "Le Fils
Héritier." <u>Mvwala</u> (pl. <u>zi-</u>) can also mean the staff
carried by such a person, itself a sign of patrifiliation, delegation and spiritual potency. As <u>mvwala</u>,
Diangienda is guided in his decisions by <u>Kimbangu</u>,
whom he sees in dreams and visions. The church
asserts that his father chose him during his lifetime
to be his successor (JM Nos. 36, 42, 43, 44; M.-L.
Martin 1975:63,146).
     The rift between Diangienda and his early asso-
ciate, Emmanuel Bamba, already explicit in 1960,
developed with respect to the government of the nascent church, and concerned both its political and
administrative aspects. Bamba, an extremely able man
from the Kasangulu area, educated by the ABFMS at
Nsona Mbata, was arrested in 1950 for religious
activity and imprisoned for three months with Kimbangu in Elizabethville. On the strength of this
connexion, he afterwards said that he knew Kimbangu's
views and that Diangienda's practice contradicted
them. The choice of Diangienda as the prophet's successor reinforced the hierarchical, patrifilial
tendency in all Kongo government (<u>kimfumu kya se</u>,
<u>kimfumu kya mwana</u>, "the authority of the father [is]
the authority of the son") and the regional focus on
Nkamba and Ngombe. The mystifications, allegedly
deliberate, of such matters as the return of
Kimbangu's remains to Nkamba (his "resurrection"),
the use of his mausoleum as a shrine, and the <u>nlongo</u>
relationship between father and son, enhanced the
power and autonomy of the Nkamba group. Bamba, on
the other hand, said that a coffin was a coffin and
<u>mvwala</u> was a stick; he said that too much money was
extracted by dubious means from the credulous, that
too much of it was spent on Nkamba, and not enough of
it publicly accounted for; he favored a religious
practice differing very little from that of the ABFMS
and an open, democratic and regionally dispersed form
of government. EJCSK's reply to these charges is
always simply that Bamba was an ambitious man, more
of a politician and a businessman (pejorative labels)
than a churchman.[3]
     As mediator between God and man, Kimbangu neces-
sarily participates in the <u>nzambi</u> spiritual hier-

archy, though at a higher level than that of a mere
ancestor (see JM No.40). Kimbanguist protests that
Kimbangu is not God (Nzambi) are occasioned at least
in part by a shift in meaning in the word nzambi,
which has only recently, under missionary influence,
come to be restricted to the highest of the series.
According to Morel, Kimbangu was known to his followers in 1921 as nzambi (Ryckmans 1970:39), and part
of the enthusiasm that he aroused was based on the
assumption that he had become the medium of a
high-ranking spirit. A government chief said he
thought that the prophets had "the sickness of God"
(mayela ma nzambi?), and he was afraid it would be
inflicted on him too if he arrested them; another
such chief was similarly reluctant because of the
prophets' n'kisi (Irvine 1974:44). The story current
in 1921 of Kimbangu's encounter with an ambiguous
figure, a man afflicted with the skin disease
makwanza, is itself a classical example of a summons
to membership in an affliction cult. The stranger
actually inflicts makwanza on "le petit Simon,"
declaring that he will never be cured of the disease
until he agrees to pray for a sick child and lay
healing hands on her (Lerrigo 1922:271; Andersson
1958:51; Raymaekers 1971:54). Kimbangu's demonstra-
tion of powers superior to those of any ordinary
healer seemed to be proof of a plenipotentiary relationship to Nzambi, and of authority superseding all
particularistic cults. People needing help therefore
abandoned their self-seeking charms in favor of a
common discipline and common promise, and many magicians, having recognized Kimbangu's superiority,
voluntarily gave up their practice.

The term nzambi (pl. zi-) evolved during the
twentieth century away from the paradigmatic sense it
retained in 1921 towards the missionary-Christian
sense of a unique God. The theory of man's possible
relationship to nzambi likewise evolved from the
notion of metonymic continuity expressed in n'kisi
cults towards the complex modern Christian ambiguities of the spirit and the flesh. This evolution in
turn is reflected in the changing meaning of mpeve a
nlongo, "Holy Spirit." Nlongo, "holy," refers to
taboo, the injunction imposed upon clients of a
charm, water spirit or the like, obedience to which
guarantees health and success. Just as modern Kongo
pastors in their sermons seek to substitute the single figure of Satan for the multiplicity of witches
and the local resentments they express, so Nzambi

subsumes all particular zinzambi and Mpeve a Nlongo
replaces the observances and guarantees of all lesser
spirits.

Kimbangu's place in the sequence of "fathers and
sons" making up the spiritual hierarchy explains certain features of the iconography of Kimbangu. A
photograph in circulation in 1960 showed Kimbangu as
an adolescent, seated on the knee of a large white
Christ. The complementary image invoked by Kimbangu
himself before Morel was that of David and Goliath.
The legends of his receipt of his commission commonly
describe him as a youth (toko dya ntwenya) or as "le
petit Simon," although he was at least 28 at the
time. A ngounzist prophecy of 1930 refers to the
coming Kingdom as that of the patrifilial child
(mwana wabutu) (Andersson 1958:98).

The community for which Kimbangu is the spiritual mediator is not united by common descent but
common locality. According to the official statements of EJCSK, this common locality is all of Kongo,
all of Zaire, all of Africa, or even the whole world;
nevertheless, the favored location and community is
that of Ngombe, the prophet's region of origin; the
sacred spot through which contact with him is best
obtained is his home village of Nkamba, the New
Jerusalem.

Dialungana, second son of the prophet, sees himself as like King David, in being the custodian of
the New Jerusalem, the New or Holy City (mbanza mpa,
velela). The focal point of Nkamba is the mausoleum
containing the prophet's coffin, which Kimbanguists
compare to the Ark of the Covenant (nkela: box, ark)
(JM Nos.42, 43; MacGaffey 1969:144). Like the Ark,
the coffin is sacred as the primary symbol of a bond
established between God and his people for their salvation, and for that reason the main feast and
sacrament of the church is that of 6 April, the
anniversary of the first manifestation of Kimbangu's
healing powers.[4] On this day, pilgrims are admitted
to the mausoleum, where they offer prayers and petitions. Here again the Biblical references legitimate
a ritual pattern whose local conceptual idiom it con-
ceals. Earth and water from Nkamba are carried home
in quantities by individual pilgrims, and are usually
available from local pastors. The water is drunk,
for vaguely defined health-giving purposes, and
water, or a mixture of earth and water, is rubbed on
the body as a therapy. Many say that witches who
drink the water at Nkamba will die on their way home.
Such practices are reminiscent of the ancestor cult

and the rite yobila tobe (annointing with grave
dirt), but Kimbangu is not an ancestor; clearly he
transcends any particular clan. In its own apologet-
ics, the church justifies the use of water by
comparison with the Catholic shrine at Lourdes; the
use of earth is not mentioned.[5]

    Although the mausoleum at Nkamba is a grave, the
fact does not identify the place as an ancestral
shrine. All points of entry to the other world are
more or less like graves, including ancient shrines
to great regional spirits (min'kisi nsi). Other
features of Nkamba of equal importance include the
little hill on which the mausoleum stands and the
healing pool ("Bethesda") at its foot. Rival
churches, such as the ECUSE of Gonda André, identify
pools and hills of their own as Bethesda, the point
of contact between Kimbangu and their own local communities (As Dialungana complained: see JM No.42,
par.63). Moreover, Kimbangu's powers and those of
his delegates are the powers of life (healing, divination) rather than the death-dealing powers of
ancestor and chief.

    In a formal sense, Kimbangu, as one who healed
in the public interest, takes the place of the
nineteenth-century simbi priest, nganga ngombo,
nganga kitomi, or nganga mbangu, but the relationship
is more than a formal similarity. I have already
mentioned the regional factor in the development of
churches (Chapter Two), the fact that a church is
thought of as providing benefits primarily for a
local community. The boundaries of such a community
are as large as possible, but always uncertain; what
defines it is its center, the pool in which the
tutelary spirit would have lived, the grave or cave
through which he could be contacted, from which power
could be drawn by authorized mediators. Nkamba
serves this function, as do other holy centers with
their hills and pools, and the analogy with Lourdes,
drawn by EJCSK spokesmen, is far-fetched.

    In addition Kimbangu is connected with the simbi
cult in a multitude of ways. The name Kimbangu
itself indicates an abnormality at birth, an initial
failure to cry which would have to be treated by the
n'kisi Kimbangu. Having no voice in this world, he
presumably had an other-worldly voice; "he was like
a dead man," said an informant. The incident might
mean nothing for the child's future, but EJCSK took
care to conceal this meaning beneath another: "It
means the sure Witness (mbangi) of the gospel of the
Lord God, the true Interpreter (mbangudi) of the hid-

den and the obscure" (Catechism, JM No.39, par.7).[6]
The legends say that as an infant Kimbangu fell into
a gully (benga) whence he was rescued by an angel;
informants have told me that the restored child was
not the original human baby but a powerful spirit of
some kind, in the same outward form. A similar incident, purportedly given in the prophet's own words,
occurred to him in a dream at a time when he was
receiving the supernatural visitations that eventually led to his prophetic vocation (Lerrigo 1922:271).
All such descents into pits and pools are regarded as
contacts with the other world.

Later in his career Kimbangu is supposed to have
triumphed over his Belgian enemies by recovering a
sort of talisman from its hiding place under a water-
fall (JM No.17, par.13; No.18, par.7). A Kimbanguist pamphlet in KiKongo cites the blessing
allegedly given by the missionary Cameron to Ma Kinzembo, the foster mother of the future prophet, as
proof that the child was from his birth "sacred"
(wawutuka wa nlongo), and was recognized as such by
the missionary (JM No.40). Just what is meant here
is obscure. According to M.-L. Martin, whose English
version of the idea has been adopted by Kimbanguist
delegates to international conferences, "Before leaving Kinzembo the missionary Cameron blessed her, and
this blessing became palpable in the person of her
grandchild (sic) Simon Kimbangu" (Martin 1968:3).[7]
The story of Kinzembo is part of the catechism of
Kimbangu, who recited it himself in 1921: "The man
(Kimbangu) thinks that probably on account of this
(blessing) he has since had a dream or vision and
been appointed by Christ as a prophet of these people, with power to heal the sick" (Graham, writing to
The Baptist Herald in 1921; quoted in Martin
1975:43). Versions of the catechism published in
other languages than KiKongo omit the story (JM
No.39).

Everybody knows that gullies and waterfalls are
where water spirits (bisimbi) live, and to say in
ordinary conversation that a child is mwana wa nlongo
means that he incarnates such a spirit, but among my
informants only the Kinenists went so far as to make
the association explicit; Kinene was mwana wa nlongo
and would call to the bisimbi in ecstasy. To recognize the association seems to deny the fundamental
doctrine that the appearance of the prophets
represented an utterly new divine dispensation of
power intended to redress the balance between Africans and Europeans. Likewise, to think of Kimbangu

as a carefully disguised <u>simbi</u> priest would be to
ignore the intervening changes in Kongo society.[8]

In the twentieth century, the conditions of
existence of local communities were determined less
by soil fertility, rainfall, and the incidence of
disease than by the transportation network, labor
demands, and the availability of schools and hospitals. Having in fact no substantial economic or
political resources of its own, Kimbanguism could not
reconstitute Kongo society; the movement therefore
dissolved into local and personal expressions (the
phenomenon of schismatic dispersal), whose cultic
practices reflected their contingency and particular-
ism in relatively dense metaphorical textures. This
development fulfilled a pattern common to religious
innovations in Kongo and in Central Africa generally.

In KiKongo, the words <u>nlongo</u>, <u>mvwala</u>, <u>mbanza</u> and
the like point unambiguously to the classical reli-
gious tradition. The ambiguities and conflicts
surrounding the use of such words in EJCSK reflect
the real difficulties involved in the translation of
meaning between two institutional contexts in a plural society. In its European-oriented francophone
presentation of itself the church minimizes these
elements or translates and explains them blandly as
"symbolic." As a result, the positive theology of
Kimbanguism is extremely vague, consisting largely of
generalized evangelical Protestant affirmations which
manage to sound timid beside the church's vigorous
denial of doctrines regarded by its opponents as
reprehensible. Nevertheless, Kimbanguists are not
only confronted by but actually live in the bureaucratic world, in which creeds and articles of
religion are needed. EJCSK has devoted much thought
to the problem. The extracts that follow, taken from
a document that was being privately circulated in
1966 (the copy I saw lacked a title page) indicate
some of the things that were being discussed then,
though not what official theology was or has since
become.[9] Parenthetical comment has been added.

## A theological working-paper

1.  Kimbanguists are opposed to ritualism. In ser-
    vices, a central place is reserved for the Bible.
    The liturgy includes confession of sins, reading
    of psalms, choral music as a means of elevating
    the soul, prayer, Bible-reading and sermon.
2.  There are only five sacraments: baptism, commun-
    ion, penitence, the consecration of priests, and

marriage. [On these the Secretary-General commented that baptism is conferred by the Spirit
only, not by water, following Mark 1:8;
confession and penitence were still being worked
out; communion had not yet been instituted; the
consecration of the priests (sacrificateurs) was
performed by the <u>Mfumu</u> a <u>Nlongo</u> at <u>Nkamba</u> from
time to time, as necessary, to give them
strength.]
3. Kimbanguists reject the mass, the worship of
saints and of Mary, sacerdotal ornaments and the
doctrine of indulgences.
4. Kimbanguism requires love of one's neighbor and
respect for the state. It condemns superstition,
idolatry, vain observance, magic, charms, curs-
ing, perjury, false witness, homicide, suicide,
dueling, theft, violation of the right of property, covetousness, hypocrisy, flattery and
malthusianism. [The Secretary-General, asked
what malthusianism might be, said he thought it
might be a typographical error for Matswanism,
which was a movement of social and political
reform in French Congo in the 1930s.]
5. The Kimbanguist conception of heaven and hell is
identical with Jewish and Christian doctrine
[which are not themselves identical].
6. Kimbanguism preaches the imminence of the blessed
day of which St. John speaks, Rev. 21:1-3. It
recognizes Christ as the intermediary between man
and God, by (par) Papa Simon Kimbangu. Kimbangu,
the missionary of Christ, is not greater than
Christ.
7. In 1921, before going to Elisabethville, Simon
Kimbangu confided to each of his three sons his
proper mission, of which Joseph Diangienda's is
to direct the church (John 5:20-23). There is,
therefore, nothing fortuitous about his appearance as its head. Recipient of a spiritual
power, His Eminence Joseph Diangienda raises the
dead, restores sight to the blind, causes the
paralysed to walk, and performs all kinds of
miraculous healing. [Asked whether Diangienda
still does, the Secretary-General said, with some
hesitation, "Whatever he once did, he still
does."]
8. Kimbanguism is not tied to any political party.
Its horizons are unlimited, and extend to the
bounds of the entire world. It has its faults,
but is nevertheless a force in the midst of this
our fourth generation.

    Asked about this "fourth generation," mentioned
in par.8, both Luntadila and Diangienda were notably
evasive; this was the only question that Diangienda
refused to answer. The idea of the fourth generation
comes from a family of European eschatologies popular
among Protestant missionaries at the end of the
nineteenth century, and since. One of them,
H. Grattan Guinness, founder of the East London
Institute, at which Henry Richards and others were
trained for mission work, wrote a book, The
Approaching End of the Age, whose first edition sold
2,000 copies within eight months of publication and
whose eighth edition appeared in the United States in
1884. The intention of the work was to prove by
astronomy and the Bible, especially the Book of Daniel, that the world would come to an end in 1900;
hence the need to send missionaries to convert as
much of the world as possible before it was too late.
H.G. Guinness, who was particularly interested in
Congo, translated and published in 1882 Brugiotti's
17th century grammar of the Kongo language. His wife
actively publicized the successes of the missions,
especially the Pentecost of the Congo at Mbanza Manteke, and undertook a personal tour of the area
(F.E. Guinness 1890).
    According to the Guinnesses, Scripture proved
that God had divided history into three stages, each
closing with a judgment and introducing a better
order of things on the way from Paradise lost to
Paradise regained. They believed that they lived in
a time like that of Noah, though the approaching
deluge would be a deluge of fire instead of water.
The last age comprised four successive kingdoms
(Guinness 1893). This sort of thing belongs to an
ancient European millenial tradition going back at
least as far as the 12th century and Joachim of Fiore
(Cohn 1961).
    Kimbangu has been widely regarded by Kimban-
guists as "the second Noah" (JM No.18, par.6). At
Nkamba Gilis was told: The Kingdom is near. We are
the Ark of the Lord before the flood. All the world
laughed at Noah, though, because he built upon the
Mountain" (Gilis 1960:78). The statement is more
accurate as a description of Nkamba than as a summary
of the Biblical story. Kimbangu is also reported to
have predicted the end of the world by fire; there
is no real evidence that he did anything of the sort,
but popular Kimbanguism is full of such legends, some
of which owe something to Salvation Army teaching
("blood and fire") (Andersson 1958:ch.5.). More

recently Watchtower, an international publication of
the Jehovah's Witnesses appearing in KiKongo as
Nkengidi, has had a certain influence on
Kimbanguists; for example, EJCSK's newspaper
Kimbanguisme, 23 December 1961, carried as a front
page article a Watchtower piece in KiKongo about the
approach of Armageddon.

Nevertheless, the presence of such ideas is not
a simple consequence of diffusion. Cosmologies all
over the world express the identity of the present
era by bounding it in time, contrasting it with a
previous and a subsequent era. At the turn of the
century, Kongo legends told how, before the present
generation began, the sky fell upon the earth and God
changed all the men of that generation into lizards
and the women into frogs. The stories envision a
future end of the world brought about by the collision of sun and moon. Kimbanguists see world history
as a sequence of three ages named for Father, Son,
and the Holy Ghost "who descended upon Simon Kimbangu," or (as in a sermon preached before Diangienda in
May 1966) for Shem, Japheth, and Ham, understood as
the Jews, the Europeans, and the Africans; in so
doing, they give a European appearance to an old
form, which otherwise appears as the ideal political
hierarchy of Father, Child, and Grandchild, and in
various other guises. The view that each age, or at
least the present one, is a cycle of four generations
or kingdoms, of which the last is herald to the new
age, likewise merely repeats the cosmological scheme
(fig. 1). As Mpadi said, in whose writing these tendencies are elaborated to extremes, "everything comes
in threes and fours." Kimbanguists at Nkamba in 1965
would say, for example "There have been four national
governments since independence, all corrupt; but in
the next government Tata Charles (Kisolokele, the
first son of Kimbangu) will be prime minister, Tata
Joseph (Diangienda) will settle permanently in Nkamba, and the New Jerusalem will have been achieved."
Others spoke of the four generations since Noah,
those of Moses, David, Jesus, and Kimbangu.

It is believed that in each age or generation
the sequence of events and the social structure are
the same. In several Kimbanguist publications the
statement recurs, "The works of God are neither old
nor new. Whatever things of God existed in the former generation (tandu kia nkulu), the same are in the
present generation, and shall be in the generation
that is to come." Kimbanguists, therefore, search the
Bible to identify the features of their world as they

appeared in other worlds: Nkamba (Jerusalem);
Mbanza Ngoyo, the prophet's birthplace (Bethlehem);
Mbanza Kongo (Babel, from which the peoples
dispersed); the colonial occupation (bondage in
Egypt); the return of Kimbangu's remains from Elisabethville ("And when the days of his mourning were
past, Joseph spake unto the house of Pharaoh,
saying ... Now therefore let me go up, I pray thee,
and bury my father").[10] The apparent conformity of
modern events to a predestined pattern strengthens
belief in the fulfillment of God's promise through
Simon Kimbangu.

Though Kimbanguists assume that the pattern is
revealed in the Bible, in fact it is imposed upon the
Bible by the reader. The consciousness that controls
the Kimbanguist reading is shaped by the cosmology of
the spiral universe, in which each turn of time
repeats and yet enlarges the previous turn. The core
of the spiral is the hierarchy of mediators between
man and Nzambi, itself modeled on the patrimonial
structure of the ideal model of customary society.

A hierarchy of terms and functions is discerni-
ble in all Kimbanguist churches, both in theology and
cult organization. As mediator, Kimbangu possesses
powers of healing and prophecy which he delegates to
his followers, who are healers, but only mediators by
delegation, and who in turn delegate the function of
prophecy (mbikudulu) to followers who are not
healers. "Every prophet tends to gather to himself
the complementary functions of these specialists, and
that itself is the sign of the emergence of a true
ngunza" (Depage 1969-70:408). This hierarchy restores the link between man and God which makes
other-worldly powers available to man to preserve him
and his community from evil, disorder, and afflictions public and private. It replaces the cults of
the dead in new social circumstances in which the
secular function of patronage is as important as
ever, though changed in content, and in which the
unitary bureaucratic framework of the state has
replaced the multitudinous politics of pre-colonial
Kongo. The linkage and its functional consequences
are simultaneously religious and political; that is
to say, both of these abstract categories are
appropriate to the phenomena.

This alliance between a religious ethic and
practice and a particular social form is not correctly understood as religious atavism or a resurgence of
paganism in sheep's clothing. Kimbangu as prophet is
the channel of God's grace to a particular community

and the symbol of its identity within the wider
Christian communion. This form of words is intelligible in Kongo terms as the supreme example of the
nlongo complex of sacred mediation, defined within
the paradigm of Kongo social philosophy as a matter
of health and social discipline achieved in
opposition to the immoral principles of witchcraft
and magic.[11] Mediation between man and God, modeled
on the pattern of chiefship (or Zairean bureaucracy)
brings salvation "on earth." The missionaries did not
allow the desires and petitions of black people to
reach God's ear, but Kimbangu created a way, and the
power of God became available among blacks, to
scatter witches and heal the sick.[12]

The redefinition of terms, together with economic changes, brought about important differences in
conception and practice between the contrast that
prevailed in the past between diviner (or "priest")
and magician, and the modern contrast between prophet
and magician. The word ngunza and the legitimating
ideology associated with it were consciously derived
from the Bible, not from classical religious tradition, no matter how much the latter shaped the
perspective in which the Bible was read. Adoption of
the new term entailed a redefinition of nganga, which
assumed almost exclusively pejorative connotations.

The introduction of general-purpose currency in
this century probably sharpened the normative distinction between public and private ends, gave it a
new symbolic dimension, and helped to link the supposed experience of witchraft with the actual
experience of capitalism.[13] In the nineteenth century, beads, brass rods, and the like had mediated
transactions in the subsistence sphere, but a nganga
was usually rewarded for his services with gifts of
food and drink. Since the seventeenth century at
least, magicians had been known as people who sought
to make a profit, but the difference between a fee
and a gift was obscured by the common use of consum-
able goods for both transactions. Nowadays, however,
money is the sign of commercial as opposed to social
relations. In social transactions, such as marriage
payments, cash is in fact usually substituted for
goods but the amounts are always referred to as "a
goat," a "suitlength," "a demijohn of palm wine," and
the like. On the other hand, undisguised cash payments are the sign of extra-social transactions with
strangers or of anti-social transactions with enemies
and exploiters; thus coins, rather than food, are
the typical bait used by modern witches, whose vic-

tims are as likely to be put to work by their masters
as eaten in the old-fashioned way. Doped change
received in commercial transactions afflicts the
unwary with suffering.

Cash, however, is not just a new utility and an
improved concept, dissolving by its intrinsic
rationality the separate spheres of the traditional
economy. It is a sign of the introduction of a new
mode of production in which labor power is a commodity and the reproduction of the relations of
production is ensured through such institutions as
taxation, public welfare, migration control, and
grade school, rather than matrilineal descent, slavery, and the hierarchy of children and grandchildren.
The ideological incorporation of cash expresses the
movement from the lineage mode of production towards
a form of capitalism via the creation and destruction
of social pluralism. The evil that the prophet
fights by means of healing is, in part, the dark side
of the capitalist economy, as the preceding chapter
showed.

## THE BLACK CHURCH OF MPADI SIMON

Whereas Kimbangu incorporated both missionary
doctrine and practical experience of colonial capitalism into an adapted form of the classical
religion, the two other responses to be considered
took different and mutually opposed directions.
Kimbangu transformed the diviner into the prophet
(ngunza), but maintained and even exaggerated the
difference between this kind of healer and the magician (nganga). Mpadi Simon, on the other hand,
rejected the term ngunza and its implicit condemnation of indigenous culture.

Mpadi Simon was born in 1909 in the village of
Ladi, Madimba territory. He regards himself as the
twin of Kimbangu, according to an obscure reckoning
based on the idea of recurrent events as the same.
Kimbangu is "the first witness"; Mpadi, "the
second." Mpadi also speaks of Kimbangu as his mpangi
(patrilateral classificatory brother) on the ground
that Kimbangu's clan and his own have intermarried
since the beginning in Mbanza Kongo. This reckoning
is based on the kind of loose association of clan
names that enables any Nkongo to demonstrate to his
satisfaction a relationship to any other Nkongo.

Reckonings of this sort and the tradition of
Mbanza Kongo were among Mpadi's earliest preoccupa-
tions, if we are to believe the account at the

beginning of a 42-page typescript dated 12 August
1933 and devoted to the history of his clan. He
reports that his elders asked him to write it and
gave him a copy of Ku Kiele, the Redemptorist missionary journal in which Cuvelier first published, in
KiKongo, the material that subsequently became his
L'Ancien Royaume du Congo (1946). The incident suggests that Mpadi and his elders were on the defensive
in some conflict of pedigrees;  only a group in trouble would have needed to write down their tradition,
or would have turned to missionary scholarship for
their sources. Under direct Catholic influence, the
romantic image of Mbanza Kongo as a national kingdom
of European feudal type became important in the evolution of Abako as a nationalistic political party,
but although most BaKongo have been so influenced in
some small degree, among churchmen only Mpadi has
taken a serious interest in the growing number of
Catholic publications on Kongo history (MacGaffey
1970b:201-08, 293-95). Mpadist sermons dwell on King
Afonso I, Bishop Henrique (consecrated in 1518) and
Beatrice, the prophet of 1704.

As Kimbangu's "twin," Mpadi was the focus, by
his own account, of much the same kind of annunciato-
ry incidents as his predecessor. At the age of two
he was raised from the dead, and other miracles
ensued. Having been trained as a catechist by the
ABFMS at Nsona Mbata and later dismissed, Mpadi
joined the Salvation Army when it first arrived in
1934. He says he was instructed to make the move in
a vision in which he was taken to a large courtyard
where he met Melchizedek, Abraham, Moses, Elijah and
Peter, who gave him, respectively, his garment of
salvation, the khaki uniform;  a book in which to
write the names of the sheep he was destined to summon from the four corners of the earth;  a shepherd's
staff (mwala ya kivungi) with which to divide the
waters of the Red Sea so that Africans might be
saved;  the oil of blessing, with which his head was
anointed, conferring supreme powers (mpungu ngolo).
Peter, the last of the line, laid his hand on Mpadi's
head and consecrated him as leader of Christ's flock.

The red flag of the Army, the initial "S," the
imagery of military discipline and spiritual battle,
and the khaki uniform, all contributed to the popular
misconception of the movement, and also left a permanent impression on Mpadi himself. In 1939, when by
strenuous effort the Army had made clear to its
adherents that it was a mission church like any
other, Mpadi asked the government for permission to

found a Mission des Noirs, a black church. He was arrested but repeatedly escaped. He spent part of his liberty in French Congo where his lieutenant and successor Mavonda Ntangu created the Khaki movement, an amalgam of Salvation Army symbols, Mpadism, Manianga <u>ngunzism</u> and Matswanism, the last a movement indigenous to KiKongo speakers in the French colony.

The excitement aroused by Khakism was enhanced by the occurrence of World War II, in which the BaKongo saw themselves as making common cause with the Germans; by Mpadi's repeated escapes, around which legends clustered abundantly, becoming partly confused with those attached to Kimbangu[14]; and by his endless output of documents reinterpreting history with apocalyptic imagery and vivid if often spurious detail. His followers say he never sleeps, and can talk forever. A peculiarity is he that tells many of his stories in Lingala, not only because, as he says, many of his followers do not speak KiKongo, but because they are fixed in his mind in that language, in which he recites them to any audience. Some of them, on the other hand, are similarly enshrined in KiKongo.

Mpadi was the first Kongo revolutionary to realize that scholarship, or the appearance of it, and written propaganda were essential weapons against a bureaucratic regime. During the Khaki period his texts were often copied by hand but since 1960 they have been mimeographed. Mpadi was not the first to see but he most effectively articulated the connection between political dependence and the relations of production, in which the BaKongo were excluded from control of technology. As the head of the Black Church in Matadi put it, staring morosely into his beer, "This glass, do I know where it comes from? No. Do I know how it is made? No." Mpadi, who at one point called his movement Mission Amerika, supposed that "Americans" would bring technology to Kongo, teaching the people how to set up their own factories (CRISP 1968:34):

Let us pray that the Governor-General of the Americans comes quickly, because when he is come he will open in this country many workshops and give much knowledge to all the Blacks. They will teach men to forge machetes, to make hoes, and to manufacture plates and cups and cloths and hats and sewing-machines and bicycles and everything you lack, they will come to teach you.

In 1970, well before Mobutu's equivocal "authenticity" campaign in favor of economic independence
and cultural and political self-determination,
Mpadi's was still the only uncompromising voice of
black nationalism raised among the BaKongo. "We want
four things," said Mpadi: "our own government, our
own wealth, our own religion, and our own science
(ngangu)." Whereas the puritanism of Kimbanguist
rules implies an internalization of the missionary
accusation of moral deficiency, Mpadi advocates polygyny, and does not forbid alcohol. He himself is
fond of Scotch, which he drinks straight. In Mpadist
services the brutality with which the colonial regime
treated its prisoners is a constant theme, and (in
1970) a whole litany of suffering, recited with the
hands clasped above the head in the old Kongo mourning gesture (sa ntala) commemorated continued
European violence in Africa. I have already noted
(Chapter Two) that most of Mpadi's adherents are of
Angolan extraction; in 1970, the Angolan war of
independence was still in progress.

Mpadi's assessment of the colonial situation is
accurate, but the categories of his thought are those
of the classical religion, not of European political
science. "The Americans" are ancestors and bisimbi,
"our own brothers," who "left our country and went to
Europe, to acquire great knowledge in all kinds of
work ... and how to govern the country." Their
supernatural help, moreover, is essential: "If the
American does not come, our rule will be in vain"
(CRISP 1968:34).

The task of extracting Mpadi's doctrine from the
flood of documents is simplified by the fact that he
repeats himself endlessly between and within texts.
Certain themes recur frequently, in various guises.
One of them is that of twinship, an uneasy balance of
alliance and rivalry between persons who are the same
yet different. In one version Mpadi and Kimbangu are
twins; Mpadi is the younger and Kimbangu's chosen
successor, yet Kimbangu's family, with whom Mpadi
should be allied, are recalcitrant and have gone over
to the enemy. The alliance Mpadi offers them is the
ancient ideal of patrilateral cross-cousin marriage,
foundation of sacred chiefship; he and the sons of
Kimbangu will exchange sisters. In another version,
Jacob and Esau, as twins, are white and black, and
Esau's loss of his birthright is a model for the
colonial expropriation (Bernard 1970:217). Mpadi
uses the Biblical story to distinguish between the
older brother, the stronger who is the natural ruler

(mfumu), and the younger, who is fit only to fabri-
cate iron implements (nganga).

A second theme is that of access to redemption,
blocked by the devices of a corrupt priesthood.
Christ and Kimbangu both play a role which in another
version of the theme goes to the apostle Peter:
"Pius I, founder of the church of Rome, saw that
Peter was preaching a message just like Christ's so
he and his colleagues, who were making a lot of money
out of religion, conspired to kill Peter, steal the
book, and found the Catholic Church (dibundu dya
Mpelo), in the year 55 after the death of Christ."

Bernard sees Mpadism as a response to disillu-
sionment, an awakening to reality. Mpadi realized,
as it were, that the colonial deck was stacked
against black people. Accordingly, in 1939 he
demanded the right to organize his own church, on the
grounds of simple parity, and thereafter upheld an
aggressive nationalism and a self-consciously African
theology. He insists that in both domains, political
and religious, African institutions are equivalent to
European institutions and as worthy. Mpadi's philosophy is as deeply embedded in the classical
religious tradition as was the Kimbanguism of 1921
but his political values are different. He rejects
the condemnation of indigenous culture entailed in
practice by the missionary denunciation of sorcery
and superstition and he does not see his religion as
a version of Christianity cleared of missionary failings. Whereas Kimbanguists trace their relationship
to God through Kimbangu and Christ, Mpadists trace it
through Mpadi and Kimbangu and regard Jesus as the
Europeans' Kimbangu. This view does not mean that
Mpadism is theologically contrary to Christianity or
that Jesus is not mentioned in Mpadist worship. The
emphasis is elsewhere: political and cultural autonomy, not theology, is what matters. The pervasive
bitterness of Mpadism contrasts with what often seems
like the naive optimism of Kimbanguism.

It follows that the whole emphasis on the prophet (ngunza) in opposition to the magician (nganga)
is missing from Mpadism, in which healing is acom-
plished largely by the use of medicines, regarded as
an ancient and valuable heritage of the African people. Kimbangu is referred to as nganga and also, in
the same phrase that the Kongo prophet Beatrice
applied to St. Anthony in 1704, as the second
nzambi. In French, Mpadi is called "Président Fondateur", but in KiKongo ntumwa, "envoy, apostle," or,
in celestial code, "T.T.A.T.," which probably stands

for <u>Tata (n)tumwa a tulendo</u>, "envoy plenipotentiary."
[15] Mpadists believe that in one of his many escapes
from the supposedly murderous attentions of his Belgian gaolers Mpadi's human spirit left him and was
replaced by some powerful superhuman force sent to
save the black race; Kimbangu and Jesus underwent
the same kind of transformation. In a public address
given in 1960, shortly after his return to Kinshasa
from exile, Mpadi summarized the spiritual history of
mankind and opposed himself and his mission to the
notion of <u>ngunza</u>, which he explicitly identified as a
derivative of mission Christianity. The following
account of the speech, though published in the
EJCSK's newspaper <u>Kimbanguisme</u> (1, 5, June 1960),
appears to represent his views fairly. The original
speech was in Lingala; the report, in KiKongo.

### <u>Report of a speech by Mpadi Simon-Pierre</u>

        God sent his son to the Jews of Israel;
at his death Jesus left his disciples behind
him. We blacks have no access to God because
the death of Jesus redeemed only the Jews; so
we have no salvation, and God is not with us.
When the white missionaries came they built
chapels, which were really prisons, in which
there were crosses and many other things that
failed to bring blacks to heaven. We were not
formerly slaves, but the first enslavement was
that we were forbidden to speak back to the
Belgians. And the second was that when a man
died he did not come into the presence of God,
for the chapel became a prison and the crucifix
its key. They closed the black man's entrance
to heaven, that he might not arrive there, and
bricked it up with mortar. When God saw that
blacks were not coming through the door any
more, he came down to Nkamba and met a woman
called Kinzembo, to whom he gave a book and
also a requirement, as follows: that though
she herself would not have a son her sister
would, and to that child the book should be
given. This message was the key that was left
with Mama Kinzembo.
        Then an acolyte stood up, removed Mpadi's
headgear, and anointed his head with oil. And
he spoke as follows: when the Lord God left
Nkamba he went to San Salvador (Mbanza Kongo)
to the Nanga clan. He left there, parted the
waters of the Inkisi River and encountered a

Pl.11: Divination, DMN-Mbumba

Pl.12: Mpadi Simon-Pierre, Founder-President
of the Black Church, Ntendesi, 1970

woman coming from her fields with a basin
containing corn, peanuts, and her hoe. When
God and his angels stood before her, the woman
trembled, but God said, Be not afraid, we are
your brethren. And she saw that God took the
appearance of her mother's brother, long since
dead, and his angels the appearance of other
deceased elders. Then God and his angels asked
her for corn and peanuts. There were only 48
ears of corn and 77 angels, yet there was
enough for one each. God said to the woman,
Are you pregnant? She denied it. He asked,
you were pregnant for five months, did you not
have a child? She said, No. Does not your
sister have a child? Yes. Then he took three
books and gave them to her and said, These are
for your nephew, a schoolboy called Mpadi
Simon, and no one else. Later, Mama Lwila
Thérèse and her husband were arrested and
interned in Oshwe.

Mpadi continued: On account of those
books that God gave to that woman a large house
is to be built, and a table put on it. On the
table the books are to be placed, and he will
come to give money and clothes to the child,
Mpadi himself. Mpadi said, I did not obtain
this work from any ngunza, nor do I know any
ngunza. I did not go to seminary to learn this
work, nor was my father ngunza or pastor. Only
God knows its origin, whereby he came to give
me a church to redeem the black people; not to
two or three, but to me alone. All who have
heard this news and have been afraid to enter
our church, enter, now that I have come, for
the way to heaven is open. We have fought the
Europeans and won. Many were arrested, but I
survived to lead you to the Father.

When he had finished speaking he sat on
his throne, and the young women gathered to
anoint his face as is the custom in the church
of Mpadi Simon.

Whereas Mpadi-Kimbangu is the black savior,
Jesus was the savior of the white race, or God's
first envoy who failed to overcome the evil designs
of the priests (the Trinity appears in Mpadist worship as "Father, Son and our Savior"). Jesus is
therefore an honored figure, but is not essential to
Mpadism. In contradiction to this assertion one
might point to a number of evangelical hymns of con-

ventional Christian character likely to be sung at
any Mpadist service. Mpadi boasts, as do the Kimbanguists, that his hymns are directly inspired from
above and owe nothing to European influence. In fact
the evangelical hymns, some of which are known to
have been in use from the 1940's to the present
(1970), are entirely European in words and music, the
latter belonging very evidently to the style of the
Salvation Army. (CRISP 1968: Document No.1.) The
distinctive musical contribution of Mpadism, though
possibly also inspired by the Salvation Army, lies in
the orchestration, which is more exciting and more
sophisticated than any other church in Kongo can provide. Distinctively Mpadist hymns, of the same
musical character, are long narrative songs, unique
among the Kongo churches, which teach the congregations the essential Mpadist legends (JM No.46).

     An Mpadist service, though it owes enough to
European influence to be called a service, could not
by its content be mistaken for a mission Protestant
service, as Kimbanguist services can be. Among its
usual features are the narrative and evangelical
hymns already mentioned, sermons expanding Mpadist
versions of history, collective recitation of prescribed texts, and prayers. For morning services, the
obligatory texts are John 3:31-end, "He that cometh
from above is above all ...," and Isaiah 61:1-6, "The
Lord hath sent me to proclaim liberty to the
captives;" in the evening, John 12:44-end, "He that
believeth on me, believeth ... on him that sent me,"
and Isaiah 53:3-9, "He is despised and rejected of
men ..." Prayers are led by three persons; a woman
begins because women (Mary, Kinzembo, Lwila) have
always been first to welcome God's messengers. Three
persons are required because one or two of them may
have sinned and their prayers would fail to get
through.

     In the Black Church as in others, services asso-
ciated with the formal organization of the church
contrast in content and personnel with the séances of
healing bands in which, after the introductory hymns
and prayers, "doctors" assume the leading roles. The
visual austerity of DMN healing is missing: white
robes and conscious dignity give way to a relative
richness of symbolic materials and an informality I
found shocking at first. At ordinary seances Mpadists wear ordinary clothes (the principal diviner in
Matadi sometimes wore a tee-shirt that said,
"Daryll's Towing") but wear red robes on special
occasions, citing Isaiah: "Wherefore art thou red in

thine apparel, and thy garments like him that
treadeth in the winefat? I have trodden the
winepress alone; and of the people there was none
with me: for I will tread them in mine anger and
trample them in my fury; and their blood shall be
sprinkled upon my garments, and I will stain all my
raiment" (Isaiah 63:2-3).

In the divination phase of the healing séance,
to be described in more detail below, the client is
usually referred to the "doctor," the resident herbalist, who administers medicines, called min'kisi.
The medicines and their administration are like those
of any nganga. The Mpadist recipes are supposedly
derived from books handed down to him from heaven,
although some in fact come from the Catholic missionary handbook Makaya ma Nsi ("Local Herbs"). Mpadi
keeps them in large ledgers which are supposedly the
books referred to in the autobiographical speech
reported above. One collection which has been published shows that the chief difference between them
and the classical recipes is the absence of earths to
invoke the power of the dead (CRISP 1968:Doc.No.6).
This apparent deficiency is explained by the fact
that the necessary connexion with the other world is
made through Mpadi himself, who ranks higher than the
ordinary dead of the cemeteries, and it is symbolized
by "the oil of blessing." Obvious sorts of trance
behavior are absent from Mpadist rituals, but the
signs of spiritual potency are there none the less in
the oil, the batons, "the Lord's Table," occasional
glossolalic mutterings and the like.

Although Mpadi, like everybody else, condemns
the self-serving use of magic, the dominant
antithesis in his ideology lies between white and
black culture rather than between ngunza and nganga,
as in Kimbanguism. Nevertheless, Mpadism is even
more strongly ambivalent about its nationalistic
assertions than Kimbanguism is. Details of healing
séances conducted in Matadi in 1970 should make this
point clear.

The chief diagnostic instrument is meza ma
Nzambi, "the Lord's Table." At Ntendesi, his headquarters, near Nsona Mbata, Mpadi keeps a large table
painted with a red cross on which clients (patients,
suspects) are sat for a kind of interrogation by
Mpadi, represented as divination, in the course of
which all sins are discovered, all evil revealed[16].
In Matadi an ordinary chair, still called meza,
replaces the table. Young girls playing the part of
the specially-trained priestesses (the barégimentes)

of Ntendesi, stand on eiher side of it, singing and
holding candles close to the shoulders of the client,
who sits on the chair stripped to the waist.   While
the choir sings with percussion accompaniment, the
healer stands in front of the client, perhaps muttering    to     himself,    communing    with    the    spirit,
"listening" to his baton, touching the client's chest
with   it.   It becomes obvious that the entire performance imitates a European doctor's consulting    room.
The muttering is in French and Flemish, and is sprinkled with medical terms, such as <u>lichaam</u>, <u>microbes</u>.
("Just hope you haven't got <u>microbes</u>," said an informant;   "<u>microbes</u>   is   terrible.")   The   baton   is   a
stethoscope.   Young   women   with   fine   breasts   are
embarrassed to expose them in public but are told not
to be ashamed, "this is a medical examination."
     The healer stops the music.   In a sneering   tone
he announces the client's failings, and then dictates
his findings, full of medical-sounding   terms,   to   a
secretary:   "She   has,   er,   <u>microbes</u>   in   her,   ah,
<u>chose</u>." He waves his baton at the choir to start   the
music again:   "<u>Pompez!</u>" He holds a candle to help him
see into the patient's eyes and nose.   Sometimes   he
cups   his hand to his ear and appears to be listening
to    a    telephone;    sometimes    he    manipulates    a
typewriter or some other imaginary machine.   Stop the
music!   He takes the patient's pulse, fires off pres-
criptions   to   the   secretary:   "Eye   medicine,   four
days;   ear medicine, two days.   Also two masses, with
12   candles."   An   afterthought:   "Also one green and
one red candle." Sometimes the "masses" are described
(in   French)   in   such terms as "mass of resistance,"
"mass   of   liberation."   Sometimes this   particular
healer offers to summon relatives suspected of witchcraft;   a friend of his, a   commissioner   of   police,
will issue the summons, to make it authoritative.   In
the course of seances he frequently plays   an   accor-
dion.
     I was not able to witness a "mass" but they   are
evidently   imitated   from   Catholic   practice.   The
patient lies wrapped in a white sheet like a   shroud,
surrounded   by   altar   candle   stumps bought from the
sexton of a nearby Catholic church for the equivalent
of   $2.00   each.   The medicines, including eye-drops,
ear-drops, medicated incisions,   and   special   treat-
ments   such   as treading on the back of the patient's
head "to extinguish witch lights," are   given   in   a
dispensary-like room.   The   doctors   are   trained at
Ntendesi, to which they return from time to time   for
more training and to collect herbs.

Thus it appears that Mpadists, too, have been unable to escape the alienating force of European judgment, and find it necessary, even while insisting on the virtues of authentic African science, to make it seem like European science and European religion.

This is the ultimate ambivalence of "the Americans," saviors-to-be who are super-Europeans as well as super-Africans. The same radical alienation, expressed in ritual that is superficially very different, characterizes the next example.

## THE UNIVERSAL CHURCH OF THE TWELVE APOSTLES

Founded in 1959, EUDA is above all a church for successful white-collar workers, none of whom experienced religious persecution in colonial times. Unlike Mpadi's, which recites praise-names and clan tradition with endless relish, the founder's autobiography makes no mention of his background in customary society. Written in French, not KiKongo or Lingala, the autobiography makes clear that his education was minimal and his employment precarious (JM No.19). Though he held various positions as clerk-typist, in 1955 when he experienced his first visions he was looking for work; the second of the visions began as a nightmare in which he was about to be crushed by a large metal object like a large house, on which was painted the name of the company from which he was seeking employment.

In the autobiography the name of Kimbangu is not mentioned nor is it ever heard in the services of the church, which conform to Protestant orthodoxy in every obvious respect. Like the regular Protestant churches in recent years, the choir, highly trained in sol-fa technique, is accompanied by percussion, tastefully employed. Communion is practised; divination of witches (bikula ndoki) is not: "Jesus didn't do it." Spiritualist manifestations are absent, although the church's membership card shows an example of glossolalia in print (cacography), the letters KCC, originally seen "like a billboard in the sky" by the founder and others, and said to mean "the new gospel." Alcohol and polygyny are forbidden. The term ngunza is not used and mothers with sick children are warned not to take them to ngunza or nganga. Members believe that Christ and his angels are neither black nor white. The Trinity is mentioned as "Father, Son, and Holy Spirit" and EUDA, unlike EJCSK, insists that the Helper left behind by Jesus was the Holy Spirit, not an incarnate form.

EUDA therefore appears to be a church whose members have fully assimilated missionary teaching to the point of replacing African with European doctrines and the elimination of syncretism. This is an orthodox Protestant church but under local control. Closer observation complicates this picture and shows that what EUDA has learned is how to disguise its beliefs in orthodox form, or rather, it has learned, better than EJCSK, that sophisticated use of the French language can express fundamental Kongo realities without need of such terms as ngunza, ndoki.

The church recruits its members chiefly by healing. A high-ranking member of the Matadi congregation explained that a friend sent him to the Founder after he had unsuccessfully consulted all kinds of healers, including a European who told him, although he was half dead, that his troubles were imaginary. Being skeptical, the informant first tested the Founder's ability on his wife, who suffered from a peculiar affliction: though she was quite young, her breasts had already fallen to her waist and the elders in the village had declared there was nothing they could do. The Founder smiled and assured the informant there was no problem; blessings on three successive days restored the woman's bosom to its pristine shape. The healing was the more remarkable in that a well-known proverb refers to its impossibility: "If a tree falls in Europe, not even the white man can stand it up again." Marvelously convinced, the informant told the healer his own problems with like success and subsequently became one of the church's leaders.

The term "apostle" designates the highest grade in the church, not restricted to 12 persons. This grade is subdivided ("Reverend Apostle Superior," for example), but consists of all who are entitled to fulfill the principal functions: healing, blessing, divination (mbikudulu), confession and preaching. Catechists (minlongi) are entitled only to hear confession and to preach. The Founder is the chief of the apostles (n'kuluntu). Only he and his deputy, who lives in Matadi, are entitled to administer communion, which is offered once a month to those who have confessed their sins and been blessed. Confession is held every Wednesday by each section (of which there were six in Matadi in 1970), meeting in private. I was not able to attend any of these meetings but apparently the confession, like "weighing" (bascule) in DMN churches, is the principal means whereby hierarchical control is maintained. Meetings are dominated by one or more people with divinatory power who make sure that penitents do not overlook any of their failings. Serious backsliding is punished by temporary loss of rank and exclusion from confession itself.

Blessing is one of the two means of healing, the other being European medicine. Blessings may be given only by apostles, who remove their shoes to do so, the better to communicate with God. Whoever reads the Bible lessons for the day also removes his shoes. This was one of the only two gestures observable at EUDA services that did not correspond to missionary practice; the other, during welcoming rites for newborn infants, was the one called kubula mpeve in which, by a sharp motion of the hand, evil spirits that may be hovering near a person's head are struck down. Ths gesture is often seen in DMN churches. Some other manual gestures used during communal prayers are of Catholic origin. Blessings for the sake of healing may be given at any time, in public or private, and involve only a laying-on of hands and sprinkling with water drawn from the tap.

Attempting to discuss kindoki, kundu and similar topics with any but the most ignorant members of EUDA leads nowhere. They are above all that. To shift to a more psychological vocabulary, however, is to elicit at once a highly articulate concern with exactly the same existential problems and the spiritual resources for dealing with them that preoccupy any DMN ngunza. For example, "what do you do if you find that the ill-will of a member of the family is upsetting others and causing health problems?" The apostles, it seems, are constantly seeing visions of angels and receiving messages, some of which they reveal; others they keep to themselves. An apostle may learn from his spiritual sources that a member of the church is about to die; he visits the person in question, and together they pray that God may change his mind. Whatever the outcome, the authority of the apostle is strengthened, obviously.

Addressing European visitors, members of the EUDA are at pains to emphasize their distance from traditional beliefs. At a church feast for newborn twins and their mothers it is explained, incorrectly, that "in the old days" twins were thrown alive into the river. In fact, like the DMN churches, EUDA has taken over the function not only of the "mothers of twins" but of any magician who treated pre-natal dif-

ficulties, and who would be rewarded by a coming-out
feast for the children successfully delivered under
his spiritual supervision.

Beneath the surface of Protestant orthodoxy,
bureaucratic efficiency and French translatability,
therefore, lies unshaken Kongo reality. The organizational form of this surface/interior dichotomy was
the contrast between the church's public, Sunday
morning services and its private Wednesday evening
confessional séances, between the "church" and the
"section" or band. The social context was that of
pluralism, in which custom is an enclave dominated by
the bureaucratic state. In the state itself the
apostles, unlike most bangunza, had been relatively
successful, at least as employees; the pastor of the
Matadi congregation was also the director of adult
education for the province of Lower Zaire.

At a deeper, psychological level, beneath the
stories of visions and healing and the exercise of
confession, lay an alienation similar to Mpadi's, an
uneasy fear of adverse judgement that betrayed the
public assertion of autonomy. The assertion of power
obtained directly from God denies and seeks to
reverse, in the manner of possession cults, the realities of political and economic power. Even these
relatively successful people were no more than minor
bureaucrats, dependent upon the potentially crushing
force of the national military-bureaucratic class
clustered around the government in Kinshasa.

EUDA therefore appears to be an independent,
bureaucratic church, but further inquiry shows that
fundamentally it shares with other prophetic movements the basic Kongo cosmology. In this respect,
the Apostles are not different from most members of
the mission-controlled Protestant and Catholic
churches, who may seek healing from a prophet in time
of need or regard the communion as a test of witchcraft. "It is often said to a catechumen, 'It is a
good thing that you will soon be baptized and will
communicate. For then your kindoki will come out and
will leave you'" (Andersson 1968:170). The difference between these other churches and EUDA is that as
mission churches they are fully integrated with the
rest of the bureaucratic sector though their schools,
hospitals, and political connexions. EUDA, a much
smaller organization, offers distinctions to individuals who might go unnoticed elsewhere and it
integrates, within a single structure, a complete
range of religious functions, including divination.

The last feature, however, has been diminishing
in importance as a convergence develops between the
prophetic tradition and mission Protestantism, led by
the Swedish mission (SMF). Andersson's account
(1968:161) of the "revival" that took place in the
mission church (EEMM) in 1947 and the remarkable part
played in it by the prophet and pastor R. Buana
Kibongi provides the best example of convergence.
"It was R. Buana who felt the opposition between the
races to be the fundamental problem, almost his personal pain." Assuming the prophetic role, he said,
"It is not for the Congolese to judge the missionary;
it is not for the white man to judge the black man.
For it is I who will judge both the one and the
other." Ordinary responses seemed inadequate to the
depth of the racial division, which evoked visions,
trances, speaking in tongues, and profound confessions. In fact, however, the division, the plural
structure, is institutional and not a function of
individual judgment, goodwill, or Christian stead-
fastness, however important these factors may be to
personal salvation.[17]

The differences among Kimbanguism, Mpadism and
the EUDA, as I have analysed them here, are that Kimbanguism, like all the mainstream of the prophetic
movement, assimilated the missionary condemnation of
indigenous "superstition" to the classical preference
for public discipline over individual pursuit of
advantage (the distinction of ends). Kimbanguists
were thus, in effect, ideologically coopted by the
colonial regime. Mpadi, on the other hand, at the
level of his own conscious doctrine and the terms he
used to define it, rejected the same condemnation.
He defined his position in opposition to all missionary values, and in Mpadism the classical disapproval
of "magic" is relegated to secondary importance. The
Apostles, superficially successful people, accepted
missionary values, including missionary condemnation
of the Kimbanguist compromise ("syncretic"). EUDA
doctrine, like Mpadism, though for opposite reasons,
rejects the term ngunza, but also rejects the whole
of the classical vocabulary.

# 8

## The Prophetic Vision

Chapters Three and Four showed that the social context of prophetism was plural, divided into bureaucratic and customary sectors, and that in distinct and specific ways prophetism responded to tensions in each of these sectors, affecting especially people who were marginal in both. In presenting this point of view I used categories of ordinary sociology, such as "plural society," "class conflict" and "institution." In these terms, the sectors of a plural society are characterized by different institutional contents: different religions, systems of government, economic relations and so on. In effect these concepts artificially break apart the phenomenon of prophetism, dividing it into its religious, political and economic aspects, for example, which then have to be reassembled to explain prophetism as a particular structure of relations between them.

Valuable and necessary though this procedure may be, I argued in Chapter Seven that to understand what religious leaders were trying to do we should employ the abstract functions of the religious commissions (kimfumu, kinganga, kingunza and kindoki), since there was evidence in word and deed that these leaders saw their own intentions in these terms. Kimfumu, kinganga, etc., cover the same ground that the sociologist would like to divide into religion, law, medicine, education and the like, although the one set of institutional categories cannot possibly be mapped on the other. The two kinds of analysis are complementary.

In this chapter I repeat and extend this process, seeking to grasp not merely the cognitive orientation of prophets but their motivation, the

engagement of their personalities in the work. The
prophetic vocation was a specific experience and its
realization satisfying, in a personal way; prophets
usually work very hard at their calling, whose material and social rewards are slight and uncertain. For
a number of individuals whose autobiographies can be
examined closely, it appears that they experienced a
particular kind of alienation which, though it originated in their social conditions, can be read in
their dreams and visions. The autobiographies proclaim both the individual's defeat and impotence,
which are to some extent real, and a miraculous
reversal of this condition, which is fantasy, at
least initially. For example: "In 1966 I fell into
a coma, and people brought blankets for my funeral;
but then I saw a bright, dazzling light, heard a
heavenly choir singing No. 461 ["Many troubles here
on earth, we suffer from sicknesses, our tears pour
down; O Spirit, come to help us!"], and I awoke to
find that I had acquired exceptional intelligence, so
that no witch could get past me." To the extent,
however, that other people can be persuaded to accept
the implicit claim of the fantasy, it becomes a real
social program, and to that extent the reversal is
also real.

For this transformation to occur the private
vision and the public social reality, the new program
and the old, must exhibit essentially the same structure and be cast in essentially the same symbolic
form, because they must be communicated. The prophet
is a theorist of his own condition and that of others
to whom he appeals; he has reflected more profoundly
and more articulately than they have on the world and
their position in it. His theory is thus, to begin
with, cosmological, describing the beginning and end
of the world, the boundaries of life and death, the
types of forces and persons in it, and the sources of
success and failure. The prophet then comments on
current events in these terms. Examples of such lectures, by Kinene and Mpadi, have already been cited.

Analysis of the prophetic theory began in
Chapter Five, in which we saw how the model of the
divided worlds was imposed upon Kongo experience of
white people in such a way that they were seen as the
dead. In this cosmology the Atlantic slave trade is
understood as witchcraft, to which modern industrial
accidents and deaths in hospitals are commonly assimilated. BaKongo are likely to regard degrees from
American universities as cultic initiations for which
the scholar may be supposed to have paid over the

souls of relatives, and expect spiritually endowed
persons, when they travel, either "in the spirit" or
as guests of the State Department, to bring back from
America news of the dead.  In other words, the other
world, inhabited by the dead, whose activities control fortune and misfortune in this world, now
includes not only the occult personalities (ancestors, basimbi) pertinent to life in the
descent-based, customary sector, but also those (Belgians, Germans, Americans, and now Zairois) who
affect one's destiny in the bureaucratic and capitalist sector, which they call nsi a mundele,"white
man's country."

The model of the divided worlds was closely consistent with the sociology of the real world of Kongo
life in past centuries.  The persistence of this
model in the twentieth century in such a way that
colonial rule was understood in terms of "the dead"
is attributable to the perpetuation, in attenuated
form, of "customary society," to the exclusion of
Congolese from autonomous participation in the
bureaucratic world they sought to understand, and to
considerable elements of both mystification and
absurdity in European colonial ideology.  On the
other hand, as we have seen, the theory of witchcraft, applied to colonial experience, leads to
conclusions that are neither absurd nor unsatisfactory as a basis for social action; the theory, that is
to say, is roughly comparable in efficiency to most
European theories applied to the same phenomena
(MacGaffey 1978).  Such theories (for example,
"modernization") are efforts to portray a world in
which the theorist does not participate, but which he
imagines, with the aid of the cosmology proper to the
structure of his own society.

From a psychological point of view, the visions
and rituals of prophets are also profoundly erotic,
as is most (perhaps all) religious symbolism.  This
quality is most obvious in the case of the short
batons or canes called n'kawa (sometimes mvwala)
which prophets often carry and to which they attribute magical potencies.  In complex ways, the
relationship between the prophet and his female followers is erotic and sometimes sexual as well.  The
more charismatic he is the more necessary it will be
that such relationships be regulated in some way,
from the sign above one office door, "No unmarried
woman may speak to the Prophet without first asking
the Secretary," to the ritualistic orgies practiced
by certain groups in the past (Andersson

1958:181-85).   Moreover, as in other pneumatic forms
of religion, the visions of the prophet and his
assertions regarding the world as he sees it commonly
exhibit such qualities of apparent delusion, hysteria
and paranoia, for example, that they would be regarded as signs of personal mental aberration were it not
for their acceptance and institutionalization in collective ritual.   Modern prophets are well aware of
this ambiguity and it is common to hear one say while
recounting his personal experiences, "they thought I
was mad, and did not realize that the Holy Spirit had
descended on me." In both of these aspects, the erotic and the delusional, Kimbanguism raises problems of
explanation to which anthropology offers long-established and thoroughly contradictory answers.
        In a tradition of social science whose philo-
sophical roots reach back to Hobbes, Locke, and the
Social Contract debates of the eighteenth century,
"the individual," studied by psychologists, and "society," studied by sociologists, are treated as
separate systems;   debate rages as to the nature of
the accommodation between these abstractions.   The
tedious circulation of the debate and its low produc-
tivity suggest that the question is malformed;   it
continues to attract attention because the energies
it harnesses are generated elsewhere in the social
system that supports social science, and have to do
with the political value of asserting or denying the
autonomy and responsibility of the individual
vis-à-vis the state.   The urgency of the political
issue ensures that social science in general will
continue to disregard the efforts of its major figures (Marx, Durkheim, Weber, Freud) to transcend this
essential opposition.
        In his discussion of magical hair, Leach (1958)
treats the erotic character of symbolism as gratuitous.   He accepts the conventional distinction
between private symbols, studied by psychoanalysts,
and public symbols, studied by anthropologists,
attempting only to bridge the gap between the two
presumptively independent systems with the Darwinian
suggestion that public symbols are effective because
they happen to engage repressed libidinal energies;
public and private meanings then coincide.
        The tyranny exercised by the abstract opposition
between individual and society is apparent in the
literature on the psychology of shamans.   As
I.M. Lewis (1971:179) explains, "one of the best
established traditions in the study of shamanism and
possession treats them as abnormalities." Shamanism

is regularly seen as the institutional equivalent, for primitive societies, of the madhouse. "An equal volume of testimony," however, "argues the precise opposite," and points out that to be effective in his difficult role the shaman cannot be a psychopath; all over the world, people clearly distinguish between mentally disturbed persons, who are a social problem, and shamans, who are valued leaders.

A third perspective seeks to resolve these conflicting interpretations by regarding the shaman as a "healed madman," a compensated neurotic. Lewis essentially assimilates this proposal to the first, saying that it is ethnocentric to dismiss shamanistic "fantasies" as what we would call mental derangement, compensated or not. His discussion leans heavily on the conventional doctrine of social anthropology, that we can learn nothing about individual mental health (his emphasis) from performances of institutionalized roles. It may be that the shamanistic role represents a culturally acceptable niche for the private neurotic proclivities of a few individuals, but the majority of people actively involved in possession cults are only mildly or temporarily neurotic "in any valid sense" (Lewis 1971:185). Of course, it is precisely this "valid sense" that is at issue, as is the relationship between the apparently neurotic behavior of the shaman and "the mass of ordinary 'normally' neurotic people who find some relief from anxiety and some resolution of everyday conflicts and problems in such religious activity." Why restrict this normal relief to religious activity? Normality itself is a function of continuous, more or less satisfactory interaction with others according to shared expectations, shared definitions of reality.

All points of view in the discussion summarized by Lewis, including his own, presuppose that personality is something the individual brings with him readymade in his encounter with society and that its normality or lack of it can be assessed independently of his engagement in any institutional context.[1] All equally fail to acount for the problematic facts at the center of the dispute. "For all that," as De Heusch remarks (1971:228), "we still have not got rid of the irritating problem of the strange similarities existing between the behavior of the western hysteric and that of a Siberian shaman or an African in a state of possession." The psychotic who for whatever reasons -- genetic, chemical or experiential -- is grossly deviant in all institutional contexts manifests behaviors that cannot be mistaken for cultural

norms; that banal truth cannot sweep away the problem of the zone of viable behaviors in which delusion
and inspiration are neighbors and in which no objec-
tive segregation of the normal from the abnormal is
possible. De Heusch continues: "It is time to seek
a common ground or discussion between ethnography,
history of religions, and psychiatry, to put forward
a perspective in which all hysteriform manifestations
would take their place in a coherent psycho-socio-
logical structure."

Such a perspective can be found in the work of
Talcott Parsons (1964), who sees the structure of the
personality and of society as continuous; the personality results from the progressive internalization
of cultural symbols. This progressive internalization is also a progressive differentiation of the
initially polymorphous social capacities of the
organism, and the structure of this differentiation,
according to Parsons, is that of the oedipus complex
(Parsons and Bales 1955). To similar effect though
from a structuralist psychoanalytic perspective, the
Ortigues write (1966:302) that the oedipus complex
describes the fundamental structures according to
which the dialectic of desire and demand, of evil and
suffering, takes shape in the society as well as in
the individual. The oedipus complex cannot be
reduced to a description of the child's attitudes to
his father and mother; it is a semantic problem, as
much social as psychological.

In psychoanalytic theory in general, the experiences of an adult serve only to reveal the dynamics
of a personality structure developed in infancy and
not subject to serious modification after the age of
about seven. Although the theory proposes, with
reference to the adult, a model of a system contained
within the individual, with reference to the development of personality in the infant it allows for
social processes in the form of the oedipal conflict.
Parsons notes the convergence here, between Freud's
views and those of Durkheim and of G.H. Mead, the
common theme being the idea of internalization (Parsons 1964:80). The difference is that for Mead in
particular the development of the personality through
the internalization of object-relations continues
into adult life. Accordingly, in theories of
interpersonal dynamics influenced by Mead, the current social situation of the adult is more than a
trigger or a facilitating circumstance revealing some
deep-seated flaw. This point of view, as Parsons
indicates, tends to integrate psychology and sociolo-

gy and has the advantage that, at one level at least, it makes possible comparative studies of personality formation in terms of the structure of adult roles in particular societies.[2]

## Basic personality

According to Parsons, personality formation occurs by progressive differentiation corresponding to "a nesting series of social interaction systems involved in socialization" (Parsons and Bales 1955:383). In this series the nuclear family, held to be universally a four-role social system, stands "somewhere in the middle," in terms both of its degree of complexity and its mediation in the life of the individual between infantile dependency and adult autonomy. "The internalization of the object systems and the values of the nuclear family and its subsystems, starting with the mother-child relation, constitutes the foundation of personality structure in all human societies. There are, of course, very important variations, but they are all variations on a single set of themes" (Parsons 1964:264).

As in other parts of Africa, the Kongo infant usually experiences an abrupt weaning at the age of two or so. His mother devotes herself to a new baby, and now that he is fully mobile and able to look after himself his other female relatives also cease to be much interested in him. He is no longer everybody's pet; he is expected to surmount his troubles more or less like an adult and nobody is likely to offer consolation except his father. From the age of about five the child fends for himself, often to the extent of having to scrounge and cook his own meals, and here again father is often the source of little gifts of food and money that help him to get by.

From these observations one would expect the Kongo child to develop ambivalent feelings toward his mother (ngudi) and to the lineage (ngudi) to which he and his mother belong. It is in fact the case that lineage members, sharing in a corporate estate, are more likely to suspect one another of witchcraft than others upon whom they are not so closely dependent. There is no ground for suggesting a causal relationship, however, and it will be sufficient to notice the congruence between childhood experiences and those of later life.

More detailed observations made by the psychologist E. Corin (1970:222, 252) among the BaYanzi, another and related matrilineal people, lead her to a

similar conclusion: the child, she says, finds in
the proximity of his father a dimension of depth and
security contrasted with the deficiency of the mother, for whom the father in his domestic role is in
some respects a substitute. This attitude remains
profoundly rooted throughout the individual's life
and is transferred to the father's lineage in relation to the mother's, father offering guarantees of
security against the overwhelming power of the matri-
clan. Presumably, however, most children have much
the same kind of experience. Those who become prophets in later life may have had unusual childhood
experience, but we know nothing of this; the view
advanced here concerning the psychology of prophets
makes no such assumption, except in the case of Mpadi
Simon.

After the latency phase of adolescent transition
the individual is emancipated from the family, with
the capacity and the right to form erotic attachments
outside it and to adopt adult roles in the political
and economic institutions of his society, all of
which presuppose a basic personality formation. "Two
of the subsidiary identifications within the family,
by sex and by generation, are to become structurally
constitutive for [the child's] status in the wider
society, and these are cross-cutting" (Parsons
1964:97). They contribute to the child's basic personality, which is the matrix for the development of
subsequent object-relations through the adoption of
more specific roles in extra-familial social systems.

In all societies, most adult roles presuppose
the masculinity or femininity of the actor, whatever
the cultural content of the sex role definition.
"Sex role thus provides a critically important path
of transition from the assumption of differentiated
roles within the family to that of roles which
transcend the family and become constitutive of the
larger social structure" (Parsons 1964:42). The
cross-cutting principle of differentiation is that of
generation, which is a relationship of both authority
and (diachronically) of succession. This sociological commonplace is well understood by BaKongo, who
conventionally divide social populations into elders
and cadets (bambuta ye baleeke) and men and women
(bataata ye bamaama). Masculinity is associated,
equally conventionally, with leadership, competence,
intelligence, auspiciousness and dexterity;
self-disparaging phrases include "We are on the left"

(ku lumonso; cf. "in the dark") and "We are as women" (tu bakento twena). To be an elder is to be in a position to command and to accept the deference of women and cadets, the hewers of wood and drawers of water, and to participate in the decisions that allocate their labor.[3]

## Mpadi Simon

Parsons suggests (1964:264-65) that all "mental pathology roots in disturbances of the relationship structure of the nuclear family as impinging on the child." Though there may be somatic factors in mental pathology, "the structure of pathological syndromes which can legitimately be called mental will always involve responses to family relationships." However, "in no society is the socialization of an adult exhausted by his experience in the nuclear family, and hence is his personality only a function of the familial object systems he has internalized." Correspondingly, mental pathology will always involve "relations to social groups other than the nuclear family and to higher levels of cultural generalization and social responsibility."

It follows that the personality, like society, can always be regarded as a formal structure of differentiating principles arranged in order of logical priority, in which each successive differentiation presupposes and enriches those that have gone before (Smith 1960:302). The basic differentiation in personality formation identifies the individual as distinct from others, and simultaneously as entering into social relations with them. The next is that of sexual identity, however that be constructed, and the next distinguishes generations. These purely formal relations enable us to compare personalities in terms of their contents. The objects internalized at the earliest levels of the socialization process have the most general consequences for the personality as a whole. Parsons also emphasizes (1964:82):

> While the main content of the structure of the personality is derived from social systems and culture through socialization, the personality becomes an independent system through its relations to its own organism and through the uniqueness of its own life experience; it is not a mere epiphenomenon of the structure of the society.

According to Parsons (1964:103):

> The reasons why neuroses, like other distur-
> bances of personality functioning, involve
> important regressive components is essentially
> that the more generalized motivational struc-
> tures--as distinguished from social values,
> where the order of generality is the
> reverse--are laid down in early childhood.
> Regression to deep enough levels, then, will
> always involve motivational structures in which
> erotic needs form an essential component.

The theory implies that disturbances of personality
functioning so disabling as to impair the
individual's viability in any social context are
explained by the content of motivational structures
laid down earliest in childhood.

The manuscripts of Mpadi Simon allow us to
explore the hypothesis of an hierarchical structure
to the personality and the complex relations between
individual motivations and social values. Mpadi's
Black Church (ENAF) deliberately asserts the validity
of indigenous institutions against foreign condemnation and upholds certain values and practices that
are not now usual among BaKongo, though they once
were. This may be the only Kongo church that advocates polygyny; like several others, it insists on
the polluting condition of menstruating women, and
segregates them in special outhouses, although most
BaKongo no longer do this.

On the other hand, the Black Church attributes
special importance to women, who are said to have
been the first to see God on crucial occasions:
Mary, Kimbangu's foster-mother Kinzembo, and Mpadi's
aunt Lwila. Women are therefore required participants in public prayers, and a corps of specially
trained girls, the barégimentes, besides playing an
important role as acolytes to Mpadi in his healing
exercises (JM p.139), are destined to be the high
priesthood of the church after his death. This exal-
tation of women is unusual, but it is accompanied by
an emphasis on the polluting aspect of women and of
sexual relations which is also unusual. Dancing, for
example, though traditional, is forbidden, not (as
among Kimbanguists and Protestants generally) because
it is an occasion of sin but because the contact may
be polluting. In certain contexts handshakes and
other personal contacts are forbidden, even within
the church; this rule is based on the risk that one

of the parties may transmit "female pollution"
(nsumukunu za bakento) acquired from a woman with
whom he has been in contact, and not, as in EJCSK for
example, on the risk of witchcraft.

Besides this ambivalence there is a diffusely
erotic quality to ENAF which earned it (in the Kasangulu area, in 1966) the sobriquet Dibundu dia
Bakento, "Womanizing Church." In Kongo, as in other
societies which reserve heroic roles to men, women's
relationship to prophets and healers often has a
noticeably erotic quality. As Burridge says
(1969:161), the commonly reported sexual attractive-
ness of prophets is a function of the conditions of
being of women in such societies (cf. Sundkler
1961:154; Janzen 1978:88-89). In certain congregations the idiosyncratic and violent trance behaviors
of some women were masturbatory and the relations
between male "weigher" and female "weighee" in the
bascule were as erotic as those of a dance-hall.
This is entirely unremarkable, but the better-organ-
ized congregations, such as those of DMNA, took care
to guard against such tendencies, insisting on discipline, due form, and proper clothing.

What was remarkable about ENAF was that its
official procedures violated decorum, especially in
the central divinatory rite, "the Lord's table"
(Chapter Seven). In a ritual environment that proclaimed the salvation made available through Kimbangu
and the virtues of African healing science, but which
in fact imitated many of the features of a European
clinic, men and women were expected to strip to the
waist in public for medical examination and discussion of their physical and social problems, including
sexual ones. Among the men who dominated the scene,
both as officiants and as audience, interest in the
nakedness of women, especially beautiful young women,
was explicit and matched the equally explicit but
unavailing embarrassment of the women being examined;
voices from the audience would tell the healer to
have the woman remove her hands from her breasts, for
example.

Indications of the source of this aberrant ero-
ticism are available in Mpadi's written rules for the
church but it is important to note that the rules are
fantasies that have never been thoroughly institutionalized. They are contained in manuscripts dating
from about 1945, when Mpadi was in his late 30's.[4]

The rules for the polygynous household include
detailed, repetitious, and sometimes incoherent
instructions about maintaining two sets of furniture

and of tableware, one for "pagans, whose mouths are
full of lies," and the other for the faithful. In
the second category, each wife is to have her own
sanctified chair, knife, fork, spoon, plate, and so
on. All these furnishings come in sets of threes and
fours. The husband is supposed to sleep with his
wives in strict rotation and to eat the food provided
by the one with whom he is sleeping that day. So
much may be ancient Kongo custom, but the rules also
provide that he have no cutlery of his own, nor even
his own chair; he is to sit on the knee of the wife
of the day, who will put food in his mouth. He is to
do this to prove to all men his submission to the
will of Almighty God.[5]
    This reversion to childhood, totally contrary to
Kongo standards, is repeated in other departments of
domestic life. The wife is to wash and dry her husband, and to shave all the hair from his body; such
shaving was formerly practised in certain rites of
passage, but not as a rule of domestic hygiene, nor
as a service for husbands. Moreover the wife is to
acompany her husband to the latrine, to watch over
everything he does and everything he says. The
instructions continue in precise detail as to the
woman's preparations for bed and her comportment
therein. She is represented as active, her husband
as entirely passive, the recipient of loving care;
in fact the text itself shifts to the first person
singular, in the woman's voice: "I, numbered wife in
the church of the apostles of the savior of the black
race, when I have placed the husband I have received
by the will of God between my breasts, and have put
his head in my elbow, and tightened the elbow ..."[6]
    After this point the text interrupts itself with
incoherent and illegible passages, although the sexual instructions are explicit and comprehensive.
Other illegible passages in which the handwriting
suggests intoxication occur when Mpadi regulates the
degree of attention the wife is to give to sewing
buttons on her husband's shirt and trousers. Another
document, tediously repetitive and formulaic, spells
out the dress code (extracts):

    No. 189.3. I have put on my khaki trousers, my
    khaki trousers of salvation given to me by God
    Almighty. Therefore I rejoice now, for God has
    provided me with my khaki trousers of salvation
    and completeness, my trousers of going to
    heaven. Isaiah 61:10 ("For he hath clothed me
    with the garments of salvation").

No.190.5. When all the buttons on my khaki
shirt of salvation and of victory have been
fastened, this is the barrier (<u>nkaku</u>) of victory and of faith, and I have fastened it
according to the commandment of Almighty God in
the midst of the great war with Satan.[7]

The compulsive concern for the buttoning of the
uniform or of whatever clothes Mpadi wears is highly
personal and of a piece with the exaggerated concern
for "purity" and with washing and shaving; it indicates uncertainty with respect to the body's outline
and hence the sense of a need to defend its boundaries. As such it is an extreme example of the
concern, general in prophetic churches, with fortifying the body and providing special boundary defences
(<u>nkaku</u>) against occult threats.[8]

Mpadi's incantatory repetition of his regulatory
formulas and his apparent anxiety about his "buttons
of salvation" are nevertheless exceptional. In the
classical psychoanalytic view, obsessive compulsions
of this sort indicate late anal fixation; the subject has trouble handling sadistic impulses, and
regresses to the anal stage when confronted with
oedipal anxieties. Mpadism emphasizes to an exceptional degree the physical brutalities suffered by
prophets during persecution and dwells on a fantasy
of black victims of Catholic priests, kept in underground caverns on all fours, loaded with chains, and
tortured with infernal injections. Within the church
the rules, real and fantastic, are backed by a sanction known as <u>punition</u> for so many days or months,
meaning that an offender is ostracized, denied domestic comforts, and forbidden to wash or shave.
References to <u>punition</u> are very frequent though it
may not often be enforced. According to the rules, a
man who spends more than the prescribed time with a
favored wife is subject to three months <u>punition</u> and
summary loss of the wife, whom the authorities give
to another husband. Failure of a wife to notice a
missing button, or of a husband to heed her mention
of it, is worthy of 12 days <u>punition</u>, and at this
point in the text "the handwriting witnesses to
increasing agitation. The wording of the paragraph
is absolutely incoherent" (CRISP 1968:50).
Thereafter in the manuscript follow two scribbled
pages, much crossed out, condemning sexual relations
after the morning ablutions.

The foregoing evidences of personal tendencies
are idiosyncratic in every respect. They run counter

to normal Kongo values and behavior, are unlike the rules and practices of any other church, and are only partly institutionalized in Mpadi's own church. They are thus not representative of Mpadism as a collective movement, and do not dominate Mpadi's public role as prophet. Nevertheless they cannot be segregated empirically from the public and institutional aspect and must have contributed substantially to Mpadi's personal motivations and hence his career. The uniqueness of Mpadism is partly a function of these particular features, summarized as a highly ambivalent attitude towards sexual differentiation, that originate at a very early level and remain inaccessible to further inquiry in the absence of biographical and psychoanalytic information. At higher levels of personality structure, however, Mpadi expresses values that rejoin both the generality of prophetism and classical Kongo culture. These values have to do with the problematic nature of the father as object, related sociologically to political features of authority and succession.

## Structural Adolescence

The oedipal crisis prefigures in the narrow world of the family the male child's subsequent confrontation as an adult with institutionalized authority and the rules of succession. "In first assuming performance functions in the family as a system, the child learns that by virtue of age he is relegated to a lower status, and the father status symbolizes this central hierarchical principle of system structure. Such a pattern principle, it should be remembered is, at this level of child development, both highly general and highly concrete" (Parsons 1964:43). The relation between family and society is not, however, one of genetic development; "If, in one aspect, a great deal of the cultural symbolization is a "projection" of experiences, especially of childhood, undergone in the family situation, it is almost equally the case that the real father is a "projection" into the family situation of the major pattern structure of the wider social system" (Parsons 1964:54).

Parson's further development of the relation of the adolescent individual to the structure of the society in which he lives is based not on structural differentiation of adult roles but on the qualitative aspects of role performance as described by the "pattern variables." His main ethnographic sources is the

modern United States, more especially the professional segment of the American middle class. Here the
roles to be adopted by the adolescent are "achieved"
rather than "ascribed," as in the family, and role
performance is "instrumental-adaptive" rather than
"expressive-integrative." It may be doubted that the
United States is as "universalistic" a society as
Parsons describes it, and his theory of it can be
said to analyze American ideology more accurately
than American society. The operational value of the
pattern variables in empirical research, especially
outside America, seems questionable. I prefer to
follow in a more conventionally anthropological
direction Parsons' basic argument: "Freud's theory
of object-relations is essentially an analysis of the
relation of the individual to the structure of the
society in which he lives" (1964:107).

    Kongo society is clearly not universalistic and
the possibilities of achievement are highly ambiguous. The ideology of Kongo institutions allows
little room for it; the emphasis is all on what is
due to and from a man, rather than on what he can
make of and for himself. In practice, as distinct
from local theory, to obtain one's due requires luck
and effort and is in no small measure an achievement.
Retrospectively, achievement is explained as
birthright ascription. In the bureaucratic institutional sector the situation is reversed. From the
beginning, Europeans preached achievement to Africans
but in practice the level and direction of African
achievement was carefully limited. Commenting in
1923 on the educational policy of the day, a contri-
butor to the journal *Congo* said the policy was to
provide blacks with the elementary instruction needed
by a laborer, cultivator, artisan or tradesman; "for
the Blacks will not be able to aspire to anything
else for a very long time. If they were given [a
more liberal] education, they would expect to become
office clerks; it is important that they know that
such jobs are not accessible to them and that they
should learn a trade" (Lacroix 1972:13).
Retrospectively, the menial role in colonial society
ascribed to Africans was explained as poor achievement (lack of economic enterprise, sense of
responsibility, etc.). The experience of most BaKongo today remains the same.

    The universality Parsons attributes to the
nuclear family is another of his more dubious assumptions, but the adolescent transition to which he
refers can be described satisfactorily using Fortes'

contrast between the domestic and the politico-jural domain. To become an adult, at whatever age a given society defines the transition, is to assume autonomy and responsibility in the social relations of production and reproduction, whatever their content may be in that society. Adult roles are defined jurally and sustained politically.

In the plural society of Belgian Congo it was possible for a man's aspirations to adulthood to be doubly frustrated. In the customary sector, as he acquired a wife and decided where to live, he might find that he was regarded as a slave, a permanent cadet. This status is a matter of one's position in the lineage structure, of which most young men (up to the age of 25 or so), have no clear idea; the identity and membership of lineages, and the traditions that legitimate their positions in house and clan, are "secrets of the elders" to which, ideally, only selected young men are initiated as they begin to show political promise. The chief reason why such information is secret is that it consists not of facts but of allegations and collusions aiding the socially powerful to manipulate the weak. Their power is literally and deliberately occult, and experience of it, as we have seen in the story of Kingani (Chapter Six), is conducive to paranoia. The prophet, as revolutionary, has real grievances, delusional though his representation of them may be, and he gains a following because in some degree others share his experience and need his services (Turner 1975:23-24):

> Since the symbolic trappings of divination and witchcraft manifest paranoid attitudes we must conclude that an influential majority of diviners are marginal men, through physiological abnormality, psychological aberrancy, or social-structural inferiority or outsider-hood .... The paranoid style does not impair the diviner's ability to sift evidence in a rational way, but it does mean that he explains misfortune by positing a complex, often logical scheme of delusory persecution ... as the evaluative frame in which he judges relationships, assigns guilt, and recommends ritual remedies. Diviners as a class may be said to exact a subtle revenge on a society which has rejected or belittled them as individuals.

Much the same comments apply to the marginality of the prophet and his followers in the bureaucratic sector, too. In both sectors he lacks control over the conditions of his own social reproduction and the nature of his exclusion is masked by ambiguous discourse. In contrast, successful people are often those who manage to parlay advantage in one sector into advantage in the other, since the two sectors are interdependent. The elders to whom the prophet is a slave, and who maintain his subjection by secret communications with the dead, are the same people as the foremen and bureaucrats who by privy arrangements with the Europeans (who are also the dead) obtain wealth and power for themselves at the expense of junior relatives whose souls they sell.

In psychological terms, "failure" in confrontation with authority and the rules of succession means that the internalization of the authoritative other does not take place; the relationship with "father" remains problematic, and the final resolution of the oedipal transformation does not occur. In this sense, the personality is "neurotic" (Parsons 1964:55):

> It would, I think, be agreed by most analysts that a personality in whom the father symbol complex as distinguished from the generic masculine role was too prominent, was probably on the neurotic side; it is, that is to say, normal to overcome the pattern of oedipal preoccupations. It seems probable that in a social system if there is undue prominence of obvious father symbolization in the cultural tradition analogous conclusions would be justified.

It is neither practical nor useful to try to decide when a symbol complex is "unduly prominent." Suffice it to say that the symbols of patrifiliation are conspicuous in prophetic discourse and ritual, and that, on the whole, they are only partly institutionalized; they are usually revealed to the prophet in dreams and their meanings are thought of as special and mysterious. References to "le petit Simon (Kimbangu)," and "photographs" showing him seated on the knee of a large white Christ are marginal to the publicly accepted doctrines of Kimbanguism. The staves (mvwala) and batons (n'kawa) with which many prophets (not all) communicate with God, heal the sick, destroy witches, listen to the Spirit, shoot

down enemy aircraft and the like, are revealed to
each one personally, each stick with its particular
properties and taboos. Some are supposed to be kept
in a red sheath when not in use. (Once when I casually picked one up, I was told I had profaned it and
that it ought now to be reconsecrated--"but since
nobody noticed, we'll let it go.")

Such sticks represent a fantasy of the power
that in real life the prophet conspicuously lacks.
They do so in a particular way that literally points
to the source of the power and establishes the relationship between the prophet and "God the Father."
Sticks are vertical, and point out the path to
heaven; sometimes, after being revealed in dreams,
they are embroidered on robes in the form of arrows.
An Mpadist hymn refers to the savior sent by God as
"the baton set upright by the father," and a prayer
represents God as saying to Kimbangu, "You will be
raised up to be the king and leader, like a scepter I
shall cause to stand from south to north for all the
Blacks" (CRISP 1968:18, 28).[9] The "arms" of ENAF
show the baton as an arrow pointing upwards and it is
said to be the weapon of a chief or warrior, like a
gun or a sword. Of the "many meanings" of the batons
carried by ranking members of the church, some, they
say, are known only to Mpadi himself; Psalm 110,
"The Lord shall send the rod of thy strength out of
Zion," is mentioned in this context.

Impotence and suffering under colonial rule were
explained by those who became Kimbanguists as results
of the interruption of their communications with the
dead ("God," "the Americans"), which Kimbangu
restores. Delusional though the sense of occult
power may be, if the prophet's claim to be the agent
of God is accepted by a substantial number of people
his social situation is in fact transformed; he
becomes the elder of an organized group for whom the
reference to God is equivalent to a lineage's reference to its ancestor, since what is emphasized is
always the manifestation of God to this particular
prophet. Intervening in the lives of his followers
by settling disputes, imposing taboos, and the like,
he behaves like an elder and negotiates with elders
as one having authority and not as a slave.
Kimbanguism certainly contributed effective forces to
the independence struggle, though we may not agree
with Kimbanguists that the prophet brought independence about.

The staff of the elder is not simply a badge of
authority. It represents a complex of assumptions

concerning the sequence of generations and the dependence of the living on their "fathers" in the other
world. In the real social world, the younger generation of men depends upon and competes with the older
generation (socially defined) for control of the primary resource, reproductive capacity. The staff
represents these virile interests, their social form,
and their perpetuation through time. In colonial
Kongo, this control was partly appropriated by laws
forbidding polygyny, limiting divorce and reallocat-
ing responsibilities for children, in conformity with
the moral and social demands of capitalism. Mpadi's
advocacy of polygyny was thus not mere
traditionalism; nor was his prophecy, that after the
coming of the Americans black men would marry white
women, mere lewdness. The most fundamental political
relations in any society regulate connubium.

Autobiographical materials by certain Kongo prophets illustrate the argument that cultural facts of
symbolism and cosmology, sociological facts of political and economic relations, and psychological facts
of subjective experience are all part of the same
system of communication and all "say the same thing."

## Nkindu

In 1966, when Nkindu was the pastor of a DMNA
congregation of Manianga people in Kasangulu, he was
remarkable for the simple, reserved and somehow trag-
ic dignity of his private consultations, and for his
authoritative and dramatic leadership of collective
rituals. His competence was recognized by his
church, which promoted him shortly afterwards to a
kind of regional inspectorship.

Nkindu's success as a prophet was balanced by
his admitted incompetence in other contexts. He
heard voices continually, which he compared with the
range of stations one might pick up on a radio; some
were the voices of angels, some of evil spirits, and
he had to be able to distinguish them. His reports
of messages received, concerning spiritual battles in
progress, in which his congregation should join with
prayer and trembling, worked wonders to exorcise
monotony from weekly services.[10] But his voices
also confused him so that he could not go to the
forest to work like other men. If he raised his
machete, the confusion in his head distracted him and
he would inevitably cut himself. He lived very simply, except for his beautifully laundered white
clothes, and his wife supported him.

In 1966 Nkindu preached a long and exciting sermon about his life. In 1969 he repeated it in
another part of Kongo and J.M. Janzen was able to
record it (JM No.51). It is evidently, like the
Ancient Mariner's, a speech that from time to time he
feels compelled to give, especially perhaps in the
presence of white witnesses. From conversations with
him we were able to fill in some details of his life.

The sermon begins with God's call to Simon Kimbangu to save suffering Africa. Kimbangu, protesting
that he is but "a small child," reluctantly accepts,
but is brutally arrested by Belgian authorities. In
asking himself how his mission will be continued,
Kimbangu's thoughts turn to his staff: Tala mvwala
ya lulendo,Bisi nza babelele yo, "See the staff of
power, the people of the earth have lost it; but
Jesus is merciful."[11] A "second Kimbangu" appears
in Manianga, Mbumba Philippe. When he too is captured, another elder is called by God to abandon
magic and become a prohet, only to be imprisoned in
his turn. Thus the sermon establishes the spiritual
hierarchy, the pedigree of the next prophet, Masamba
Esaie, founder of this particular church. Masamba is
described as one who had no father and was abandoned,
but an exchange of glances with Nkindu reveals to the
latter, who comes from the same village, that Masamba
was "a child of Kimbangu," and thus his true successor.

Nkindu's sermon continues with an account of his
own humiliation ("You're an animal") as houseboy in
the service of the Governor General. Like Masamba,
he too is eventually imprisoned, but the promise of
salvation is renewed in the revelation to Masamba,
while in prison, of a book entitled The Prophet Who
Was Strengthened with the Staff of His God. The sermon leads into a hymn composed by Masamba in praise
of Christ's redemption of mankind, and ends with an
account of Nkindu's own achievements, not in DMNA but
as a captain in the Salvation Army. The point of
these achievements (which are at least partly imaginary) is to report that at last, after independence,
Nkindu earned the respect and praise of Europeans.

In real life the ideal fusion of redeeming grace
and social success did not come about. During the
1950's, after his release from whatever imprisonment
he suffered, Nkindu entered the Salvation Army seminary but was also a member of a clandestine prophetic
band. He says that the Spirit would warn him of sur-
prise bedchecks and enable him to return 60 km. to
his dormitory in 30 minutes to avoid being caught

out. Eventually, in 1961, after independence, he
attempted to merge bureaucratic and customary religion by performing pneumatic healing during Salvation
Army services and was dismissed.

In the context, vividly described, of colonial
violence, the sermon traces a partially successful
resolution of the conflict between black and white in
terms of God's salvific intention working itself out
through a succession of prophets from the beginning
to the present, which is itself marked by patrifiliation and the staff of power and delegation. The
irrationality of the colonial system, with its
self-proclaimed benevolence and its practical brutality, its exhortations to achievement and its
simultaneous denial of opportunity, corresponded to
the classic type of a "double bind" (Bateson
1972:Pt.III). To judge by his own words, Nkindu's
troubles were linked with his experience of oppression; his vocation as prophet was a way of
salvation, spiritually and socially.[12] However, his
sermon tells us nothing directly about the intervention of the Spirit in his own life.

## Dizolele

A younger man than Nkindu, who had not
participated in the great struggles of the prophet
movement, built his own church in 1959, in the midst
of the nationalist ferment that led to independence
in 1960. His autobiographical account of the events
leading up to his commissioning as a prophet makes
little mention of colonial circumstances as such. A
white man appears in it only at the very end, a Protestant missionary who recognizes the genuineness of
Dizolele's state of grace and rather superfluously
authorizes his baptism. Thus this career, like Nkindu's, culminates in vindication before the European.

The context and content of the first and second
visions Dizolele reports indicate that in 1955, a
time of economic depression in Belgian Congo, he was
distressed by his inability to find work (JM No.19);
the parallel with Kimbangu's experience is close.
The first vision begins with a journey across a
landscape often encountered in the legends of questing heroes on their way to find "God the Father."[13]
While deeply asleep, Dizolele is called by name and
finds himself suddenly leaving the house in the company of a stranger, although the door remains
unopened.

On the road we took we entered an immense forest before crossing a very large expanse of grassland in the middle of which I saw a crossroads and a man coming towards us. Heading for me, he saluted me by raising my arm with his hand and saying, "Blessed be the womb that bore you and the breasts you sucked." When I looked behind me I found that my guide had disappeared and I was alone wth the one who had greeted me. Fixing his eyes on me he said, "Follow me," and I obeyed.

On arriving at the top of a small hill he showed me a deep well of very pure and clear water in which I saw beautiful fish swimming. The depth of the well was like the distance between earth and sky. "Do you see?" he asked; and I replied, "Yes." "Look," he said, "in this water you will find your good fortune. When you need clothes, you can get them here. When you are hungry or wish to feed strangers, come here. When you arrive to fish here is what to do." And he plunged the index finger of his right hand into the water; one of the fish came and bit on it. He pulled, but the fish was so long, so infinitely long that, being unable to pull it completely out of the water he put it back in. "Put in your finger too," he said. This I did, and a fish seized it, but being unable to withdraw it from the water because of its endless length, I too put it back.

My companion led me past the well to where we saw a great river, like Nzadi. "In this river," he said, "all the fish collect that I have just shown you in the well, but you may not touch any fish in this river, nor drink of the water." After that we went back to the well and my companion said, "Take a good look at this place and put a sign so that you will be able to come here daily." When all this was done, we returned to the crossroads where I met him. He knelt down to pray. I stood at his left. While he prayed, he gritted his teeth. At the same moment, a great light from the sky surrounded us. My mind was opened and I knew that he was asking God for the heavenly dew and the blessing on me.

Having prayed, he stood up, and went off to heaven. Left alone, not knowing what to make of this event, and not realizing that I

still inhabited my own flesh, I supposed that I
must be dead and situated in the land of the
dead. Then I went a little way and saw a road,
and women on the road fetching water ....
After much thought I grew calm and remembering
that yesterday evening a man had called at the
house I realized that I had seen a vision.
Thereupon I went to the house in which I had
been sleeping but found the door shut on the
inside so that I could not open it.

Standing out there in front of the door
and reflecting on my absence during many hours
of the night, I asked myself many questions:
"Won't Michel, who is still asleep, reprove me?
If he asks me where I've been, what will I say?
Won't he imagine that I've been out to steal or
to look for women, won't he break off our
friendly relations? In spite of this, I rapped
on the door so firmly and with such a bold air
that my friend opened it without asking me
whence I came. I went back to bed.

The road through a forest, across a grass wild-
erness and a crossroads to a river and the top of a
hill is the road to the land of the dead, traversing
the habitats associated with the several categories
of spirit: the ancestors, land simbi, water simbi,
sky spirits. The river is "like Nzadi," and lest the
point be lost on us the author says, "Not knowing
what to make of this event, and not realizing that I
still inhabited my own flesh, I supposed that I must
be dead and situated in the land of the dead." The
abundance of good things available at the well (whose
depth is "like the distance between earth and sky")
suggests the phrase ngudi a nkama, "source of
wealth," used by missionaries in a phrase referring
to heaven, nkembo a ngudi a nkama, "The glory of the
Lord." The river, as opposed to the well, is the dangerous, undifferentiated world of the dead, its
riches available to Dizolele only through his own
particular canal, on which he is to put a sign. The
gritting of teeth (kweta meeno) is a traditional sign
of an authoritative person, although Dizolele's companion remains anonymous.

As cosmology, the furniture of the dream is
common cultural property. It is also very obviously
erotic; the relationship between the worlds is
modeled on a sexual encounter, and conventionally one
approaches the grave, as to the vagina, "naked as he
was born." The sexual source of the dream material is

stressed by the author himself, in effect, when he
supposes that his friend will imagine he has "been
out to steal, or to look for women." The subheading
for this vision is "Birth."[14]
      In his next vision, Dizolele reveals his ner-
vousness about his unemployment:

> The next evening, at about midnight, when we
> were all asleep I heard outside a great strong
> voice of one crying, "Isaac!" As I replied to
> him I found myself outside without having
> opened the door. There I found a crowd of peo-
> ple sitting in a circle with myself standing in
> the midst of them. From the sky there came
> down a large metal object like a large house,
> on which was painted in large gold letters the
> word "FORAKAM." As we all looked at this thing
> we saw it slowly descend in the direction of my
> head. Although from fear I wanted to run away,
> it followed me until it touched my head and
> then descended to the ground.
>       Trying to find out where this thing came
> from, I called one of the people sitting around
> to pull on the chain by which it had been
> lowered. We pulled and pulled until a voice
> came from heaven saying, "Let be!" and we
> shouted, "Stop, it is a thing come from God."
> After so shouting, I saw that I was alone,
> there was no one else, nor yet the thing.
>       When I approached the door of the house I
> tried to push it but saw that it had been shut
> from the inside as it had been the first day,
> and from that I concluded that I had seen
> another vision.

      FORAKAM was the name of the company from which
he hoped to obtain work. The situation is made all
the more ominous by the group of people sitting
around; routine dream interpretation immediately
recognizes table ronde, or manenga, a conclave of
witches. The threat is removed after divine intervention. Later, Dizolele continues, he noticed a
change in his attitude; he was no longer interested
in the things of this world, but rather in heavenly
things. He began to read the Bible and to attend
Protestant services, though he had been educated as a
Catholic. Meanwhle he experienced, as his "third
vision," a voice calling him once again by name and
commanding him to read Psalm 136, an exercise that
miraculously lasted all night.

A few months later he performed his own first miracle by praying to God to cure a sick friend. So unobtrusively was this done that only one person realized who was the author of it, but Dizolele forbade him to speak to anyone about it. This and a number of other phrases scattered through the text draw an implicit parallel with the work of Christ.

The second miracle was public and it announced a power superior to that of magicians. The sick child in question suffered from fainting fits, a simbi affliction, and had accordingly been subject to a taboo keeping him away from hearths, which are antithetical to water spirits, but to no avail. Dizolele derogates the taboo and heals the child; since then, "the parents, having believed in Jesus Christ, follow me and participate in our Religion."

Behind the apparently unpredictable sequence of gratuitous events, Dizolele's spiritual career marches in step with that of other questing heroes, bringing him from a condition of marginal impotence and distress to an honorable position as head of a corporate church and delegate of Christ. The transformation proceeds by the gradual identification of the hero with an impressive but initially anonymous otherworldly figure able to provide him with all that he lacks. In the first vision God is prayed to but does not reveal himself; in the second, he speaks from concealment, mysteriously impelling Dizolele to turn to the Bible; in the third vision, direct contact is established, and the sequence of miracles begins thereafter. The autobiography does not stop there, however. Dizolele is commanded to show himself to the clergy of the Protestant mission, first the blacks and then the missionary himself, whose permission for baptism testifies to the authenticity of Dizolele's calling.[15]

The autobiographical sequence also corresponds to the order of psychological events that Silverman (1967:23-24) regards as common to both shamanism and schizophrenia. The primary condition is a feeling of fear, failure and guilt, with "seriously damaged self-esteem" resulting from "incompetent behavior in life situations that are acknowledged as crucially important." The "preshaman becomes preoccupied with his personal situation and experiences isolation and estrangement leading to self-initiated sensory deprivation, with consequent inevitable difficulty in the differentiation between phantasy and nonphantasy .... The already unstable and weakened 'psychological self' is disorganized by this drastically altered

environment and is unundated by lower order referential processes such as occur in dreams .... The
world comes to be experienced as filled with super-
powerful forces and profound but unimaginable
meanings." Psychological resolution of this state,
involving a reorganized set of perceptions and conceptions of reality, depends on the contingencies of
individual existence.

Silverman's paper has the merit that it allows
for the intrusion of social factors at two points in
the individual's history, the onset of the neurosis
and its resolution, but he goes on to argue that
because in our culture the individual experiencing
such anxieties receives little cultural support for
his new view of reality, he becomes a schizophrenic
rather than a shaman. In one culture, it is socially
viable behavior to communicate directly with spirits
and to exhibit "grossly non-reality-oriented idea-
tion, abnormal perceptual experiences, profound
emotional upheavals, and bizarre mannerisms;" in
another, it is not (Silverman 1967:29, 22).

This conclusion appears to be ethnocentric and
tautological; in "our culture" people do not become
shamans, but after experiencing anxiety processes
they may achieve positions of creative leadership in
politics, art, religion and many other fields, based
on acceptable new symbolizations of reality. They
may even claim to communicate directly with spirits,
but the acceptability of the behavior guarantees that
it will not be classified as abnormal, bizarre, or
unreasonably emotional. Acceptability in turn is not
simply a function of culturally specific canons of
reality-orientation but of political and economic
forces at work among the public at a given time;
collective paranoia is neither a permanent nor a peculiar characteristic of "primitive" societies.

In any society there are also persons unable to
overcome their anxieties, and whose delusions are not
supported by the public. Such people fail to some
extent to be socially viable in any institutional
context except a custodial one. In Kongo the verb
lauka covers both of these situations; it refers to
possession by occult forces, but only the outcome
reveals whether the forces are benign or not, and
whether the victim will emerge as one endowed with
socially valued power. When Ntinu Lukeni, the legendary founder of Mbanza Kongo, was about to become
king, "he went out of his mind" (laukidi), indicating
in this instance that he had been chosen by spirits
for initiation (Cuvelier 1946:15). Kimbangu also,

when God first called him, went out of his mind
(laukidi) (JM, p.150).
       On the other hand, BaKongo usually explain
bizarre and delusional behavior affecting social viability as resulting from improper traffic with the
occult. "He acquired charms to pass his exams, or to
favor his business, but when he failed to hand over
souls as the fee for them, they turned on him and
affected his head," one is told.  The Holy Spirit,
too, when it summons a prophet, must be obeyed, lest
it cause madness.  The distinction between the forces
at work, thought of as empirical, is in fact retrodictive and depends on the outcome.[17]

Ndo Mvuzi

       I have been arguing that the prophets in general
experienced in acute form the contradictions of the
society in which they lived.  Burridge (1969:160)
compares the prophet and the anthropologist as persons who experience contrasting systems of meaning:
"Mind and emotions are confused; two different
worlds have met in each person. One alternative is
insanity.  Another is to comprehend one world in
terms of the other." The present argument deals with
a set of factors present in Belgian Congo and in the
social characteristics of prophets and their followers that is much more specific than a meeting of
worlds and is as much a matter of political and
economic structures as of cognitive experience and
confusion.  In both the customary and the bureauratic
sector, prophets belonged to the stratum of failures
as defined by social structures that insisted upon
such stratification.  Possibly because of some additional constitutional predisposition, they reacted to
their experience by incorporating the structure of
the problematic relationships into their personalities.
       The evidence of personality disorder is a
communicative or pseudo-communicative practice in
which the accepted symbolic ordering of social life
is denied.  Communication itself is restructured as
the non-conforming individual attempts to take control on his own terms (Haley 1963). This is what
Turner (1975:24) calls the diviner's revenge.
Glossolalic speech or any other hocus-pocus is a
pseudo-communication which "says": "I am speaking to
you, but you are unable to respond as you usually
would, and therefore you cannot define me as you usually would; I am an other person than you thought."

Such discourse always includes oblique indications of this other personality; it is never mere nonsense. The incomprehensible spiritual language that the prophet André Gonda sometimes prayed in, for example, was an excellent imitation of the pretentious elocution of French-speaking announcers on the Kinshasa radio; it asserted that he belonged to another and more prestigious sphere than he in fact did. Such a move will succeed only if the references are understood and if a number of other people find that conforming to the would-be prophet's demands seems to solve their problems, too.

In 1966 a man whom I shall call Ndo Mvuzi, having some pretensions as the founder of "The National Prophetic Movement," sought recognition from governmental authorities in Matadi. The file of correspondence relating to him is the only record of these pretensions. His name does not crop up in lists of prophets or in other correspondence and in 1970 no other trace of his activities could be found. His letters, besides being inflated and megalomaniac, are incoherent in both style and substance. Commenting on them, an official wrote, "As for me, I do not know what to make of a movement led by a prophet that seeks to develop in its midst a whole traditional government and a workers' union, not to mention a litany of the law."

Yet Ndo Mvuzi's texts, doubly ambivalent in their continuous reference to the real and to the occult worlds, and to indigenous as opposed to bureaucratic institutions, simply aggregate the main popular themes of the independence movement of the 1950s. To say, as some anthropologists would do, that they are the utterances of a religious fanatic does nothing to explain them; pigeonholing is not an explanation and religious utterances do not usually have this character in Kongo or elsewhere. Explanation must refer to the texts themselves and the context of their utterance.

The letters and other documents in the file draw their peculiar character from the confusion of terms drawn from four different realms of discourse: prophetism, tradition, ethnography, and bureaucratic government. Prophetism and tradition (kinkulu, the traditional histories of the clans) belong historically and sociologically to the indigenous or customary sector of the plural society that is modern Zaire. Ethnography and bureaucracy belong to its bureaucratic sector. In all four realms, language is used in a highly ritualistic manner, parading symb-

olic forms overtly or latently related to the distribution of power in society, or, in a word, to
luyaalu.
      For the customary sector the rhetoric of tradi-
tion and prophecy has been discussed in previous
chapters. In the bureaucratic (European) sector the
ethnography of Kongo has been ritualistic in a double
sense. First, it has focused almost exclusively on
tradition and related matters which are in fact part
of the symbolic apparatus of Kongo society but which
have been regarded by the ethnographers as authoritative accounts of what actually happens or used to
happen. The principal topics, all more mythological
than sociological, include the former kingdom of
Kongo, chiefship, the migrations of the clans, and
their socio-political role. Secondly, during the
colonial period and to some extent since, ethnography
has provided the mythical charter for the Belgian
version of indirect rule and for the tutelary relationship between the bureaucratic sector and the
customary. BaKongo were constantly confronted by a
grotesque, carnival image of their society and culture, supported by the combined authority of
missionary, district commissioner and literate scholarship.[18]
      In bureaucratic governments everywhere, many
details of routine serve the latent ritual function
of defining the status of officials individually and
collectively with respect to the rest of the population. In Lower Zaire Province after independence the
ritualistic function of symbolic assertions inherited
from the colonial regime was exaggerated as the
government's real powers declined. In this respect
government was similar to, and was much imitated by,
the many little prophetic congregations whose corporate existence consisted in little else besides
ritual gestures (see Chapter Four).
      Ndo Mvuzi's apparently incoherent juxtaposition
of terms drawn from these four different realms follows conventional practice with respect to the use of
words in ritual, magic, and power-related contexts.
In praise-names, traditions and magical recipes, the
BaKongo rely on a punning technique in which similar
or homonymous terms serve to link concepts from different natural and social domains. They see the
resulting metaphoric relations between heterogenous
concepts as sources of both power and intellectual
satisfaction. They regard the range of both
knowledge and ingenuity needed to comprehend or to
originate such powerful discourse with some awe as an

occult faculty. The observer may find that the hidden meaning assigned to words is merely idiosyncratic, and the claim to occult power mystifies only its author unless social factors in the environment are engaged with it in some practical way.

A sample of Ndo Mvuzi's most magniloquent style shows the interweaving of bureaucratic forms with exotic elements whose source is not always evident. The translation given here from the French original is as literal as possible, but to understand the references it is often necessary to reconstruct an underlying KiKongo sentence (JM, pp.13-17).

> I the undersigned, in the name of the Governor
> of the Province/LUS/NP/66--Matadi City Hall,
> and in my personal capacity as High Official of
> the Administration of the Savanna--Policy of
> Greatness ...

The evocation of City Hall's filing systems immediately after the Governor's title has an effect like that of playing the national anthem. "Policy of Greatness" is a reference to General de Gaulle, whose speech in Brazzaville on 24 August 1958 encouraged nationalists to increase their demands for political emancipation. In the context of the nationalist movement, therefore, Ndo Mvuzi associates himself with the Governor in a joint claim to greatness. "The Administration of the Savanna" is the revival, in the form of the government now installed in Matadi, of the Kongo Kingdom, one of the Kingdoms of the Savanna about which J. Vansina had written in a book published locally at this time (Vansina 1965b). The next selection from this letter makes it clear that Ndo Mvuzi's claim to be associated with the kingdom is that of a simbi priest:

> Continuing my work of making contact with
> higher authorities and to preserve intact the
> Potential of the Unlettered Scientist, Guardian
> Spirit of the Country, Occult Warrior in the
> Strength of Native Intelligence. With
> reference to Article 39 of the Congolese
> Constitution of 1 August 1964.
> B/A. Regular/abbreviated as/V.S.M.E.K.-III-!!!
> /New Regime/E/D/M/1/3.3.66. Union of all the
> Peoples of the Black Continent.

"Guardian spirit of the country" (génie du pays)
translates simbi kya nsi (local spirit), although it
also connotes the "genius" of the "scientist," that
is, savant, a French word adopted in popular KiKongo
to refer to possessors of occult knowledge, such as
prophets or magicians. Guerrier-occulte en Valeur de
la Sûreté Indigène refers both to the secret police,
whose hidden operations preserve the country against
subversion, and to the prophet, "warrior in the
occult," who offers security against witches. The
savant, despite his bureaucratic fanfares, is
illettré, because his knowledge is indigenous, not
drawn from books like the white man's. The "union of
all the peoples" is both nationalistic and bureaucratic (trait d'union, "hyphen").

In a further communication, Ndo Mvuzi provided
the by-laws of his organization, differing from other
documents of the kind only in its greater gusto.
Some extracts:

> Statute of the Traditional State, supreme
> head of men wise in traditional language, and
> in international languages.  26 October 1945.
> Emblem--Insignia:  Lightning-Thunderbolt.
> Flag of seven stars.  National Prophetic
> Movement proceeding from the prophetic Epiphany
> of 1921, Symbol of the Independence of
> Congo-Leopoldville.
> Occult Minister of the Committee for the
> News Service in Traditional Language, His
> Supreme Excellency Mr. Masenga Jean.
> President General of the Epiphanous
> Association of the Middle Classes and Congolese
> Independents, Mr Mussanda Samuel.

As before, the bizarre character of the statements results from the condensation of references to
several domains at once. The stars signify the prophetic revelation of Kimbangu in 1921, an Epiphany
foreshadowing the independence of Belgian Congo
("Congolese Independents").  The "wise men" of this
epiphany are masters not only of KiKongo and tradition but of glossolalia, the languages of occult
inter-mundane communication ("international languages"); in other words, they are mim'bikudi, prophets or soothsayers, who provide "news service" by
"traffic" (commerce) in traditional language with the
angels." The lightning-bolt (ndingi) is a symbol of a
diviner's revelation.  "October 26, 1945," is presumably the date of Ndo Mvuzi's own prophetic calling.

Ndo Mvuzi thus declares himself to be a broker
or interpreter making contact both between the traditional and the bureaucrat worlds, KiKongo-speaking
and French-speaking, and between the living and
"higher authorities," the dead. This function is
exercised in the historical context of the Kimbanguist movement, the nationalist struggle, and the
present bureaucratic regime. He and his colleagues
are occult mediators, an "epiphanous middle class,"
but here it is necessary to recall that in Belgian
Congo "middle class" had a special sense, referring
to a commercial bourgeoisie who would mediate between
civilized Europe and backward Africa (see Chapter
Three). So "traffic" with the other world is
commerce.
    The file also includes a form of laissez-passer,
both an identity-document (praise-name) and a pass.
It begins in a mixture of French and KiKongo:

> Publication of the Clans. -- Voluntary
> Code and Corps of Volunteers. Grandson of a
> great-grandson, or bankakulaka beto. We came
> from the land of Greece. The name of the clan
> in that country was Mundele a Moanda, now
> called Mpudi a Kongo, Mpanzu a Nzinga,
> Mvul'anene Ne Noki, Ancien Royaume de la
> Savane: 1) Nsanda Kongo 2) Mbinda Kongo
> 3) Mboma za Kongo
>     I call upon the authorities both civil and
> military, doctors of medicine, doctors of
> Roses, and Lodges of the ancestors, to take
> care for the safety of the Unlettered
> Scientist, Genius of the Country. See File No.
> 192/I/62/DM/NGP/66, in Nzanza Commune.

"Publication of the clans" (Editorial des Clans)
translates ndumbululu a zimvila, "proclamation of
praise-names." A praise-name begins with the owner's
genealogical descent and a declaration of the origin
of his clan (MacGaffey 1970:ch.2; JM No.27); in
this instance, Ndo Mvuzi shows himself to have been
influenced, like many others, by Catholic missionary
ethnography, which taught that the Bantu-speaking
peoples originated near the Mediterranean. After
this relatively orthodox beginning, Ndo Mvuzi's praise-name shifts into typically Kongo semi-serious
braggadocio: mvul'a nene means "heavy rain," though
it echoes mvil'a nene, "important clan;" Ne Noki
means "Lord Downpour," though it echoes the name of
Noki (Noqui), a place on the Zaire near Matadi at

which many of the clans crossed in their legendary
migrations; Ancien Royaume de la Savane combines
L'Ancien Royaume de Congo (Cuvelier 1946) and Les
Royaumes de la Savane (Vansina 1965b), with a reference to "the traditional authority of the savant."
The three names that follow are the constituent
houses of Ndo Mvuzi's clan, Mpudi a Kongo.[19]

The rest of the document is highly ambivalent,
in that it is a request for a laissez-passer from the
authorities, itself couched in the form of a
laissez-passer (cf. Janzen 1978:57-59), and full of
word-plays situated somewhere between French and
KiKongo. The "doctors of medicine" are banganga;
"doctors of Roses" are Rosicrucian experts, members
of a form of mail-order magic popular among educated
BaKongo; "roses" and "lodges" sound much the same in
Kongo pronunciation; and the file number is correct.

Ndo Mvuzi's sonorous self-praise and strident
claims for recognition, couched in language that
violated all categorical order, provoked a flutter of
correspondence in the upper reaches of government.
To keep control and still respond to the situation in
due form, officials countered his display of ritual
symbols with displays of their own, as in this letter
from the mayor of Matadi:

Monsieur le Gouverneur,
    With reference to your letter No.11/020/Off. Gov.
    Prov./02573/LA/04 of 30 November, in re the topic
    cited in the margin hereof, and basing myself on
    my Decision No.16/AK/N.6/NG/66 of 26 September
    1966, forwarded to you in my letter No.2533/AK/
    NG/66 of 3 October last, I have the honor...

In the end the government proscribed Ndo Mvuzi's
group, basing itself upon the Constitution of the
Republic, the law of 14 August 1962 creating the Province, various decrees respecting public order,
several whereases, and (finally) the urgency of the
situation. In a vain last appeal, straight-forwardly
written in the vehicular KiLeta of the city, the prophet spoke for all the unlettered and oppressed while
still preserving, if I read him correctly, a sense of
the absurdity of the whole exchange:

    About that File, I want to ask you to give me a
    stay of execution. Read Article 18 of the
    Congolese Constitution ... You people in
    government are not supposed to forget us, you
    have to obey the Law!

In Ndo Mvuzi's sentences we find an inventory of all the factors, bureaucratic and customary, that constitute what BaKongo call luyaalu, "(mystically empowered) government," and the rhetorical conventions appropriate to each factor, but all so cryptically scrambled as to be totally ineffective as communication.[20] As in the traditional wisdom of the elders, a sense of mysterious potencies is created by portmanteau expressions piling multiple references upon each other within a partially articulated social and cosmological theory. The claim that one commands hidden forces is converted into real power to the extent that people accept it, but it is self-defeating when no one can perceive the meaning or is willing to concede the claim. The curve of the ratio of incantation and success is therefore parabolic.

In some prophetic writing we find cacography, or glossolalia in print, a transitory non-communication which, like the diviner's meaningless interjections, asserts the superior validity of the part of the message that is transmitted in clear (JM, p.27). Some prophets go a stage further, covering pages with meaningless scribble; the fact that they gloss it as "heavenly language" does not make it any less meaningless, although on another level the scribble plainly indicates the author's struggle with a world in which written documents are an expression and means of overwhelming power. Failure in this struggle is readily put down to the individual's personal incompetence, but we should rather recognize the gross absurdity or irrationality of the bureaucracy itself, in which (in Kongo in the 1960's) virtually nothing worked the way it was supposed to work and everything that worked did so covertly, by compromise, collusion and chicane. In this respect, the modern world was not much different from the traditional; in both sectors, losers fought back with manipulative improvisations and inflated rhetoric of their own. In short, in the most sober sense, Kongo is a world of kindoki (witchcraft).

# Conclusion

This book began historically, with the Protestant missionary efort of the 1870's, and led into a
description of contemporary (1970) beliefs and practices. This movement reverses the direction in which
I myself traveled, from direct experience to the pursuit of the past. When I arrived in Zaire (then the
Democratic Republic of Congo) in 1964, it happened
that members of the Church of Jesus Christ on the
Earth by the Prophet Simon Kimbangu (EJCSK) were the
first people to take an interest in my work, though I
thought of myself at the time as more concerned with
politics than religion. They were the first to
introduce me, in Matadi and at Nkamba, to milieux in
which the use of the KiKongo language predominated.
In so doing, they hoped to serve the Church's
interests; they knew that the weight of influential
opinion was against them and were anxious to invite
government officials and potentially influential
foreigners to witness their activities and testify to
their respectability. At the same time few
foreigners had been to Nkamba and there were some
missionaries who made it clear that in their eyes my
visit there amounted to recognition of an illicit
regime. These attitudes have since changed, but this
book is written under the unavoidable burden of
knowledge that not only Kimbanguism in the 1960's but
the entire process of describing and understanding
religions comparatively has been corrupted by the
intrusion of moral judgments linked to political
interests.

Most Protestant missiological commentators on
Kimbanguism are preoccupied with the question of its
status as Christian or non-Christian. Presented as a
question of theology and spirituality, this issue is

in fact largely political. Andersson (1968), for
example, approves of pentecostalism within the mission church but suspects it of being merely disguised
paganism ("syncretism") when its practitioners defy
mission authority. M.-L. Martin (1975) uses the same
imprecise criterion with different results; as Fernandez says (1978:222), her book seeks to judge
whether the theology, liturgy and good works of the
Kimbanguist church qualify it for admission to the
World Council of Churches; she concludes that they
do, and reserves the pejorative term "syncretic" for
Kimbanguisms that defy the authority of EJCSK.
      Political considerations of a different sort
enter into the judgment of Martial Sinda (1972), himself a Nkongo from Brazzaville. Sinda maintains that
Kimbangu was a nationalist. He regards religion in
general as a form of irrationality unfavorable to
modernization and effective politics, and blames
EJCSK for distorting the prophet's originally political intention. Sinda draws his information on
Kimbangu mostly from Belgian sources in which the
movement's threat to colonial rule is hysterically
exaggerated. Sinda also accepts (1972:95) the
Catholic missionary view that the European impact had
reduced Kongo religion to a welter of superstitions
incapable of motivating any movement. His information on and interpretation of the secular movement,
Matswanism, are much more reliable.
      Sinda's view, that Kimbanguism owes little to
indigenous Kongo religion, contradicts that of the
missiological commentators, who dwell on its syncretic character. On the other hand, the missiologists
tend to take the colonial and post-colonial political
situation for granted and to isolate the spiritual
dimension for consideration. None of these writers
pays much attention to social structure, customary or
bureaucratic, and the specific position of the prophets within it.
      G. Balandier, in his The Sociology of Black
Africa (1970, orig. 1955) offers us the most serious
attempt to explain Kimbanguism historically and
sociologically. Insufficiency of means betrays
Balandier's intention. Unlike Andersson and Sinda,
Balandier does not know KiKongo; his interpretations
of central terms are absurd. For example, he
says(1970:415), without the slightest justification,
that ngunza means "all these at once" and therefore
expresses the prophet's relationship to the Trinity
as the KiKongo equivalent of "messiah." Balandier is
well informed about the African quarters of Brazza-

ville, but his acquaintance with rural Kongo and with
Kimbanguism is derived mostly from colonial files and
the work of missionary ethnographers such as Van Wing
and De Cleene. Accordingly, his understanding of
Kongo social structure (clan, slavery, patrifiliation, kinkazi) is seriously deficient, as is his
conclusion (1970:389) that the most serious crises of
Kongo society are due to "its relations with the outside world, the dominant colonizing society, rather
than to its internal relations."

Reviewing the approaches to religious movements
current in the 1970's, Fernandez (1978:204) deplores
their reductionist tendencies and attributes their
demise to the increasing influence of historians, who
advocate "descriptive integration of specific events
with overall dynamics." The historian D.W. Cohen,
however (1977:16), is less satisfied with his colleagues' achievements. He says that historians, like
the anthropologists from whom they learned about
African institutions, have been insufficiently aware
of "the representational or 'modeling' aspects of
their enterprise," the extent to which social reality
is transformed by the categories in which it is
represented, rather than directly depicted. It follows that many representations of reality are
possible and that, in particular, the student should
be aware of the different sources of his own account
and that which members of the society might organize
within their own "mental compartments." Moreover,
according to Cohen, historians "have misperceived
social structure and culture as the contexts within
which event, change and development occurred," and he
speaks of the "meretricious separation of culture,
context and structure from change and development."
Models, then, are constituent parts of changing
institutions.

The present study, written by an anthropologist,
is inevitably historical because the phenomenon, Kimbanguism, itself demands of its interpreters that we
understand "what happened in 1921," and because the
study itself has been in progress during nearly
20 years of change in both Zairean reality and
anthropological theory. Like Cohen's account of
Bunafu, it attempts "to present context and change as
both moving and one—to tell and inform within one
structure of presentation." Like historical testimony, it is itself to be seen as "the outcome of a
variety of processes that essentially constitute the
modes of communication of information" in our world
(Cohen 1977:189).

It has been argued here that the plural structure of colonial society governed social action in
1921, pluralism itself being an organic condition and
not, as some would have it, a mere juxtaposition of
old and new. Congolese were assigned roles in both
sectors of this plural society. To understand Kimbanguism we must consider its adherents concretely in
terms of their specific situations and prospects
within the context.

As distinct though interdependent societies, the
European and African sectors of Belgian Congo institutionalized different cosmologies and epistemologies
as prerequisites of social action. This discrepancy
imposed strains on Congolese in addition to those of
economic and political repression.

The prophets, notably Simon Kimbangu, proposed a
reformulation of social relationships grounded in an
analysis of history. Although European commentators
paid attention exclusively to the threat this reformulation posed to their own control of social
relationships in church, state and workplace, the
threat to the existing order in the customary sector
was equally marked.

Kimbanguism in 1921 drew primarily on the indigenous cosmology to interpret both the Bible and the
contemporary social situation. It was not therefore
any less Christian than, say, modern European as
opposed to early Syrian Christianity, both of which
were deeply implicated in the history of their times.
Although the intellectual content of Kimbanguism
deserves attention, that content can neither be
separated from its expression in social action nor
readily classified as theological, political, or
sociological.

Like many modern African intellectuals, whose
efforts have not always been recorded in print, Kongo
prophets endeavor to reconcile the still incompatible
principles of customary and bureaucratic social
organization and to solve the problem of political
and intellectual autonomy in a world system dominated
by Europe (MacGaffey 1981). They offer their followers, as Buakasa puts it, a reading of the
contradictions of modern society, a translation of
its culture. The result is inevitably a compromise,
full of paradox, ambivalence and the need for continued adjustment.

This account does not try to explain away these
tensions, but situates them in an holistic, historical study integrating event, individual action and
motive with culture and structure. In the process it

has shown that modern prophetism in Lower Zaire
includes the following forms, among others: two
that, by their own criteria are Christian but not
Kimbanguist, one led by a European (the Pentecost of
the Congo) and one by an African (EUDA); the Kimbanguism of 1921, EJCSK, and the DMN group, to all of
which the term kingunza properly applies, and which
are both Christian and Kimbanguist; and the Black
Church, which is Kimbanguist but not Christian.

## Postscript:  EJCSK in 1980

From its beginning, Kimbanguism has had to
struggle with conflicts internal and external. In
the process it has changed; it has produced a major
church, internationally recognized, and to that
extent is no longer a movement. In conversation,
educated leaders of EJCSK give the impression, in the
1980's, that they no longer remember the enthusiastic, pre-bureaucratic Kimbanguism of colonial times.
They deny that in becoming a church the movement has
changed its character and, specifically, that its
roots in popular sentiment and culture have withered
to any important extent.

Yet the evidence of change is given not only in
the comments of observers and elderly adherents of
the movement, whose growth they have witnessed, but
in documents. The fifth edition of Essence de la
Théologie Kimbanguiste, a mimeographed document of
some 25 pages signed by Diangienda ku Ntima, Chef
Spirituel, and circulated in 1980, shows the distance
traveled since the preparation (ca. 1963) of the
document discussed in Chapter Seven.[1]

The new document distinguishes explicitly
between the movement of 1921 and the church legally
recognized in 1959. The document's political horizon
is much wider than that of its predecessor, and its
theology more sophisticated. It joins the majority
of modern African theologians in insisting that
knowledge of God in precolonial times amounted to a
proto-gospel. EJCSK's own theology may differ from
that of some other churches, but its support for ecu-
menism is firm.

EJCSK prefers the Biblical to the scientific
account of creation, and believes in the eternal
Trinity. Grace, faith and good works are all necessary to salvation, and man should not presume that
God, though all-loving, is all-forgiving. The Church
thinks of the Communion of Saints as a large but
select group around God's throne. It accepts the

existence of Hell, but denies that Christ harrowed
it; the righteous dead up to that time had been kept
in a place of their own from which the Crucifixion
released them. The Kingdom of God is a heavenly
kingdom, to be established on earth at the second
coming of Christ.

The Church practices four sacraments: baptism,
administered at about age 12; communion, to be cele-
brated annually on 25 December, 12 October
(anniversary of Kimbangu's death) and 6 April (anniversary of the opening of his ministry);
ordination of clergy; and marriage. Ministration of
holy water to the sick is not a sacrament, nor is the
penitential rite, though in 1963 it was. EJCSK's
creed, "inspired by the Nicene creed," makes no mention of the Virgin or of Pontius Pilate; it is not a
regular part of Kimbanguist services.

In its theology of baptism and of salvation,
EJCSK aligns itself with evangelical Protestantism,
yet in accepting the doctrine of the Real Presence of
Christ in the Eucharist it explicitly dissociates
itself from that tradition. In fact, like Easter
itself, Communion remains fundamentally alien to Kimbanguism. The Spiritual Head is the only person
authorized to administer the sacrament, which many
Kimbanguists have received only once, if at all,
since its institution in 1971.

All of the features of apparently traditional
Kongo belief that attracted attention in the first
version of the theological summary have disappeared
from the fifth. Moreover, an annex to the fifth edition, replacing the organizational statute (Nsadulu)
of the 1960's, presents the structure of the Church
as a purely administrative hierarchy from which the
political-charismatic elements (commented on in
Chapter Four) have also disappeared; the basadisi or
sacrificateurs of Nkamba and the three brothers, the
zimvwala, together with their spiritual and healing
functions, are not mentioned (cf. JM No. 43), nor are
the Spiritual Head's exceptional powers to heal the
sick.[2] Among the sacraments, the renewable sanctif-
ication of the sacrificateurs by the Spiritual Head
gives way to a rite of ordination for ministers.
Another annex prints the catechism, a single text
which replaces the two catechisms (of Christ and Kimbangu) current in the 1960's and greatly abbreviates
the stories of Ma Kinzembo and of Kimbangu's early
ministry (cf. JM No. 39).

Fieldwork in 1980 showed the persistence of
traditional elements not mentioned officially, but

also that these elements play a diminishing part in the continuing evolution of popular Kimbanguism.

Kimbanguists observe a number of rules in addition to the Ten Commandments. One forbids them to eat pork, a taboo which the official documents explain by reference to the Gadarene swine, into which Jesus caused evil spirits to enter. The Gospel paradigm covers a traditional belief that Kongo witches change their victims into domestic pigs; the documents do not mention that Kimbanguists may eat wild pig, nor that there is also a taboo against eating monkey. Asked about this taboo in 1966, Diangienda said, without elaborating, "There are two kinds of monkey; one of them is forbidden, but the other we may eat." The permitted species, makaku, live in bands, but nsengi monkeys, which go in pairs like man and wife, are believed to be transformed human beings (bituzi) (Andersson 1958:176). In Upper Zaire, in 1980, Kimbanguist natives of the region observed the rule with respect to local species, having confirmed, they said, that what the BaKongo told them about these animals was true.

The Kimbanguism of Lower Zaire drew its religious strength from rural life and customary institutions. Since EJCSK is now a national and international church, the culture and social structure of the BaKongo could scarcely continue to define its beliefs. Strong cultural continuities extending along the ancient trade routes into Bandundu and Kasai Provinces provided and continue to provide a matrix for a multitude of movements historically related to Kimbanguism (Munayi 1976), but in the north and east cultural resemblances are considerably attenuated. In Kisangani, capital of Upper Zaire, Kimbanguism has generated no offshoots. EJCSK exists there partly on the strength of its role as a nationally recognized body with educational and other public functions, partly as a benevolent association for elements of an urban proletariat lacking close ties to their rural societies of origin (MacGaffey 1982a). Kimbanguism in Kisangani owes its origin specifically to the nationalist ferment that developed there after World War II, whose most famous product was the Mouvement National Congolais of Patrice Lumumba. Kimbanguism never developed strong local leadership. In 1980, pastoral responsibilities were still in the hands of BaKongo from Kinshasa who complained, with reason, of the shallow implantation of the faith; they regarded themselves as missionaries to the heathen.

Though this is a different Kimbanguism from that
of Lower Zaire in its quality and social relations,
it is not devoid of vitality nor of a popular culture
proper to the Church, best seen in the productions of
its theatrical group. Vivid plays put on once a
month in 1980, in association with fund-raising
drives (<u>nsinsani</u>), clearly displayed Kimbanguist
theology. A hierarchy of delegated authority and
responsibility links God the Father through the Son
and Simon Kimbangu to Diangienda, shepherd of the
flock. At the Day of Judgment the righteous will be
saved, the sinners and hypocrites handed over to the
Devil and his assistants. As in other versions of
this great drama, the Devil gets all the best lines,
and provokes much laughter. His costume caricatures
that of a witchdoctor, the indigenous healer and
diviner whom many in Kisangani are in fact tempted to
consult. But behind the laughter there is fear, and
not only fear of falling into temptation, because the
costume of the devils is also that of the Simbas, the
rebels whose bloody occupation of the city in 1964 in
fact brought hell to some Kimbanguists and many others (Verhaegen n.d.).

Besides such themes interpreted in the light of
frightful memories there were others, imported from
headquarters in Kinshasa, which popularized legends
concerning Kimbangu and the period of colonial persecution. In 1980 these themes stressed the fidelity
and chastity of the prophet's wife Marie Mwilu, and
her role as heavenly mediator and source of consolation. They were evidently imitated from Catholic
models and deliberately intended to counter the moral
decay of the family; nothing of the sort was current
in Lower Zaire during the 1960's.

The context for these developments includes the
evolution of Zairean society from the pluralism of
the colonial regime towards an institutionally homogeneous nation state, an end deliberately pursued by
the government in its "policy of national integration" (MacGaffey 1982b). This policy favored
capitalist development and central control of
resources at the expense of the local social forma-
tions sheltered by indirect rule, and created a new,
uniform family code and system of local government to
replace customary institutions which, in most of the
country, had long since ceased to provide adequate
social regulation. The problems faced by EJCSK, and
the resources on which it drew, were increasingly
like those of other churches and national institutions. The elders of 1921 and the Kongo religious

tradition they represented were no longer effective elements of the Kimbanguist Church, which depended more and more on educated men able to function bureaucratically than on the mystical functions of divination and healing.

# Notes

## INTRODUCTION

1. For example, Malinowski's survey of Trobriand culture in the second chapter of Argonauts (1961:49-80) lists the institutions in order from material to ideal: domesticity, production, government, religion.
2. "The traditional rubrics, such as religion, myth, ritual, kinship, economics, and so forth, are all defined either in terms of our own ethnocentric (mis)interpretation of our own social system, or in the functional terms which have dominated anthropological work during the last seventy-five years or so" (Schneider 1976:210).
3. "I should make it clear that ethnocentric categories are not wrong in themselves. What is wrong is to compare things that are not comparable and to analyze things by categories that do not apply. Indeed, the whole enterprise in cultural analysis starts with our own society as a point of departure, not only because we know it (or can know it) in both accuracy and depth, but because it is precisely our own society which is problematic in our lives ...
   "If we start with the question of meaning and how it is symbolized, we must first ask how each culture slices the pie of what is defined as reality, its experience. I would insist that this is no less an analytic scheme, a theoretical statement, than any other." (Schneider 1976:211). This perspective does not exclude the existence of universals, but requires their presence to be verified empirically.
4. This distinction is derived from Fortes (1970:99), but is not identical with Fortes' usage. In practice, Fortes uses the concept of "domain" much as Smith does; what concerns him chiefly is the difference, in the study of kinship in particular, between the politico-jural (public) and domestic (familial) domains. But in his definition a "domain" resembles Smith's institution, and he speaks of the domains of law, economy, religion, and family, among others. "Institution" is not a technical term in Fortes' usage (1969:95-99).

## CHAPTER ONE

1. The BaKongo, identified by a common social structure and language, include a number of "tribes" of uncertain boundary which owe their identities chiefly to the accidents of ethnographic reporting. They include the BaVili of Loango

on the coast, the BaKunyi in the north, and perhaps the
BaPende to the east. In the ethnography of the center we
find groups to which the designation BaKongo is commonly
restricted, including BaYombe (in Mayombe) BaSundi (in
Manianga) and BaMpangu (in the east), all within the modern
Region (province) of Lower Zaire. For these Zairean groups
a central dialect has been standardized by Protestant mission usage to serve increasingly, in the twentieth century,
as their common language, KiKongo. This language is to be
distinguished from the crude vehicular language of the
colonial administration in the area, called KiLeta,
"language of the state". A still more restricted ethnic
grouping, bounded on the north by the Zaire, roughly speaking, consists of those who call themselves esi Kongo,
"people of Kongo," and relate the term to their supposed
common origin in Mbanza Kongo. The dialects of this restricted group are the basis of modern KiKongo, of which
BaYombe in particular will speak, with considerable exag-
geration, as though it were a different language
altogether. The provinces of the old kingdom have no significance in the twentieth century. People identify
themselves, according to context, as belonging to this or
that village, to a region unified by the commercial truck
route that serves it, or to some emergent political faction. The largest of such factions consists of the BaKongo
of Lower Zaire ("Kongo") as opposed to the rest of the
country, known to them as Bangala. When the context is
vague, people are more likely to designate their language
narrowly, as KiManteke, KiManianga, KiNdibu and the like.
In common modern usage, and for the purposes of this study,
the main central groups are BaYombe (near Tshela), BaMboma
(north of Songololo and in southern Mayombe), BaNdibu
(around Mbanza Ngungu (Thysville), and usually including
the Besi Ngombe in the north, near the Zaire) and BaNtandu
(east of the River Inkisi). (Van Wing 1959; Soret 1959;
Vansina 1965:ch.8).

2. The early history of Kongo, summarised here as it is usually understood, is being radically revised by new studies of
the relations between the Kongo and Portuguese kingdoms.
See Hilton (1981) and Thornton (1981).

3. Baptist Missionary Magazine, Boston, Nov. 1886, March
1887, March 1980, January 1903.

4. See the Redemptorist missionary reports in La Voix du
Rédempteur 1900–1910, passim, and Minjauw (1949).

5. The appearance of Halley's comet in 1910 had occasioned
conversions and millenarian excitement in Northern Kongo
(Andersson 1968:52).

6. The biography was captured at Nkamba in 1921 and "freely"
translated into bad French to be included in a symposium of
documents relating to "l'affaire Kimbangu," intended for

government use. Copies of the original, mimeographed
KiKongo text have not come to light but presumably remain
in circulation in Kimbangust milieux. The biography is
obviously the basis for much of the popular tradition
respecting Kimbangu and also for EJCSK'S official "catechism of Simon Kimbangu," (JM No.39).

7. "Cult of affliction," a term defined by V.W. Turner
(1968), refers to a religious configuration, common in Central Africa, in which sickness and misfortune are
interpreted as spiritual commands to join an association of
individuals, previously afflicted in the same way, who can
cure the affliction by mediating the power of the spirit
responsible for it.

8. A MS. note of this date, to this effect, existed in the
Archives of the Cataracts District in 1966, but there is
evidence, some of which may never be published, that Kimbangu was in fact received into the Catholic Church shortly
before his death. The matter has been much discussed in
Zaire (Bontinck 1981).

9. Joseph Kasa-Vubu, a MuKongo, past president of Abako, was
President of the Republic from 1960 to 1965.

CHAPTER TWO

1. I was assisted by Bakwa Mwelanzambi, a native of the town
and at the time an anthropology student at the National
University, Kinshasa.

2. After 1972, as a result of government decrees, there existed only three Christian churches, the Protestant, Catholic,
and Kimbanguist. Islamic, Jewish, and Orthodox communities
also existed, but were of small importance. Several of the
organisations listed here, notably the DMNA, sought admission to the United Church of Christ in Zaire (ECZ) but
generally without success.

3. EUDA, founded in Matadi in 1959, is not related to churches
of similar name elsewhere in Africa.

4. I visited other congregations, besides those listed in
Table 2, as follows: EJCSK in Mbanza Manteke, Kinzolani
(Kemba), Nkamba, Kinshasa, Kimpese, Thysville (Mbanza Ngun-
gu), Kasangulu, Kisantu; DMNA in Nzieta (Manianga) and
Kasangulu; DMN-Mbumba in Kinshasa and Kasangulu;
DMN-Nlandu in Mativa (Mbanza Manteke); EC-Gonda in Kasan-
gulu and Kinshasa; EJCDT at Mbanza Ngoyo; ENAF at
Ntendesi; Witnesses in Kasangulu; EECK in Mbanza Manteke,
Nsona Mpangu, Kinshasa, Kimpese, Kasangulu and elsewhere;
Catholics in Kisantu, Lemfu, Kasangulu and elsewhere;
Salvation Army in Kasangulu; Eglise Congolaise (E.Bamba)
in Kasangulu and Kinshasa.

5. J. Diangienda, "Eglise et politique," <u>Messager</u> <u>du</u>
   <u>Kimbanguisme</u>, 7 April 1972, reprinted in <u>Cahiers</u> <u>de</u> <u>la</u>
   <u>Réconciliation</u> May–June 1966, Nos. 5–6.
6. "The more strongly-based and entrenched religious authority
   becomes, the more hostile it is towards haphazard inspiration" (Lewis 1971:34). "As early as September 1934 there
   were in Yalala two groups of prophets. One held to the
   word of God as authority and means of edification, the
   other, on the other hand, was so emancipated that it no
   longer considered it had any need of the Bible" (Andersson
   1958:110).
7. Edouard and his personal friends knew of a large "traffic
   circle" constructed in another village by a Kimbanguist
   visionary as a site for spiritual encounters and eventually
   for the second coming of Kimbangu. A photograph of this
   construction appears in Thompson (1981, fig. 122), together
   with a discussion of its cosmographic significance. The
   cosmology implicit in Edouard's vision is explained in
   Chapter Five.
8. Mandelbaum (1966) describes them as the "transcendental"
   and the "pragmatic," but "transcendental" invokes theological complexities. The term "universal" is commonly used by
   Kimbanguist churchmen themselves in this context. Depage,
   in an excellent study of the organization of Kongo prophetism (1969–70), uses the terms "formal" and "informal," and
   speaks of "church" and "sect" where I have "church" and
   "band."

CHAPTER THREE

1. Pauwels (1971) lists and comments on statutory interven-
   tions in the realm of customary law, the development of a
   national legal doctrine, and the fusion of the customary
   and statutory judical systems decreed in 1968. In 1980, an
   official commission produced a new civil code (MacGaffey
   1982b).
2. Richards to Duncan, 28 January 1847. At the time, a pound
   sterling was equivalent to about $5. Axelson (1970:ch. 8)
   and Mahaniah (1975) explore the economic and social structure of Protestant missions. I know of no comparable work
   on Catholic missions.
3. In these villages people spend much of their time out of
   doors. The house is reserved for storage, sleeping, and a
   few other specially private functions; it is lived out of,
   rather than lived in. A veranda of overhanging eaves pro-
   tects the fabric from the rain and provides shade and
   shelter for people. Verandas are not a feature of European
   architecture and are omitted from Manteke houses built in
   the European style, greatly diminishing their utility.

4. "The European element... has undergone striking transformations. All were called upon to assume in one way or
another--sometimes even without being aware of it--duties
involving authority, and tasks of an educational nature. A
new psychology was created, and thus a special form of
European society adapted to African conditions came into
being" (Inforcongo 1959:41-42).

CHAPTER FOUR

1. Cartiaux to District H.Q., Boma, n.d. (1921).
2. In 1886, similar conditions contributed to the prophetic
movement called the Pentecost of the Congo, of which the
prophet was Henry Richards. In this movement, the order of
conversion corresponded roughly to the inverse order of
social rank in local society, beginning with slaves purchased by the missionary and with an accused witch called
Lutete, and ending with Na Ndumu a Mvula ("The Thundering
of the Rain"), head of Nkazi a Kongo, the most powerful
clan in the area.
3. It would be interesting to know the relationship between
Kimbangu's lineage and that of the catechist Mvwala (see
Chapter One). Mvwala came from Kinzinga village.
4. According to Diangienda, interviewed in 1966, there was
some tension at Nkamba at that time over questions of land
tenure, some elements of the Mpanzu clan seeking to reclaim
land taken over by the church, but he expected no serious
difficulty because most of the "fathers" were themselves
Kimbanguists and therefore subject to his authority.
5. The difference between 'normal' and 'revolutionary' divination among the Tigray and Guji Oromo in Ethiopia is
discussed by Bauer and Hinnant (1980).
6. This deflection is least evident in ENAF. Mpadi wrote:
"All the suffering of sickness which surrounds us is due to
the terrestrial authorities that reign over us and govern
us badly in everything. They are like the men that have
been given to the black race (to govern it). The
sicknesses of every kind from which we suffer most are (1)
arrests, (2) interrogations, (3) flogging, (4) prison, (5)
forced labor, and witches who kill and eat us; all this is
of a piece" (CRISP 1968:31).

CHAPTER FIVE

1. The explorer Coquilhat wrote, concerning the Bangala:
"Some of the natives assert that I get cowries, pearls, and
mitakou from the depths of the earth. Others say that
these fine things come from the bottom of the sea; to them
the white man is an aquatic being, and I myself sleep beneath the waves. But they are all agreed in considering me

related to <u>Ibanza</u>, the god or devil of whom they often talk. The more I deny my supernatural ancestry, the more firmly do they believe in it." He was asked to control the weather (cited in Levy-Bruhl 1923:377).

2. To "speak good KiKongo" it is more important to be familiar with rhetorical conventions and etiquette than to have good pronunciation and grammar.

3. Apparently the rule of thumb in Zaire for distinguishing between black whites and real whites is like that used by the Polynesian Tikopia to classify birds, according to the mode of action of the individual: "A bird that behaves normally is 'just a bird;' one that behaves abnormally -- as by coming towards a man instead of running from him -- is regarded as likely to be a spirit" (Firth 1966:10). The truly significant figures, potent for good and ill, are not whites as such but ambivalent figures who cross the boundary.

4. A Khakist prayer: "We pray in the name of Tata Matswa and of Simon Kimbangu, in the name of Mavonda Ntangu and of Bula Mananga and in virtue of our fathers and mothers in America (<u>mu lulendo lwa atata za Melika</u>) and in virtue of our deceased fathers and mothers" (Andersson 1958:199, his translation). Note the set of four prophets; their names are arranged in an order appropriate to a congregation in French Congo (Brazzaville).

5. "But woe unto you, scribes and Pharisees, hypocrites! for ye shut up the kingdom of heaven against men: for ye neither go in yourselves, neither suffer ye them that are entering to go in."

6. "But the chief priests and elders persuaded the multitude that they should ask Barabbas, and destroy Jesus."

7. "But what went ye out for to see? A prophet? Yea, I say unto you, and more than a prophet (<u>m'bikudi</u>). For this is he, of whom it is written, Behold, I send my messenger (<u>ntumwa</u>) before thy face."

8. This man went on to say, "Our forebears, like Joseph, were sold into Egypt" (cf. MacGaffey 1969:145). The mediating role attributed to the Americans was also given as early as World War I to the Germans, against whom the Belgians were then fighting. A Pende legend speaks of a particolored person, half white and half black, who lived under the ocean, belonged to both worlds at once, and was called Jamanyi (Germany) (Gusimana 1970:59).

9. This explanation of missionary destruction of charms as a way to render the Congolese powerless was already being offered in 1700 (Cuvelier 1953:130).

10. "Everything that exists [here] on nseke a mpanga exists also [there] in nsi a vinda ... There is, however, this difference: that no-one inhabiting nsi a vinda may eat pepper ... If anyone should eat pepper he returns to the

earth and becomes visible to the living" (Laman 1962:17). Though it is said the dead have neither salt nor pepper, there is also the idea, still current among KiKongo speakers in the Caribbean, that eating the salt of the other world (America) prevents one's soul from returning to Africa.    In modern Kongo, pepper is a good all-purpose medication against ghosts and witches. People bury it under doorsills and carry it in their wallets to safeguard their money.

11. The meaning of death is not a simple matter of observation in America either.    American courts have recently been asked to define life and death more precisely, in connection with both abortion and the rights of the terminally ill.   At modern American funerals it is not at all clear that the corpse has in every way ceased to be a person.

12. The corresponding Ovimbundu term is _ohasa_, the malevolent power of an enemy and the power by which the king combats the enemy. No wonder, says the ethnographer (Hauenstein 1970:163), that many Ovimbundu cannot tell the difference between magic and religion.   But perhaps, he says, the "contradictory definitions" of _ohasa_ are a "mystery" of the Bantu soul one just has to accept.

13. "The essential distinction lies in the use to which the power is put ... how any particular case is labelled depends upon the viewpoint of the speaker" (Wilson 1959:66).

14. In their own discussions, BaKongo do not distinguish the categories of the dead as tidily as this. The conceptual distinctions are maintained by the social reality of cult performance, including accusations of witchcraft, which endows the different spiritual categories with their apparent reality.   There is no articulated, shared "system of thought." See Weber (1963:10) and MacGaffey (1977b).

15. This artificial stabilization, relating the accidents of nature to the order of culture, reflects a perception of the intimate links that in fact obtain between social structure and disease;   for example, the terrible epidemics of sleeping sickness that raged between 1890 and 1920 were directly related to social reorganization, as the authorities moved the people into new environments for colonial purposes (Sabakinu 1974).

## CHAPTER SIX

1. Andersson (1958:203) quotes a man who said, with respect to Munkukusa, "There are two kinds of sickness, that which comes from God and that which is produced by wicked people. The first you whites have also, but not the second."

2. On the wall of his office he kept a photograph of a Mau-Mau general under arrest, whom he said was Kimbangu. Another

photograph, a negative print, showed "white" people who
were, according to Makanzu, Europeans who had come to him
to be healed.

3. Kiernan (1976), describing the meetings of Zulu Zionists,
emphasizes their "syncretism," the combination of Biblical
revivalism with African traditional practices relative to
affliction. Despite a clear temporal and even spatial division between the preaching and the healing phases, they
form part of a single event and a single framework of
action. Each phase is dominated by different personnel,
notably the minister amd the prophet, but this is a complementary division of leadership, characterized as
"constitutive" and "allocative," respectively. In Kongo
prophetic groups, this symmetry is replaced by a relationship in which the prophet is unquestionably dominant; the
preaching phase is merely a prologue to his entry, often
made spectacularly, and when the administration of medication follows divination the prophet himself or a third
party, not the minister, bears this responsibility. In
Kiernan's terms, the Kongo prophet exercises both constitutive and allocative functions.

In Kongo, therefore, the prophet is always identified
with a church, however ephemeral that organization may in
fact be, but among the Zulu there may be "pirate prophets,"
operating individually and beyond the restraint of ministers. In Zionist eyes, such a prophet is no better than a
diviner (isangoma) or herbalist (inyanga), "whose activities are regarded as commercial, anarchic, and malevolent"
(Kiernan 1976:363). "Not being tied to an ideal of communal effort, his powers belong to him alone, to be disposed
of as he wishes and he is free to exploit them for personal
gain. When Zionists condemn such malpractice, they single
out the commercial emphasis for comment, but they are
equally concerned with its implication, namely, the private
nature of the transaction and its lack of any institutionally inspired altruism." These concerns, expressed in
similar language, are also those of the BaKongo; in
Chapter Five they were designated "the distinction of
ends."

4. "What is good, for Ndembu, is the open, the public, the
unconcealed, the sincere" (Turner 1975:239). Among Zezuru
(Shona), as long as the spirit medium has public support,
he is regarded as the paragon of moral virtue, in contra-
distinction to his rival the nganga. The openness of the
spirit medium, his association with the ancestors and
heroes, which are the pillars of collective morality, and
his rejection of medicines, which are morally tainted, contrast sharply with the nganga, whose secrecy and
involvement with medicine associate him with those who work
against the collective ideals, the sorcerers (Fry 1976:17).

5. The technical discreteness of kinganga and kingunza is graphically demonstrated in Janzen 1978, Fig. 12.
6. "Foundation" sometimes refers simply to the "founder's" arrest by the Belgians for "subversive" activity.

## CHAPTER SEVEN

1. In the seventeenth century, n'naki meant prophet, from the verb naka, "to predict," now obsolete (Van Wing and Penders 1928). We have no description of a n'naki. In Masonukwa Manlongo, the translation of the Bible attributed mainly to Laman and used by the ABFMS, the word for prophet is m'bikudi. Unlike ngunza, m'bikudi is an ordinary KiKongo expression based on the verb bikula, "to reveal, foretell." The prophets active in Mbanza Nkazi in 1908 were known as mim'bikudi, and the term is still applied to any prophet in his capacity as seer, or to one of his assistants, usually a woman, who specializes in this faculty. Catholic Bible story books avoided reference to the prophets, whom they referred to as profeta and m'bikudi; ngunza was not used officially by Catholics until after 1960 (JM, p.15).
2. The last of a man's children, male or female, is priest of his father's grave, because it is to him in particular that the spirit of the deceased passes (Doutreloux 1967:97; MacGaffey 1970b:158; JM No.36).
3. In 1961 Bamba founded his own Eglise Congolaise, supported only by people from his own region (Kasangulu). He was a successful businessman, and in 1962 was Minister of Finance in the Adoula government. In 1966 he took part in a naive conspiracy to overthrow Mobutu, and was publicly hanged. His church, which was dissolved immediately afterwards, did not practice communion but was in other ways apparently similar to ABFMS, though with a strong nationalist tendency. Bamba gave therapeutic blessings to people who sought them, however, and his followers told many stories of his miraculous powers. In 1980 a church dedicated to his name had recently been revived in Kasangulu; its members' veneration of Kimbangu and Bamba clearly expressed their hostility to the government of the day: "where is the independence we were promised?"
4. In 1965, at Nkamba, I was erroneously told that 6 April was the anniversary of the return of the prophet's remains, though in fact that anniversary falls three days earlier and is not a feast in its own right. The distinction is slight, since the mausoleum is the sign and means of the continued availability of the mediation first opened in 1921. In 1965, 6 April fell about a week after Easter, a feast to which Kimbanguists, like many other Protestants,

pay little attention, and which in that year was virtually ignored at Nkamba.

5. "Declaration" by J. Diangienda, Kimbanguisme, 1 May 1960, in French; in English in M.-L. Martin 1968:27.

6. The only Kimbanguist text known to me that mentions the covert explanation is by a student at Dr M.-L. Martin's Kimbanguist Theological Seminary.

7. Dr. Martin has been kind enough to explain to me that this phrase means, "the word of blessing became not just a transitory word but an effective action of God in the world." That Kinzembo is described in some texts as Kimbangu's grandmother results from mistranslation of the Kongo expression grande mère, which means "mother's older sister." The missionary was not in fact Cameron but Percy Comber (Bontinck 1976:155).

8. There is no indication that Kimbangu controlled the weather; in this respect he was less like a simbi priest than Henry Richards. The hypothesis of a categorical association between the simbi cult and prophetic movements is supported by the deliberate attempt of one simbi priest to convert his shrine into an independent church in the 1920's (MacGaffey 1977c).

9. This chapter represents Kimbanguist theology as it was in the 1960's. Changes apparent in 1980 are discussed in the Conclusion to this book.

10. In 1702, Beatrice, who said Christ was born in Kongo, and saw various local towns as "Bethlehem," "Nazareth," and so on, was apparently governed by the same conception (Chapter Two, and MacGaffey 1969:141-47).

11. This point of view became part of the official policy of cultural authenticity. "Nous avons retenu les valeurs culturelles qui sont une source d'inspiration pour notre vie nationale au xxme siècle, et nous rejetons certaines coutumes qui relevaient plus de l'ignorance des siècles passés que de nos valeurs culturelles. Ainsi, nous avons retenu la référence à nos ancêtres qui procède de la métaphysique animiste bantoue mais nous rejetons le fétichisme qui n'est qu'une manifestation d'ignorance" (Sakombi Inongo 1973:213).

12. Andersson justly remarks, "The Biblical message of a living God who was infinitely superior to anything in the way of ancestor spirits and nkisi-gods corresponded to the deepest need in the African's heart. This contrast sometimes led to a realistically conceived struggle for power between Nzambi Mpungu and the whole host of minkisi. The later form of Ngunzism had to a certain extent reverted to the old conceptions according to which Nzambi is not, certainly, a Deus otiosus, Who is completely inaccessible to all appeals and cultic acts, yet is nevertheless a god who has withdrawn from the struggle and strife of this world, and

Who can therefore not figure in the front rank of the powers to whom man in need must address himself" (Andersson 1958:108).

13. "Money seems to be the most <u>frequent</u> and convenient axis on which millenarian movements turn. Money points up the difference between qualitative and quantitative measures of man in relation to his moral stature. Money is significant in the colonial situation, and in the collision between a subsistence and complex economy." Also, "much of what a prophet has to say hinges on the handling of money. Either he tries to make money a relevant measure of man, or he denies that money can measure anything but itself" (Burridge 1969:146, 155),

14. The legends of Mpadi's and Kimbangu's triumphs over death are interchangeable, except that whereas Kimbangu, loaded with chains, may be imprisoned underground with only "one banana" to sustain him, Mpadi is usually left with "only a bottle of whiskey."

15. Mpadi quotes Matthew 11:9-10, "But what went ye out for to see? A prophet (<u>m'bikudi</u>)? Yea, I say unto you, and more than a prophet. For this is he of whom it is written, Behold, I send my messenger (<u>ntumwa</u>) before thy face, which shall prepare thy way before thee."

16. Every Mpadist household is supposed to have its own holy table, or "table of submission," at which prayers are to be said, and where family disputes are to be settled, with the aid, if necessary, of the section leaders (<u>basudes</u>). Mpadi adduces Psalm 23 in support of the ritual configuration of staff, table and oil: "Thy rod and thy staff they comfort me. Thou preparedst a table before me in the presence of mine enemies: thou anointedst my head with oil; my cup runneth over."

17. A student thesis (Muloki 1975) by a DMNA sympathiser mentions several groups of <u>bangunza</u> who remained within the SMF mission church after the secession of DMNA in 1961. They include Nsadidila, "the remainder," also called Mantela, "those who stand (for prophetic worship);" and Manzakala, "those who sit," a group that practices neither spirit possession nor weighing and permit themselves to use alcohol and tobacco.

## CHAPTER EIGHT

1. This common perspective is that of the labor recruiter for industry, interested only in the de-socialized or impersonal interchangeability of normal individuals; it is precisely in this perspective that the concept of mental illness first took shape in seventeenth-century Europe (Foucault 1965:61).

2. Compare Marx (1975:299): "Above all we must avoid postu-
lating ´society´ again as an abstraction vis-à-vis the
individual. The individual is the social being. His manifestations of life ... are therefore an expression and
confirmation of social life. Man´s individual and
species-life are not different, however much -- and this is
inevitable -- the mode of existence of the individual is a
more particular or more general mode of the life of the
species .... Man, much as he may therefore be a particular
individual (and it is precisely his particularity which
makes him an individual, and a real individual social
being) is just as much the totality -- the ideal totality
-- the subjective existence of thought and experience
society presents for itself .... Thinking and being are
thus certainly distinct, but at the same time they are in
unity with each other."

3. Van Wing (1959:63) quotes an elder´s praise-name: "The
chief Nsako ... has his residence (vunda). Those who do
not know the way to vunda (to rest) are slaves, who are
sent for wood and water." In Makanzu´s casebook (Chapter
Six), 28 percent of his diagnoses of affliction mention
either slavery disputes in the clan or disapproval of the
client´s marriage by his (her) elders, patrilateral or
matrilateral. A further 14 percent mention disputes with
the elders over other or unspecified matters, including the
client´s choice of residence. These figures are evidence
of the extent to which BaKongo are conscious of elderly
authority, and resentful of it.

4. Some of these manuscripts were lent to me by people close
to Mpadi, or given to me by Mpadi himself. Others were
published in a French translation by H. Matota, in the
Travaux Africains No. 80-81 (1968) by CRISP, with an introduction by B. Verhaegen. Comments cited below, on the
character of the handwriting, are by Matota.

5. CRISP 1968, Doc.No.4, "Règlements pour l´entretien des mai-
sons des apôtres."

6. CRISP 1968, Doc.No.5, "Règlement des femmes mbandambanda."

7. Mpadi, M.S. Nsiku mia Mvuatulu Kaki, "Rules for the Khaki
Uniform." The khaki uniform, derived from the Salvation
Army (though Mpadists say Mpadi designed it for the Army),
signifies, for the BaKongo as for the British, spiritual
"warfare." It is still favored by Mpadists, although in
1970 it had been replaced, for men and women, by red clerical garb copied from the Catholic Church. See pl. 12.

8. See Chapter Two, on "fortification." The body-image
boundary corresponds in some ways to a screen on which is
projected the individual´s basic feelings about his safety
in the world. "In the absence of a body-image boundary
capable of supplying a minimum constancy in new situations,
the individual finds it necessary to create exterior condi-

tions which will artificially provide a substitute boundary" (Fisher and Cleveland 1958:354-55).

9. South African Zionists refer to their long white staves as "weapons," because they are used to ward off malevolent forces. Conferring the staff expresses the dependence of the recipient on his leader. The staff also stands for the person who carries it, and it is buried with him (Kiernan 1976:343).

10. Kiernan, discussing Zionism (1976:355), speaks of "the effects of carefully nurtured tension and of organized enthusiasm upon relationships of dependence within the group. Tension is induced in order to strengthen the control exercised by a leader."

11. <u>Bela</u>, "to lose," as a race or a lawsuit; not "to mislay."

12. In Matadi in 1970, a couple of DMN prophets, of a different church, wore the dates of their imprisonment by colonial authorities for prophetic activity embroidered on their robes. They were both highly eccentric. One of them lived as a client and talisman of the military base; he was supposed to be able to catch enemy bullets for them in his hands.

13. "A prophet is an adventurer, and his revelation often bears the hallmarks of any traveller's tale" (Burridge 1969:159). See JM No.31, the story of Tsimona-Mambu, and MacGaffey (1974), the story of the son of Nzambi Mpungu. A version of the quest, casting Kimbangu as the hero in search of power, is the Mpadist text, "The twelve persons of Simon Kimbangu" (Andersson 1958:195-96). The essence of the movement (<u>lateral</u>, then <u>vertical</u>) corresponds to the genealogical distance between Ego and Father, who belongs to another clan ("village") and to the ascendent generation. See Fig. 3 and the story (in Chapter Two) of Edouard's visit to America.

14. The vaginal pool and the extensible finger recur in legends concerning Kimbangu's "rebirth," no longer as an ordinary human being but as some kind of extraordinary spirit in human form. See also Sundkler (1961:155).

15. Though much less detailed and revealed only in self-reported vision, this progress is similar to that of a Senegalese boy described by E. Ortigues (1964). The boy's psychological troubles are eventually solved by the revelation of ancestral spirits, whose priest he becomes.

16. For an unsuccessful bid, see the story of Edouard, in Chapter Two. A three-day visit to the land of the dead is a commonplace in legends of famous magicians of the past, as of modern prophets.

17. In psychiatry, likewise, the distinction between "process schizophrenia," often found in organic, degenerative disease, and "reactive schizophrenia," which is "primarily a disorder of living," is similarly retrodictive. The dis-

tinction, by H.S. Sullivan, is cited by Silverman
(1967:22), whose paper is concerned only with schizophrenia
of the reactive type. Worldwide, the symptoms of process
schizophrenia are remarkably similar (Murphy 1976). The
problem with the schizophrenic configuration appears,
superficially, to lie not in describing it but explaining
it. Explanations turn out, however, to be legitimations
for, and thus the ideology of, the social process of reaction to schizophrenia on the part of others. Since it is
only through such reaction that the deviant behavior is
recognized and categorized, the explanation is not "of" the
event but "part of" it. In no such event, however, is the
reaction the sole constituent; some people are mad in any
and all environments.

18. MacGaffey 1970b:ch.11. For examples, see Philippart
(1920); De Cleene (1946); Domont (1957).

19. Another Matadi religious group superimposed social science
and traditional science to the extent of calling itself
IRESOCO, "Institut de recherches scientifiques d'occultisme
congolais," after the Institute of Social and Economic
Research (IRES) at Kinshasa University. The statutes of
IRESOCO give its objectives as:

> Scientifically cultural, derived from ancestral Congo-
> lese tradition. Most of the members generally are
> practitioners of the art of healing on the model of the
> elders, witchdoctors, so-called occultists in foreign
> magic, and others who are interested. The association
> is concerned also with removing undesirable elements
> detrimental to morals, that is, it will where necessary
> warn the authorities of every evil, self-proclaimed
> witchdoctor, healer, or quack who resorts to harmful,
> immoral, or scandalous practices.

IRESOCO envisaged publications based on its work, but
it too was banned, on the tenuous ground that the elections
(1970) were approaching.

20. "La conscience individuelle n'est que le point de rencontre
des temps collectifs" (Halbwachs 1947:29).

## CONCLUSION

1. A summary of this text has been published by Dubois (1981).
2. The annex is signed by the Spiritual Head's chef de cabi-
net, Bena Silu. As recently as 1975, in a similar document
prepared for an international conference, Bena Silu included the charismatic elements at the head of the
organisational table.

# Chronology

1878    Protestant mission to Mbanza Kongo.

1879    Henry Richards settles in Mbanza Manteke.

1885    Congress of Berlin. Congo Free State founded.

1886    The Pentecost of the Congo.

1908    Free State becomes Belgian Congo.

1921    Kimbanguist movement begins.

1939    Mpadist or Khaki movement.

1953    Abako founded.

1957    Re-emergence of Kimbanguism.

1960    Belgian Congo becomes Democratic Republic of Congo.

1965    Mobutu Sese Seko seizes power.

1971    Democratic Republic of Congo becomes Republic of Zaire.

1971    Suppression of independent churches.

# Abbreviations

Abako       Alliance des Bakongo.

ABFMS       American Baptist Foreign Missionary Society.

BMS         Baptist Missionary Society (British).

Cah.        One of the numbered notebooks (cahiers) in the Laman
            archive. See Janzen (1972).

CRISP       Centre de Recherches et de Documentation
            Socio-Politiques. Brussels.

DMN         Dibundu dia Mpeve a Nlongo, Church of the Holy Spirit.

EC-Gonda    Eglise Chrétienne Union Saint Esprit (ECUSE).

ECZ         Eglise du Christ au Zaire.

EECK        Eglise du Christ au Congo Kinshasa.

EEMM        Eglise Evangélique de Matadi et du Manianga.

EJCDT       Eglise de Jésus Christ par Deux Témoins.

EJCSK       Eglise de Jesus Christ sur la Terre par le Prophète
            Simon Kimbangu.

ENAF        Eglise des Noirs en Afrique (Black Church).

EUDA        Eglise Universelle de Douze Apôtres.

JM          J.M.Janzen and W.MacGaffey, 1974. An Anthology of
            Kongo Religion.

LIM         Livingstone Inland Mission.

MPR         Mouvement Populaire de la Révolution.

SMF         Svenska Missionsförbundet, Swedish Missionary Union.

# Note on Orthography

The standard adopted for spelling KiKongo is Laman's Dictionnaire Kongo-Francais, although quoted spellings, dialect variations, place names important enough to appear on maps, and personal names have been left as one finds them. Tone indications have been omitted, because Laman's conventions are unsatisfactory and no alternative has been developed; in modern KiKongo tone has lost much of its importance. Vowel length, however, though omitted from the orthography in general use in Zaire, is indicated by Laman's conventions as follows (Laman 1936:xi):

A radical syllable is long when a semi-vowel precedes or a nasal group follows the radical vowel. Eg.,bwaka, byeka, kanga. lomba. If such a syllable is short, the long consonant is doubled to distinguish words that are otherwise identical. Eg., bwakka, byekka, kanga.

The vowel is doubled if its length is the sole difference between words otherwise identical, but differing in meaning or grammatical use.

# References

## Periodicals

*Baptist Missionary Magazine*, Boston.
*Cahiers de la Réconciliation*. Paris: Mouvement International
de la Reconciliation.
*Congo Mission News*. Leopoldville.
*Kimbanguisme*. Leopoldville: EJCSK. Newspaper, French and
KiKongo.
*Kongo dia Ngunga*. Leopoldville: Abako. Newspaper, French and
KiKongo.
*La Voix du Redempteur*. Redemptorist newsletter.
*Salongo*. Kinshasa. Newspaper, in French.

## Unpublished and Fugitive Materials

Bahelele, J.N.  1964.  *Kinzonzi ye Ntekolo andi Makundu*
(Kinzonzi and his grandson Makundu). 3rd ed. Matadi:EEMM.
B[ayuvula] B. Benammis. 1963. *Oh! Premier Congrès des
Prophètes Bangunza*, 1960-62. Mimeo.
Corin, E.  1970.  *L'Image du père chez les BaYanzi
matrilinéaires*. Doctoral dissertation in psychology,
Catholic University of Louvain.
Dialungana K. Salomon. 1959. *Nsikulusu za Dibundu*
(Strengthening the Church). EJCSK. Mimeo.
Diangienda ku Ntima. 1979. *Essence de la théologie
Kimbanguiste*. 5th. ed. Kinshasa: EJCSK (mimeo.).
Diantezila, N. 1970. *Munkukusa, vo Kimaledimba* (Munkukusa, or
Kimaledimba). Mimeo.
EJCSK.  n.d.  *Nsadulu ye Ntwadusulu ya Dibundu dia
"Kimbanguisme"* (Practices and organisation of the
Kimbanguist Church). Privately printed.
Mahaniah, K.  1975.  *The Background of Prophetic Movements in
the Belgian Congo*. Doctoral dissertation in history, Temple
University.
Martin, M.-L.  1968.  *Prophetic Christianity in the Congo*.
Johannesburg: Christian Institute of Southern Africa.
Muloki wa Mutweba.  1975.  *La communauté du Saint-Esprit en
Afrique [DMNA] et son influence dans la communauté
evangélique du Zaire*. Mémoire, Institut Supérieur
Théologique de Kinshasa.
Mpadi Simon-Pierre. Letter to Mavunza Dragon, 14 May 1940.
Mimeo., in Lingala.
——————————. n.d. *Nsiku mia Mvuatulu kaki* (Rules for
the khaki uniform). M.S.

Stuart, C.H. 1969. The Lower Congo and the American Baptist Mission to 1910. Doctoral dissertation in history, Boston University.

## Books and Articles

Andersson, E. 1958. Messianic Popular Movements in the Lower Congo (Studia Ethnographica Upsaliensia VI). Uppsala.
------------. 1968. Churches at the Grass-roots. London: Lutterworth.
Axelson, S. 1970. Culture Confrontation in the Lower Congo. Falkoping, Sweden: Gummesons.
Balandier, G. 1970.The Sociology of Black Africa. London: Deutsch.
Bateson, G. 1972. Steps Towards an Ecology of Mind. New York: Ballantine.
Bentley, W. Holman. 1887. Dictionary and Grammar of the Kongo Language. London: Baptist Missionary Society.
Bernard, G. 1970. Diversité des nouvelles églises congolaises. Cahiers d'Etudes Africaines 10, 2:203-27.
Bittremieux, L. 1922-27. Mayombsch Idioticon, 3 parts. Ghent: Erasmus.
------------. 1936. La Société Secrète des Bakhimba au Mayombe. Brussels: IRCB.
Bontinck, F. 1976. Histoire du Kimbanguisme (Review article). Cahiers des Religions Africaines 10, No. 19:153-61.
----------. Kimbangu: légende et histoire (Review article). Revue Africaine de Théologie 5, No.10:251-67.
Buakasa, G. 1968. Notes sur le kindoki chez les Kongo. Cahiers des Religions Africaines, 2:153-69.
----------. 1972. Le discours de la 'kindoki' ou 'sorcellerie.' Cahiers des Religions Africaines 6:5-67.
Burridge, K. 1969. New Heaven New Earth. Oxford: Blackwell.
Cavazzi de Montecuccolo, J.A. 1968. Descrição historica dos tres Reinos do Congo, Matamba e Angola. 2 vols., trans. and ed. G. Graciano Maria de Leguzzano. Lisbon: Junta de Investigaçoes do Ultramar.
Chomé, J. 1959. La Passion de Simon Kimbangu. Brussels: Présence Africaine.
Claridge, G.C. 1922. Wild Bush Tribes of Tropical Arica. London: Seeley Service
Cohen, D.W. 1977. Womunafu's Bunafu. Princeton: Princeton University Press.
Cohn, N. 1961. The Pursuit of the Millenium. 2nd ed. New York: Harper.
CRISP. 1968. Documents de Simon Mpadi. Brussels: CRISP.
Cuvelier, J. 1946. L'Ancien Royaume de Congo. Brussels: Desclée de Brouwer.

Cuvelier, J. 1953. Relations sur le Congo du Père Laurent de Lucques (1700–1717. Brussels: Institut Royal Colonial Belge.

De Cleene, N. 1946. Le clan matrilinéal dans la société indigène, hier, aujourd'hui, demain. Brussels: Institut Royal Colonial Belge.

Depage, A. 1969–70. L'organisation du prophétisme kongo. Cultures et Développement (Louvain), 2:407–26.

Desroche, H. and P. Raymaekers. 1976. Départ d'un prophete, arrivée d'une église. Archives de Sciences des Religions 42:117–62.

De Heusch, L. 1971. Pourquoi l'épouser? Paris: Gallimard.

Domont, J.M. 1957. La Prise de conscience de l'individu au milieu rural Kongo. Brussels: Académie Royale des Sciences Coloniales.

Douglas, M. 1963. The Lele of the Kasai. London: Oxford University Press.

Doutreloux, A. 1967. L'Ombre des fétiches. Louvain: Editions Nauwelaerts.

--------------. 1971. Review of Fukiau, N'Kongo ye nza yakun'zungidila. Africa 41:172–3.

Dubois, J. 1981. Les Kimbanguistes vus par eux-mêmes. In Ngindu, ed., Combats pour un Christianisme Africain. Kinshasa: Faculté de Théologie Catholique.

Dufonteny, R.P. 1924. Relation sur le Kibangisme. Bulletin trimestriel de la Ligue pour la Protection et l'Evangélisation des Noirs (Liège). 12e. année, 2:5–31.

Dupré, M.-C. 1975. Le système des forces nkisi chez les Kongo d'après le troisième volume de K. Laman. Africa 45:12–28.

Evans-Pritchard, E.E. 1937. Witchcraft, Oracles and Magic among the Azande. London: Oxford University Press.

Feci, D. 1972. Vie cachée et vie publique de Simon Kimbangu. Brussels: Centre d'Etudes et de Documentation Africaines.

Fernandez, J.W. 1978. African religious movements. Annual Review of Anthropology 7:195–234.

Feyerabend, P. 1975. Against Method. Atlantic Highlands, N.J.: Humanities Press.

Firth, R. 1966. Twins, birds and vegetables: problems of identification in primitive religious thought. Man (N.S.) 1:1–17.

Fisher, S. and S.E. Cleveland. 1958. Body Image and Personality. Princeton: Van Nostrand.

Fortes, M. 1969. Kinship and the Social Order. Chicago: Aldine.

---------. 1970. Time and Social Structure. New York: Humanities Press

Foucault, M. 1965. Madness and Civilization. New York: Mentor.

Fox, R.C., W. de Craemer and J.M. Ribeaucourt. 1965. The
    second independence: a case study of the Kwilu rebellion in
    the Congo. Comparative Studies in Society and History
    8:78-110.
Fry, P. 1976. Spirits of Protest. London: Cambridge
    University Press.
Fu-Kiau, A. 1969. Le Mukongo et le monde qui l'entourait
    (N'Kongo ye nza yakun'zungidila). Kinshasa: Office
    National de la Recherche et du Développement.
Gilis, C.-A. 1960. Kimbangu, Fondateur d'Eglise. Brussels:
    Librairie Encylopédique.
Goody, J. 1977. Production and Reproduction. Cambridge
    Studies in Social Anthropology, No. 17. Cambridge:
    Cambridge University Press.
Guinness, F.E. 1890. The New World of Central Africa. New
    York.
Guinness, H.G. 1884. The Approaching End of the Age. 8th.
    American ed. New York.
Guinness, Mr. and Mrs. H.G. 1893. Light for the Last Days.
    London.
Gusimana, B. 1970. La révolte des Bapende en 1931. Cahiers
    Congolais 16, 4:59-70.
Halbwachs, M. 1947. La mémoire collective de le temps.
    Cahiers Internationaux de Sociologie 2:3-31.
Haley, J. 1963. Strategies of Psychotherapy. New York:
    Grune and Stratton.
Hauenstein, A. 1970. Le roi Pomba Kalukembe et le problème de
    l'ohasa. Anthropos 65:154-165.
Hilton, A. 1981. The Jaga reconsidered. Journal of African
    History 22:191-202.
Horton, R. 1971. African conversion. Africa 41:85-108.
Horton, R. 1975. On the rationality of conversion.
    Africa 45:219-35.
Inforcongo. 1959. Belgian Congo (Vol. 1). Brussels: Belgian
    Congo and Ruanda-Urundi Information and Public Relations
    Office.
Irvine, C. 1974. The birth of the Kimbanguist movement in the
    Bas Zaire, 1921. Journal of Religion in Africa 6,1:23-76.
Janzen, J.M. 1972. Laman's Kongo ethnography.
    Africa 42:316-28.
-----------. 1977. The tradition of renewal in Kongo
    religion. In N.S. Booth, Jr., ed., African Religions:
    A Symposium. New York: Nok.
    _____ 1978. The Quest for Therapy in Lower Zaire. Berkeley:
    University of California Press.
Janzen, J.M. and W. MacGaffey. 1974. An Anthology of Kongo
    Religion. (University of Kansas Publications in
    Anthropology, No. 5.) Lawrence: University of Kansas.
Jewsiewicki, B., Kilola Lema, and J.-L. Vellut, 1973.
    Documents pour servir à l'histoire sociale du Zaire: Grèves

dans le Bas-Congo (Bas-Zaire) en 1945. Etudes d'Histoire africaine 5:155-88.

Johnston, H.H. 1884. The River Congo. London.

Kiernan, J.P. 1976. Prophet and preacher: an essential partnership in the work of Zion. Man 11:356-66.

------------. 1977. The work of Zion: An analysis of an African Zionist ritual. Africa 46:340-56.

Kimpianga Mahaniah. 1981. Le munkukusa comme structure de guérison chez les Kongo. In Ngindu, ed., Combats pour un Chistianisme Africain. Kinshasa: Faculté de Théologie Catholique.

LaBarre, W. 1971. Materials for a history of studies of crisis cults: a bibliographic essay. Current Anthropology, 12, 1:3-44.

Lacroix, B. 1972. Pouvoirs et structures de l'Université Lovanium. Cahiers du CEDAF No. 2-3. Brussels: Centre d'Etude et de Documentation Africaines.

La Fontaine, J.S. 1970. City Politics: A Study of Leopoldville, 1962-63. London: Cambridge University Press.

Laman, K.E. 1936. Dictionnaire Kongo-Francais. Bruxelles: IRCB.

----------. 1953. The Kongo I. Studia Ethnographica Upsaliensia, IV. Uppsala: Almqvist and Wiksells.

Laman, K.E. 1957. The Kongo II. Studia Ethnographica Upsaliensia, VIII. Uppsala: Almqvist and Wiksells.

----------. 1962. The Kongo III. Studia Ethnographica Upsaliensia XII. Uppsala: Almqvist and Wiksells.

----------. 1968. The Kongo IV. Studia Ethnographica Upsaliensia XVI. Uppsala: Almqvist and Wiksells.

Leach, E. 1958. Magical hair. Journal of the Royal Anthropological Institute, 88, 2:147-64.

Lemert, E.M. 1962. Paranoia and the dynamics of exclusion. Sociometry 25:2-20.

Lerrigo, P.H. 1922. Rock-Breakers: Kingdom-building in Kongo Land. Philadelphia: Judson.

Lévi-Strauss, C. 1968. Introduction à l'oeuvre de Marcel Mauss. In M. Mauss, Sociologie et Anthropologie, 4th. ed. Paris: Presses Universitaires de France.

Levy-Bruhl, L. 1923. Primitive Mentality. New York: Macmillan.

Lewis, I. 1971. Ecstatic Religion: An Anthropological Study of Spirit Possession and Shamanism. Baltimore: Penguin.

Mabie, C.L. 1952. Congo Cameos. Philadelphia: Judson.

MacGaffey, W. 1968. Kongo and the King of the Americans. Journal of Modern African Studies 6:171-81.

------------. 1969. The beloved city: commentary on a Kimbanguist text. Journal of Religion in Africa 2:129-47.

------------. 1970a. The religious commissions of the BaKongo. Man 5:27-38.

MacGaffey, W. 1970b. Custom and Government in the Lower Congo. Los Angeles: University of California.
——————. 1971. Congo (Kinshasa): the view from Matadi. Africa Report 16, 1:18-20.
——————. 1972a. Comparative analysis of Central African religions. Africa 42, 1:21-31.
——————. 1972b. The West in Congolese experience. In P.D. Curtin, ed., Africa and the West. Madison: University of Wisconsin Press.
——————. 1972c. Review of A. Fu-Kiau, N'Kongo ye nza yakun'zungidila. Journal of Asian and African Studies 7,1-2:23-4.
——————. 1974. The Black Loincloth and The Son of Nzambi Mpungu. Research in African Literatures 5, 1:23-30.
——————. 1977a. Economic and social dimensions of Kongo slavery. In S. Miers and I. Kopytoff, eds., Slavery in Africa. Madison: University of Wisconsin Press.
——————. 1977b. Fetishism revisited: Kongo nkisi in sociological perspective. Africa 7:140-52.
——————. 1977c. Cultural roots of Kongo prophetism. History of Religions 17, 2:177-93.
——————. 1978. African history, anthropology, and the rationality of natives. History in Africa 5:101-20.
——————. 1979. African religions: types and generalizations. In I. Karp and C.S. Bird, eds., Explorations in African Systems of Thought. Bloomington: Indiana University Press.
——————. 1981. African ideology and belief. African Studies Review 24, 2-3:227-74.
——————. 1982a. The implantation of Kimbanguism in Kisangani, Zaire. Journal of African History 28:381-99.
——————. 1982b. The policy of national integration in Zaire. Journal of Modern African Studies 20, 1:87-106.
Malinowski, B. 1961. Argonauts of the Western Pacific. New York: Dutton.
Mandelbaum, D.G. 1966. Transcendental and pragmatic aspects of religion. American Anthropologist 68:1174-1191.
Maquet-Tombu, J. 1952. Le Siècle Marche. Bruxelles: Office de Publicité SA.
Markowitz, M.D. 1973. Cross and Sword: The Political Role of Christian Missions in the Belgian Congo, 1908-1960. Stanford: Hoover Institution.
Martin, M.-L. 1975. Kimbangu: An African Prophet and His Church. London: Heffer.
Marx, K. 1975. Economic and Philosophic Manuscripts of 1844. In Karl Marx Frederick Engels Collected Works, Vol. 3. New York: International Publishers.
Masamba ma Mpolo. 1976. La libération des envoûtés. Yaounde: Editions CLE.

Masonukwa Manlongo [Holy Scriptures]. Leopoldville (Kinshasa):
    Les Sociétés Bibliques au Congo, 1962.
Mauss, M. 1968. Sociologie et Anthropologie. 4th ed. Paris:
    Presses Universitaires de France.
Middleton, J. 1970. The Study of the Lugbara. New York:
    Holt, Rhinehart and Winston.
Minjauw, L. 1949. Les Rédemptoristes au Bas-Congo, 1899-1949.
    Louvain: Imprimerie Saint-Alphonse.
Monnier, L. 1971. Ethnie et Intégration régionale au Congo.
    Paris: EDICEF.
Monteiro, J.J. 1875. Angola and the River Congo. 2 Vols.
    London.
Moerman, D.E. 1979. Anthropology of symbolic healing.
    Current Anthropology 20,1:59-80.
Mudimbe, V.Y. 1981. Visage de la philosophie et de la
    théologie contemporaines au Zaire. Brussels: Centre
    d'Etudes et de Documentation Africaines.
Munayi Muntu-Monji. 1976. Nzambi wa Malemba: Un mouvement
    d'inspiration kimbanguiste au Kasai. Cahiers des Religions
    Africaines 10, No.20:219-40.
Murphy, J.M. 1976. Psychiatric labeling in cross-cultural
    perspetive. Science 191:1019-28.
Mwene-Batende, G. 1971. Le Phenomène de dissidence des sectes
    religieuses d'inspiration kimbanguiste. Brussels: Centre
    d'Etudes et de Documentation Africaines.
Ortigues, M. 1964. Le message en blanc. Cahiers
    Internationaux du Symbolisme, 5.
Ortigues, M.C. and E. 1966. Oedipe Africain. Paris: Plon.
Parsons, T. and R.F. Bales. 1955. Family, Socialization and
    Interaction Process. New York: Free Press.
Parsons, T. 1964. Social Structure and Personality. New
    York: Free Press.
Pauwels, J.M. 1971. L'adaptation du droit africain par voie
    jurisprudentielle: expérience et projets au Congo. Revue
    Congolaise de Droit (Kinshasa) No. 1:61-87.
Philippart, L. 1920. L'Organisation sociale dans le Bas
    Congo. Congo I, 1 and 2:46-66; 3 and 4:231-52; 5:505-19;
    etc.
Phillips, R.C. 1888. The Lower Congo: a sociological study.
    Journal of the Anthropological Institute 17:214-237.
Randles, W.G.L. 1968. L'Ancien royaume du Congo des origines
    à la fin du XIXe siecle. Paris: Mouton.
Ranger, T.O. 1968. "Introduction," in Ranger, ed., Emerging
    Themes of African History. Nairobi: East African
    Publishing House.
-----------. 1976. From humanism to the science of man:
    colonialism in Africa and the understanding of alien
    societies. Transactions of the Royal Historical Society,
    5th series, 26:115-41.

Raymaekers, P. 1971. Histoire de Simon Kimbangu, prophète, d'après les écrivains Nfinangani et Nzungu, 1921. Kinshasa: BOPR, Université de Kinshasa.

Rotberg, R.I. and A. Mazrui, eds. 1970. Protest and Power in Black Africa. New York: Oxford.

Rubbens, A. 1945. La solution de l'intégration des élites. In A. Rubbens, ed., Dettes de Guerre. Elisabethville: Essor du Congo.

Ryckmans, A. 1970. Les Mouvements Prophétiques Kongo en 1958. Ed. P. Raymaekers. Kinshasa: Université Lovanium.

Sabakinu Kivilu. 1974. Notes sur l'histoire de la maladie de sommeil dans la région de Kisantu, 1900–1912. Likundoli (Lubumbashi) 2,2:151–63.

Sahlins, M. 1976. Culture and Practical Reason. Chicago: University of Chicago Press.

Sakombi Inongo. 1973. L'Authenticité. Cultures au Zaire et en Afrique (Kinshasa) 1:211–63.

Sautter, G. 1966. De l'Atlantique au Fleuve Congo: Une Géographie de Sous–peuplement. The Hague: Mouton.

Schneider, D.M. 1976. Notes towards a theory of culture. In K.H. Basso and H.A. Selby, eds., Meaning in Anthropology. Albuquerque: University of New Mexico Press.

Silverman, J. 1967. Shamans and acute schizophrenia. American Anthropologist 69:21–31.

Sinda, M. 1972. Le Messianisme congolais et ses Incidences politiques. Paris: Payot.

Slade, R.M. 1959. English–speaking Missions in the Congo Independent State, 1878–1908. Brussels: Académie Royale des Sciences Congolaises.

Smith, M.G. 1960. Government in Zazzau. London: Oxford University Press.

———————. 1974. Corporations and Society. London: Duckworth.

Sohier, J. 1966. Du dynamisme léopoldien à l'immobilisme belge. Problèmes Sociaux Congolais No. 73:41–71.

Soret, M. 1959. Les Kongo Nord–Occidentaux. Paris: Institut International Africain.

Stanley, H.M. 1879. Through the Dark Continent. 2 Vols. New York: Harper.

———————. 1885. The Congo and the Founding of its Free State. 2 Vols. New York.

Sundkler, B. 1961. Bantu Prophets in South Africa, 2d. ed. London: Oxford University Press.

Thompson, R.F. 1981. The Four Moments of the Sun. Washington, D.C.: The National Gallery.

Thornton, J. 1981. Early Kongo–Portuguese relations: a new interpretation. History in Africa 8:183–204.

Troesch, J. 1961. Le nkutu du comte de Soyo. Aequatoria 24ème annee, No.2:41–49.

Tuckey, J.K.   1818.   <u>Narration</u> <u>of</u> <u>an</u> <u>Expedition</u> <u>to</u> <u>Explore</u> <u>the</u>
   <u>River Zaire</u>.   London
Turner, V.W.   1967.   <u>The</u> <u>Forest</u> <u>of</u> <u>Synmbols</u>:   <u>Aspects</u> <u>of</u> <u>Ndembu</u>
   <u>Ritual</u>.   Ithaca and London:   Cornell University Press.
-----------.   1968.   <u>The</u> <u>Drums</u> <u>of</u> <u>Affliction</u>.   London:   Oxford.
-----------.   1975.   <u>Revelation</u> <u>and</u> <u>Divination</u> in <u>Ndembu</u>
   <u>Ritual</u>.   Ithaca and London:   Cornell University Press.
Vansina, J.   1965a.   <u>Introduction</u> <u>a</u> <u>l'Ethnographie</u> <u>du</u> <u>Congo</u>.
   Brussels:   Editions Universitaires du Congo (CRISP).
-----------.   1965b.   <u>Les</u> <u>Anciens</u> <u>royaumes</u> <u>de</u> <u>la</u> <u>savane</u>.
   Leopoldville:   Institut de Recherches Economiques et
   Sociaux.
-----------.   1973.   <u>The</u> <u>Tio</u> <u>Kingdom</u> <u>of</u> <u>the</u> <u>Middle</u> <u>Congo</u>
   <u>1880-1892</u>.   London:   Oxford University Press.
Van <u>Wing</u>, J.   and C.   Penders.   1928.   <u>Le</u> <u>Plus</u> <u>Ancien</u>
   <u>Dictionnaire Bantu</u>.   Louvain:   Kuyl-Otto.
Van <u>Wing</u>, J.   1958.   Le Kibangisme vu par un témoin.   <u>Zaire</u> 12,
   6:563-618.
-----------.   1959.   <u>Etudes</u> <u>Bakongo</u>.   2d.   ed.   Brussels:
   Desclée de Brouwer.
Verhaegen, B.   n.d.   <u>Rébellions</u> <u>au</u> <u>Congo</u>.   Brussels:   CRISP.
Ward, H.   1890.   <u>Five</u> <u>Years</u> <u>with</u> <u>the</u> <u>Congo</u> <u>Cannibals</u>.
   London:   Chatto and Windus.
Weber, M.   1963.   <u>The</u> <u>Sociology</u> <u>of</u> <u>Religion</u>, trans.
   E. Fischoff.   Boston:   Beacon.
Weeks, J.H.   1908.   Notes on some customs of the Lower Congo
   people.   <u>Folklore</u> 19, 4:409-437.
-----------.   1914.   <u>Among</u> <u>the</u> <u>Primitive</u> <u>Bakongo</u>.   London:
   Seeley Service.
Willame, J.-C.   1972.   <u>Patrimonialism</u> <u>and</u> <u>Political</u> <u>Change</u> <u>in</u>
   <u>the</u> <u>Congo</u>.   Stanford, California:   Stanford University
   Press.
Wilson, M.   1959.   <u>Communal</u> <u>Rituals</u> <u>of</u> <u>the</u> <u>Nyakyusa</u>.   London:
   Oxford.
Young, C.   1965.   <u>Politics</u> <u>in</u> <u>the</u> <u>Congo</u>.   Princeton:   Princeton
   University Press.

# Index and Glossary